Selfless Minds

Selfless Minds

A Contemporary Perspective on
Vasubandhu's Metaphysics

MONIMA CHADHA

OXFORD
UNIVERSITY PRESS

OXFORD
UNIVERSITY PRESS

Great Clarendon Street, Oxford, OX2 6DP,
United Kingdom

Oxford University Press is a department of the University of Oxford.
It furthers the University's objective of excellence in research, scholarship,
and education by publishing worldwide. Oxford is a registered trade mark of
Oxford University Press in the UK and in certain other countries

First Edition published in 2023

Published in the United States of America by Oxford University Press
198 Madison Avenue, New York, NY 10016, United States of America

British Library Cataloguing in Publication Data
Data available

Library of Congress Control Number: 2022947762

ISBN 978–0–19–284409–5

DOI: 10.1093/oso/9780192844095.001.0001

Printed and bound by
CPI Group (UK) Ltd, Croydon, CR0 4YY

For my Papa

Contents

Contents

Acknowledgments

My work on this book was made possible through invaluable research support from the Australian Research Council (DP200103557), and the Monash Centre for Consciousness & Contemplative Studies (M3CS), generously funded by the Three Springs Foundation.

I am grateful to many researchers from around the world for inspiration, fruitful discussion, and generous comments. I owe the largest debt to Shaun Nichols. Over the last few years Shaun has been a frequent collaborator and a valued friend. Shaun encouraged me to write the book, and he has discussed, read, and commented extensively on various ideas and chapters of this book. I have spoken to Shaun about every aspect of the book and part of our joint work figures in Chapter 5 of the book. I am extremely grateful to Shaun for his academic generosity. Tim Bayne, my friend and colleague at Monash, likewise went well beyond the call of duty and offered generous comments on various parts of the book. I have benefited greatly from many discussions and Tim's incisive comments. I have also benefited greatly from many stimulating and encouraging discussions and comments on parts of the book from Jonardon Ganeri. Jonardon offered fruitful and much needed resistance to my interpretations of Vasubandhu's work. Manuela Kirberg read the penultimate draft of the book and her input improved the manuscript in innumerable respects. Thank you, Manu, your work saved me from numerous errors.

I would like to thank the commissioning editor at OUP, Peter Momtchiloff, for his confidence and interest in my proposal. His selection of reviewers and help with every stage of the process has been invaluable. Anonymous readers for Oxford University Press offered a host of insightful comments and criticisms on the book proposal that have helped to shape and improve this book.

I have had the good fortune of having excellent teachers and mentors in my philosophical journey which started at Delhi University and brought me to Monash. I'd like to single out several people whose dedication to philosophy has done much to shape my philosophical dispositions: Nirmalangshu Mukherji, Frank Jackson, Aubrey Townsend, John Bigelow, Lloyd Humberstone, Michael Smith, Edward Khamara, Richard Holton, and Rae Langton. I would also like to thank my colleagues at Monash, in particular Jakob Hohwy and Jennifer Windt for their support. I have presented this material at various philosophy seminars and conferences in Australia and overseas. I thank all the audiences for their comments.

There is one person without whose unfailing love and encouragement this book could not have been written: Ajay Raina, thank you.

Some of the material has appeared in publication elsewhere. I am grateful to the publishers for permission to use the material from the following articles:

- Chadha, M. (2015). Time-Series of Ephemeral Impressions: The Abhidharma-Buddhist View of Conscious Experience. *Phenomenology and the Cognitive Sciences*, 14(3), 543–60.
- Chadha, M. (2017). No-Self and the Phenomenology of Agency. *Phenomenology and the Cognitive Sciences*, 16(2), 187–205.
- Chadha, M. (2018). No-Self and the Phenomenology of Ownership. *Australasian Journal of Philosophy*, 96(1), 14–27.
- Chadha, M. (2019). Reconstructing Memories, Deconstructing the Self. *Mind & Language*, 34(1), 121–38.
- Chadha, M. and S. Nichols (2020). Experiential Unity Without a Self: A Buddhist Response to the Case of Synchronic Synthesis. *Australasian Journal of Philosophy*, 99(4), 631–47.
- Chadha, M. (2021). Eliminating Selves and Persons. *Journal of the American Philosophical Association*, 7(3), 273–94.

Introduction

Philosophical traditions in classical India agreed on one thing: We are not what we think we are. They disagreed, however, on the answer to the question: What are we? The disagreement, despite the agreement, is curious. And that drew me to Indian philosophy.

The self is central to our ordinary understanding of the mind. We ascribe mental states and activities to selves. We think of the self as the source of agency and the subject of experience. The dominant Hindu view of the self (*ātman*) as an eternal conscious substance trapped in the cycle of birth and rebirth sounded excessive to me. This Hindu view had many critics in ancient India, most famously the Buddhists. They argued that there are no such selves; we are nothing more than a bundle of constantly evolving physical and mental states. This no-self view sounded no less excessive. It is difficult to conceive of ourselves as mere bundles of physical and mental states without a self. The conflict between these irreconcilable views motivated me to probe deeper. The question in my mind was whether either of these classical Indian views is philosophically defensible. I spent a decade or so trawling through the classical Hindu-Buddhist controversy looking for an answer. Discussions of these issues in the classical texts always seemed to end in a stalemate. To get a purchase on philosophical issues which would help to make progress on the Hindu-Buddhist debate about the self, I found myself looking to contemporary philosophy for inspiration.

No-self views are becoming increasingly popular in contemporary philosophy, facilitated by the influence of the cognitive sciences. However, most contemporary views focus on the denial of the "self" as real entity, whether it is identified with a mind/brain, a persisting Cartesian substance, or some intermediate notion. But they are content to settle for metaphysically deflated notions of the self: self-models (Metzinger 2003), virtual selves (Bayne 2010), self-representations (Nichols 2014), etc. These surrogates, arguably, are introduced to do some of the work of the self. Metzinger claims that there is no such thing as a substantial self, but only a dynamic, ongoing process: a phenomenal self-model that is responsible for specific representational and functional properties. Bayne grants that experiences do indeed have "owners" or "bearers," but the owner of an experience is nothing "over and above" a virtual object. Similarly, Nichols argues that although the self-representation associated with episodic memory is not a good basis for a metaphysics of personal identity, it can and does serve as a trigger for self-conscious emotions, for example guilt.

Selfless Minds: A Contemporary Perspective on Vasubandhu's Metaphysics. Monima Chadha, Oxford University Press.
© Monima Chadha 2023. DOI: 10.1093/oso/9780192844095.003.0001

This book is a major departure from these approaches. It develops a radical no-self view without the need to employ surrogates to do the work of the self. My point of departure is the insight, first formulated by the Abhidharma Buddhist Vasubandhu, that the self is causally inefficacious. This insight is not given the recognition it deserves in contemporary philosophy. Instead, philosophers inspired by Buddhist thought sometimes defend process views of the self as the subject of experience and the agent of action (Thompson 2014), and at other times favor minimal views of the self as the subject of experience (Krueger 2011; Strawson 2017). On occasion when they do accept that there is no room for the self in Buddhist philosophy, they introduce conventional persons to do the work of the self (Siderits 2019; Ganeri 2017).

Vasubandhu (4th–5th century CE), arguably the most prominent Abhidharma Buddhist philosopher, deeply influenced three major Abhidharma traditions: Vaibhāṣika, Sautrāntika, and Yogācāra. His *magnum opus*, the "Commentary on the Treasury of the Abhidharma" (*Abhidharmakośa-Bhāṣya*), is to this day the primary resource for knowledge of the Hinayana Buddhist philosophy that flourished in Northern India in the first millennium. In the *Abhidharmakośa-Bhāṣya*, Vasubandhu argues against his Hindu opponents that the self (*ātman*) conceived of as substantive essence of the psychophysical complex is causally impotent. He also argues against fellow Buddhist Pudgalavādins that persons conceived of as the whole psychophysical complex exist in name only; they too do not do any causal work. This rejection of self and person is the central theme of this book.

If we grant that there is no self, we are left with deeper questions about how the sense of self or self-representations is implicated in our ordinary everyday experience and thought about the world and ourselves. A sense of self is involved in all kinds of experiential phenomena: episodic memory, unity of consciousness, sense of ownership, sense of agency, etc. And if we grant that there are no persons, questions remain about the status of our person-related concerns and interpersonal practices. My objective in this book is to answer these questions on behalf of the Abhidharma Buddhist. Inspired by a line of reasoning in the *Abhidharmakośa-Bhāṣya*, I shall develop a no-self and no-person philosophy of mind with the help of tools, techniques, and empirical findings from the cognitive sciences. The convergence of cognitive sciences and contemporary philosophy of mind that has emerged in recent years is what makes this possible. I believe this approach would be welcomed by Vasubandhu and other classical Indian philosophers who creatively develop insights from the *Vedas* and *Nikāyas*; it is possible to hear an echo of the creation hymn in the *R̥gveda* in the atomism of the Nyāya-Vaiśeṣika philosophers.

The Abhidharma Buddhist tradition is known for its radically revisionary no-self ontology. It is also well known for sustained, in-depth inquiry into the phenomenological structure of conscious experience. Unfortunately, the results of this inquiry are not that well known in contemporary philosophical circles.

The Abhidharma present a picture of world and mind in which the only ontologically real primitives are momentarily existing mental and physical *dharmas*, best understood as tropes or quality-particulars. In this worldview, the work of the self is transferred to the mental *dharmas*. This *dharma* ontology replaces the (inner) self as the homunculus that observes, manages, and controls the cognitive processes as well as the central processor that produces experiences and thoughts. The mind, according to the Abhidharma, is nothing more than a multi-layered series of causally related and interacting *dharmas*. There is no longer a self in charge of the mind-body complex, nor is there an executive in control of cognitive and intentional processes and actions. And there is no longer a person who is the bearer of moral concern and responsibility. As Vasubandhu puts it, there is no owner of experiences, no agent of actions, and no bearer of burdens.

This sparse *dharma* ontology clearly has much work to do. So, the Abhidharma philosophers continuously debated the number, groups, and varieties of *dharmas*. These debates appear to be disagreements about the details of the nature and classification of basic constituents of reality (*dharmas*). They reveal that the classical Abhidharma philosophers were deeply concerned with the "observational adequacy" (to borrow a term from Chomskyan linguistics) of the *dharma* ontology in accounting for the constitution of mental and physical states.

Any systematic no-self philosophy of mind must, however, account for the data of experience. This raises questions about the descriptive adequacy of the Abhidharma no-self view. Does the underlying *dharma* ontology adequately account for the phenomenology of conscious experience and thought in a self-less world? The Abhidharma project is concerned not only with cataloguing *dharmas* but also with explaining how the *dharma* ontology may account for conscious experience, thought, and action. These explanations turn out to be insufficient and in need of further work. It is here that I draw on resources from the cognitive sciences to complement the Abhidharma Buddhists' insights to produce a satisfactory explanation of the data of experience.

Furthermore, the no-self and no-person view is not just a descriptive thesis about the world. It also has normative implications. These call for a major reconfiguration of our ordinary person-related concerns and practices. The Abhidharma Buddhists are not interested in saving these practices because they claim that these concerns are misguided as they are borne out of the false belief in the self. And, that belief, they aver, is the root cause of suffering. Although these are fairly new hypotheses in contemporary philosophy, the ancient Indian Abhidharma Buddhist tradition has explored them in detail. In the *Abhidharmakośa-Bhāṣya*, Vasubandhu provides us with an advanced point of entry into this topic of contemporary philosophical interest, which I will use as my starting point for exploring these hypotheses.

A natural strategy to account for descriptive adequacy might be to argue that one can have the sense of self or self-representations without a self. This, however, is not the strategy adopted by Vasubandhu. He is not just an eliminativist about the self but also an illusionist about the sense of self and all kinds of self-representation. His argument is that one can account for all the mental phenomena that need to be explained without positing self-representations or the sense of self. This is the strategy I will pursue here. The aim is to reconstruct Abhidharma explanations for a wide range of experiential and cognitive phenomena without implicating self-representations: conscious experiences, diachronic and synchronic unity of experiences, sense of ownership, and sense of agency.

A common approach among contemporary philosophers inspired by Buddhism is to introduce conventional persons to serve as a basis of person-related concerns and interpersonal practices like ascribing blame and apportioning punishment (Siderits 2019; Ganeri 2017). Although classical Abhidharma philosophers grant the conventional reality of persons, they do not think that merely conventional entities can carry the causal burden of the self. Rather than reconstructing persons from the remnants of the no-self view, the Abhidharma Buddhists recommend a wholesale revision of our person-related concerns and interpersonal practices.

Most contemporary philosophers writing on Buddhism think that the main problem plaguing the no-self view is that we are left without an explanation of the phenomenology of our ordinary conscious experiences. They are not troubled by the problems facing our ordinary person-related practices, because while they eliminate continuing selves they leverage the Buddhist distinction between the *Two Truths* to leave conventional persisting persons as part and parcel of the world. To reconstruct persons to do at least some of the work of the selves is, I think, to misunderstand the strategy employed by Vasubandhu. To pursue his argumentative strategy, we need to explain conscious experiences, thought, and action in a self-less and person-less universe. This, however, leaves us without a basis for our ordinary person-related concerns and interpersonal practices. But, as said, the Abhidharma Buddhists are not interested in saving these practices and concerns, their aim instead is to fundamentally overhaul them. This is what motivates their revisionary metaphysics.

This book defends the hypothesis that it is possible to salvage much of our experience, thought, and action without implicating the self. But I hesitate to follow the Abhidharma Buddhist recommendation that we need a wholesale reconfiguration of our person-related concerns and interpersonal practices. Since Peter Strawson there has been an assumption in contemporary philosophy that our person-related practices are sacrosanct, "not something that can come up for review" (1962, p. 14). I question this assumption. I believe that the revisionary Buddhist metaphysics provides philosophers with an occasion to re-evaluate our person-related practices, attitudes, and concerns.

The main aims of the book, then, are to explore the descriptive adequacy and the normative implications of Vasubandhu's no-self view. The first chapter sets the scene by placing Abhidharma philosophy in the historical context of Buddhist thought, briefly recounting key divisions, seminal texts, and philosophers of its scholastic traditions, and introducing our protagonist, Vasubandhu. In the second chapter, I situate Vasubandhu's no-self view against the background of conceptions of the self in contemporary analytic philosophy, following which I explicate his argument for the no-self and no-person metaphysics. The rest of the book is largely dedicated to the defense of this Abhidharma Buddhist ontology of mind.

The biggest challenge for Vasubandhu, as I see it, is to give an account of the phenomenology and the subjective character of our ordinary conscious experience in the absence of selves and persons. This will be the focus of Chapters 3 through 7. The no-person view leaves us without a basis for our person-related concerns and interpersonal practices. This, I argue in Chapters 8 and 9, requires a major overhaul of our ordinary person-related concerns and interpersonal practices. Should we be willing to go that far with the Abhidharma Buddhists? I do not answer this question here but specify the costs and benefits of following the Buddhist Path. I do not endorse a wholesale rejection of our ordinary practices; that is practically impossible. The hope is to invite contemporary philosophers to commence a review of our ordinary practices in the light of Buddhist metaphysics.

This book sets forth a revisionary conceptual scheme envisaged by the ancient Indian Buddhist philosophers. I lay out the revisionary metaphysics and its normative implications as an alternative vantage point to challenge what we ordinarily assume and intuit. That said, I recognize the danger of losing sight of the fact that the Buddhist alternative is no less in need of philosophical scrutiny. As philosophers, we should be willing to scrutinize both conceptual schemes and their normative commitments and be prepared to "rebuild our ship on the open sea" (Neurath 1959, p. 201). The best way forward, I think, is to question the priority relation between metaphysics of identity and ethics. Rather than aiming to establish the true metaphysics of selves and persons before applying it to ethics, as most philosophers tend to do, or constructing the metaphysics of selves and persons constrained by our ethical concerns as, for example, Marya Schechtman (2014) does, I recommend that we build theories of "what we are" and "how we should live" that are mutually constrained by some forms of reflective equilibrium.

Note to the Reader

No one has the time to read a whole book these days, especially one this long. Here is a suggestion for those looking to dip into the book. Readers unfamiliar with the Abhidharma Buddhist tradition in classical India would be advised to read Chapter 1, while those familiar can skip it. Those interested in Vasubandhu's no-self and no-person view are advised to read Chapter 2. Readers interested in issues about conscious experiences without a self—say, experiences of agency and ownership—would be advised to begin with Chapter 2 before turning to Chapters 6 and 7 in which these issues are examined. Similarly, readers interested in the unity of consciousness should read Chapter 2 and then turn to Chapters 4 and 5. Finally, readers with an interest in what happens to person-related concerns and interpersonal practices would be advised to read Chapter 2 followed by Chapters 8 and 9. The chapters of this book are designed to be stand-alone and complete. This means that a reader interested in a particular topic, say episodic memory without the self, may read only Chapter 4. This comes at a cost, however. Some material, especially key quotes from translations of primary texts and their discussion, is repeated in various chapters. Those reading the whole book might find this tedious. However, in my experience, revisiting key passages in the primary texts aids the understanding and often offers fresh insight. I hope my readers will enjoy and develop these insights.

A final observation. This is a book about the Indian Abhidharma Buddhist tradition (as opposed to the Pāli Abhidhamma tradition) from a purely philosophical point of view rather than from the perspectives of history of philosophy or comparative philosophy. While I am concerned to do justice to Vasubandhu's thought, I do not wish to become embroiled in questions of philology and exegesis. So, I will simply use the standard translations of the Sanskrit texts and avoid lengthy digressions on the interpretation of disputed terms and stanzas. In a way, this work may be understood as a contribution to cross-cultural philosophy, "philosophy without borders" as Chakrabarti and Weber (2015) call it. A borderless philosophy straddles geographical areas and cultures, contexts, and times and "instead of preserving, quoting and juxtaposing [one's sources], one picks up a concept, a line of reasoning or some, however, minor point arising out of years of imaginative rearrangement and cross-fertilization of the ideas retrieved from different cultures, periods, texts, and disciplines" (Chakrabarti & Weber 2015, p. 231). This book is a "line of reasoning" from Vasubandhu's *Abhidharmakośa-Bhāṣya*.

1

Historical Introduction to Abhidharma Buddhist Philosophy

1.1 Introduction

Buddhism is a rich and long tradition originating with the historical Buddha, Siddhartha Gautama, in 450 BCE in north-central India. From there it spread, over the next millennium, first southwards to Sri Lanka and beyond, then to Southeast Asia, then to Northwest India towards present-day Pakistan and Afghanistan, then to China and Tibet, and, finally, to East Asia all the way up to Japan. Its interactions with local and competing philosophical traditions led to plural and often competing accounts of the Buddha's teachings in multiple material forms—texts, dialogues, poetry, monastic manuals, and meditation practices— and languages: Sanskrit, Pāli, Sinhalese, Chinese, Tibetan, Japanese, etc.

Buddhist philosophy is founded upon the historical Buddha's first sermon *Four Noble Truths*: there is suffering; suffering has a cause; suffering can be removed by removing its causes; and following the "Buddhist Path" can lead to the cessation of suffering. The *Four Noble Truths* seem simple at first sight, but such an impression is misleading. The first truth, for example, is not restricted to a given mental episode, physical condition, person, or living being; it is a fact of the condition of existence. In this sense, it is a contentious claim that may require explanation and justification. It is, however, universally accepted by all ancient Indian traditions except the Chārvākas. The Hindu sage Patānjali echoes it in *Yogāsūtras* when he says that: "to the discriminating mind all is nothing but pain" (Woods 1915, p. 40). The philosophical agreement among the ancient Indian traditions as far as the *Four Noble Truths* are concerned, however, ends here.

The second noble truth invites substantial disagreement between the Hindus and the Buddhists about the nature of the world and our place in it. The Buddhist identifies the cause of suffering as craving (*tṛṣṇā*, literally: thirst). The reason craving leads to suffering is because it is premised on the false assumption that the object and the subject of craving are permanent. Craving supports the idea of a continuing self. But that is not how the world really is: the object and the subject of craving are both impermanent. According to the Buddhist, the root cause of suffering is *mistaking the impermanent elements to be permanent*. In this way craving is linked with ignorance. For the Hindu, however, it is ignorance per se

Selfless Minds: A Contemporary Perspective on Vasubandhu's Metaphysics. Monima Chadha, Oxford University Press.
© Monima Chadha 2023. DOI: 10.1093/oso/9780192844095.003.0002

that is the root cause of suffering. According to the Hindu, the root cause of suffering is *mistaking the permanent self to be the impermanent elements.*

The third noble truth suggests that to end suffering, we must get rid of craving. The cessation of suffering is to be brought about by literally extinguishing craving and with it, desire, hatred, greed, etc. These can be extinguished, in the strong sense of being logically uprooted once and for all, by getting rid of the illusion of the permanent self. If there is no self, the pre-condition of the possibility of desire, craving, and the resulting negative emotions are uprooted. Here, liberation from suffering is enlightenment (*nirvāṇa*). Conversely, the ancient Hindus suggest enlightenment (*mokṣa*) is achieved through knowledge of the *Vedas* and its teachings of action (*karma*), duty (*dharma*), and knowledge of the eternal self (*ātman*).

The fourth noble truth is that the way to achieve enlightenment is to follow the *Eightfold Path*. It is described as the middle path between that of the indulgent householder and that of the ascetic monk who engages in excessive self-mortification through penance, fasting, bodily torture, etc. According to the Hindus, both extremes were permissible, perhaps even positively obligatory during certain stages of one's life (depending on one's caste). In Buddhism, on the other hand, liberation is best understood in psychological terms, as a mental discipline having to do with the transformation of the mind by inculcating the right kind of emotions and internalizing vows that will naturally dispose one to right action (in all its forms: mental, verbal, and bodily actions). The *Dharmacakra Pravartana Sūtra* lists the *Eightfold Buddhist Path* in terms of the following elements:

(1) Right view.
(2) Right intention.
(3) Right speech.
(4) Right action.
(5) Right livelihood.
(6) Right effort.
(7) Right mindfulness.
(8) Right concentration.

The numerical order of the eight elements does not signify an order in which they are to be followed and practiced. Rather, the idea is that these are to be developed more or less simultaneously; they are all linked, and each helps in the cultivation of the others. Some of the elements may seem self-explanatory, but a precise and succinct explanation of the intended sense of each may be helpful. The elements of the Path fit neatly into three categories: the first two are about wisdom and knowledge; the next three are about morality or ethical conduct; and the last three are about mental discipline.

Of the elements of knowledge, the right view implies seeing and knowing things as they really are.[1] The *Four Noble Truths* and the *Eightfold Path* are included in the right view as they represent the wisdom of the Buddha. Right intention is explained as intention that is free from attachment to worldly pleasures, selfish desires, ill will, hatred, and violence. Of the elements of ethical conduct (*śīla*), right speech is defined as that which is not false, divisive, hurtful, or mere idle chatter. Right action is refraining from harming living things, from destroying life, from stealing, from dishonest dealings, and from illegitimate sexual intercourse (for nuns and monks, celibacy). Right livelihood means that one should abstain from making one's living through a profession that brings harm to others, such as trading in arms and lethal weapons, intoxicating drinks, or poisons, killing animals, cheating, stealing, etc. Of the elements of mental discipline, right effort consists of preventing unwholesome states of mind (for example, greed, hatred, and delusion) from arising, to get rid of unwholesome states that have already arisen, to produce wholesome states of mind (for example, compassion, non-attachment, loving kindness) that have not yet arisen, and to hold on to wholesome states of mind already present. Right mindfulness is to be diligently aware, mindful, and attentive with regard to the activities of the body (*kāya*), sensations or feelings (*vedana*), activities of the mind (*citta*) and real things (*dharmas*). The last element, right concentration, indicates four stages of deep meditation (*dhyāna*), sometimes also referred to as absorptions. In the first stage of *dhyāna*, passionate desires and certain unwholesome thoughts like sensuous lust, ill will, languor, worry, restlessness, and skeptical doubt are discarded, but the feelings of joy and happiness are retained as are certain mental activities. In the second stage, all intellectual activities are suppressed, though the feelings of joy and happiness remain. In the third stage, the feeling of joy, which is an active sensation, also disappears, while the disposition of happiness still remains in addition to mindful equanimity. In the fourth stage of deep meditation, all sensations, including those of happiness and unhappiness, disappear; only pure equanimity and awareness remain. There are other meditations which concern inculcating positive emotions like loving kindness, compassion, sympathetic joy, and finally equanimity. These emotions, in turn, lead to right intentions, which are crucial for right action. The *Eightfold Path* thus outlines a way of life for all Buddhists. It is a rigorous method that involves mind and body, thought and action, and the practice of meditation.

---

[1] The catch-phrase "knowing things as they really are" is used extensively in all Buddhist philosophy, but it needs to be interpreted cautiously. Buddhist revisionary metaphysics is not aimed at capturing the structure that the world really has (or as is revealed by science), rather it aims at providing a structure that aims to reduce suffering. Furthermore, there is no settled meaning for this phrase as the conception of "real" changes as Buddhist philosophy evolves. How it evolves in the Abhidharma tradition will become clear later in this chapter.

The Hindus, instead, recommend four alternative (though overlapping) paths to liberation (*mokṣa*): the Path of Action (*karmayoga*), the Path of Knowledge (*jñānayoga*), the Path of Devotion (*bhaktiyoga*), and the Path of Meditation (*dhyānayoga*). The Path of Action is based on a duty-oriented ethics where duties (*dharma*) are determined by one's caste and stage (*Varṇāśrama*) of life. Thus, unlike the Buddhist egalitarianism—same prescriptions for everyone—the Hindu prescriptions differ based on caste. These philosophical disagreements between Hindu and Buddhist traditions led to the composition of the finest works of Indian philosophy. The most important Buddhist philosophical theories and arguments were formulated after the first century CE in highly charged debates with the Hindus. Classical Indian Buddhist philosophy, I think, owes most debt to its most ardent Hindu critics.

1.2 The Place of Abhidharma Philosophy in Buddhist Tradition

Buddhist philosophy can be roughly divided into three major traditions: Early Buddhism, the Abhidharma, and the Mahāyāna. The teachings of the Buddha and his immediate disciples are found in the *Nikāyas*, the earliest texts of the Buddhist tradition. The central aim of *Nikāya*-texts and of the Buddha's teaching is to eliminate suffering. Some Buddhist philosophers argue that the *Nikāya* framework in the *Nikāyas* is anti-metaphysical in that the Buddha shuns ontological questions about the status of persons, rebirth, and the external world. This is true to an extent because there is a set of questions, which the Buddha declares cannot be answered because "the terms do not apply"[2] (trans. Ñāṇamoli & Bodhi 1995, p. 594). For example, in response to the question about where the person who has achieved liberation would be reborn, the Buddha's response is to say that the question does not fit the case. Just as it does not fit the case to ask where a fire, burning in front of one, has gone once the fuel is used up and the fire is extinguished.[3] However, to say that *some* questions do not fit the case does not imply that the Buddha was anti-metaphysics. The Buddha never claims that *all* metaphysical questions are meaningless. Metaphysics is central in the Buddha's quest for the elimination of suffering. The first sermon that the Buddha delivered concerned the *Four Noble Truths*. The second sermon, the *Anātmalakṣaṇa Sūtra*, sets out the doctrine of no-self. Later *sūtras* in the twenty-second chapter of the *Saṃyutta Nikāya* (part of the discourse on the "aggregates") note that the first step towards eliminating suffering is to get rid of conceptualizations that are responsible for the proliferation of wrong views. The most prominent example of a wrong view is rooted in the use of the word "I," which leads us to imagining a

---

[2] *Majjhima Nikāya, Aggi-Vacchagotta Sutta 72.*
[3] *Majjhima Nikāya, Aggi-Vacchagotta Sutta 72.*

continuing self as its reference. The second step is to *see* (that is, experience during meditation) the selfless and impermanent nature of our being (Bodhi 2000). This suggests that rather than ignoring metaphysics, the message of the *Nikāyas* is that we must be ontologically conservative. We should not take it for granted (as, for example, the Hindu Naiyāyikas did) that every term in a language refers to an existing real entity. Terms like "I," "ego," and "self" (and even the *skandhas*, or mental and physical aggregates, according to the *Mahāvarga*) are to be understood as conceptual fictions that result from verbal proliferation (*prapañca*). In the *Nikāyas*, however, we are only given examples; we are not offered a criterion for distinguishing between terms that refer to real entities as opposed to those that refer to conceptual fictions. This distinction forms the basis of the famous Buddhist doctrine of *Two Truths* formalized by Abhidharma philosophers, to which I return later.

The second major tradition of Buddhist thought began with the rise of Abhidharma philosophy in India from the third century BCE. It was mainly a scholastic (as opposed to monastic) enterprise to systematize and organize Buddha's teachings in the *Nikāyas*, which were preserved in the form of sermons. Abhidharma texts form part of the Buddhist canon along with the Buddha's discourses (*Nikāyas*) and the rules of monastic discipline (*Vinaya*), which are said to have been composed around the time of Buddha. The stated aim of the Abhidharma is to present an account of conscious experience to provide the theoretical counterpart to the Buddhist practice of meditation. This is achieved by offering an exhaustive list of "what there is" in terms of a reductionist ontology of *dharmas*, the impartite mental and physical events that are the fundamental building blocks of the universe. The striking difference between the *Nikāyas* and the Abhidharma methods is that the *Nikāyas* are full of analogies, examples, and images, while the Abhidharma exposition presents the Buddha's teachings in technical terms that are carefully defined to ensure analytical exactitude. Furthermore, the Abhidharma texts also offer arguments to defend the Buddhist theses against the objections raised by the Hindu schools. Thus, for example, the Abhidharma formalize the *Two Truths* by offering a criterion to distinguish between real entities and those that are considered mere conceptual fictions. In the seminal Abhidharma text *Abhidharmakośa*, Vasubandhu explains:

> That which does not have a cognition when it has been broken is real in a concealing way (*saṃvṛti sat*); an example is a pot. And that of which one does not have a cognition when other *dharmas* have been excluded from it by the mind is also conventionally real; an example is water. That which is otherwise is ultimately real (*paramārtha sat*).[4]   (trans. Ganeri 2007, p. 170)

---

[4] *Abhidharmakośa* 6.4.

This criterion simply says that which disappears under analysis is not ultimately real, since when it is divided into parts it can no longer be cognized. A broken pot is no longer seen as a pot, a body of water analyzed by the mind into constituent atoms is no longer thought of as water.

The Mahāyāna is the third major tradition in Buddhist philosophy. Mahāyāna literally means "great vehicle" and was founded by Nāgārjuna in the second century CE as a movement to restore the Buddha's original message. Nāgārjuna, perhaps the greatest Mahāyāna thinker, argued that the Abhidharma philosophers have lost the message of the Buddha in their ontological profligacy of positing innumerably many *dharmas* and types of *dharmas*. The Mahāyāna monks prided themselves on retreating to the wilderness to practice meditation and on following the more rigorous path of the *bodhisattvas* in imitation of the Buddha himself. Nāgārjuna generalized the Buddha's critique of language and conceptual thought, as originally formulated in the *Nikāya* version of the no-self theory, to all of language and conceptual thought. Part of his project was to deconstruct the Abhidharma reductionist ontology of *dharmas*. The Madhyamaka philosophers argued that the complex Abhidharma network of *dharmas* and their causal relations are conceptual fictions like those of the self and the aggregates (*skandhas*), which, at best, can only comprise conventional truths. What, then, is ultimately true? The early Mahāyāna answer is intriguing: Nothing. All things are empty. Madhyamaka interpreted this answer to assert that all things are devoid of essence (*svabhāva*). *Dharmas*, too, are empty and lack an essence.

This "rough" division of Buddhist philosophy into three traditions follows Siderits' "basic division into three distinct phases in the development of Buddhist philosophy" (2007, p. 14). It is rough because it runs orthogonal to the early history of Buddhist thought in India. To place the Abhidharma tradition historically in Buddhism, we must make a digression. Although the information on the early evolution of Buddhist thought in India after the death of Buddha is scant, uncertain, and often contradictory, it is nevertheless well-established that the first division in the Buddhist community took place about two centuries after the Buddha's death, in the third century BCE, with the emergence of the Sthaviras and the Mahāsāṅghikas. It is sometimes suggested that this division was prompted by differences in their ordination practices, which later led to doctrinal disputes among them. This, in turn, led to the evolution of the various Buddhist philosophical schools (Cousins 1991). However, there is no consensus on this. For example, the *Mahāvibhāsā* account claims that the division was prompted by a dispute over "five points" advanced by a monk named Mahādeva. In any case, by the end of the second century BCE there were already eight divisions among the Mahāsāṅghikas, although the Sthaviras were as yet undivided. By the end of the first century BCE, traditional Buddhist accounts report eighteen Sthavira schools. This might have to do with the fact that the number eighteen is conventional in Buddhist historiography, rather than the reality (Obeyesekere 1991). Often Buddhist sources offer different lists which mention many more schools. It is likely that, as Buddhism spread over the entire Indian subcontinent and parts of Central Asia and Eastern Asia, multiple branches of monastic Buddhist communities (*saṅghas*) sprouted in various regions. The *saṅghas* tended to assimilate with the people, customs, language, and territories of the place, which caused distinctive schools to develop (Ronkin 2005).

This explanation, however, falls a little short. It does not take cognizance of the fact that each of the Buddhist schools claims to be *the* true follower and *the* authentic interpreter of the *Nikāyas*, the original teachings of the Buddha.[5] But the *Nikāya* literature, much like the Hindu *sūtras*, lends itself to diverging interpretations, which, in turn, created the different schools. As said earlier, *Nikāya* texts are impregnated with metaphysical doctrines, but at this stage in their development, the Buddhist theses were nebulous and mostly explained by analogies, examples, and metaphors. This is particularly important because the Buddha used his sermons as dialectical devices that were suited to the audience being addressed. In the *Nikāya* literature we do not find any clear statements or arguments for the distinctive Buddhist metaphysical doctrines. For example, *Saṃyutta Nikāya* 8.392 says:

> Having traversed all quarters with the mind,
> One finds none anywhere dearer than oneself.
> Likewise, each person holds himself most dear;
> Hence one who loves himself should not harm others.
>
> (trans. Bodhi 2000, p. 171)

The message of compassion put forward in this quote is not in terms of denying the existence of the self, rather it is suggested that compassion is an extension of self-love. This passage is open to various interpretations and was indeed used as a basis for many distinct readings of the Buddhist no-self doctrine. Some suggest that the terms "self" and "self-love" in this context are merely didactic devices to make sure that the audience understand the virtue of compassion (Stoesz 1978). Others suggested that even though the Buddha denies the ultimate reality of self, he does not deny conventional persons (Siderits 2015).[6] It is also important to note here that the motivation for clarification and defense of particular interpretations of the *Nikāyas* came not only from fellow Buddhists, but also, and more importantly, from their Hindu critics. This led to the Sthaviras eventually morphing

---

[5] It is for this reason of fidelity that the *Nikāyas* are referred to as the Sūtrānta literature. It is identical in the Hindu philosophical schools, where each claimed to be *the* authentic interpreter of the *Vedas*.

[6] This point is discussed in detail in Chapter 2; in the discussion of the proof for the non-existence of the self, Vasubandhu dismisses such texts as misinterpretations of the message of the Buddha.

into the systematic Abhidharma schools consolidating Buddhist teaching into an ordered philosophical theory with its own specialized epistemology, metaphysics, and logic. The Mahāsāṅghika school similarly evolved later into the Mahāyāna doctrine as well as becoming the source for the development of tantric Buddhism.

Within the Abhidharma tradition, Sarvāstivāda (advocates of the doctrine that all things exist) and Theravāda (doctrine of the elders) emerged as independent schools early at the *Third Buddhist Council*, which is generally believed to have been held in 236 CE. The Sarvāstivāda became established in Northern India, mainly Kashmir and Mathura, whereas the Theravāda spread to Southern India, Sri Lanka, and Southeast Asia. Over time, other Abhidharma schools also flourished in India, the most noteworthy among which are the Sautrāntika (those who rely on the *sūtras*), the Pudgalavāda (those who affirm the existence of the person), and the Yogācāra (those who practice yoga) schools, the last being of special interest here. Yogācāra appeared around the middle of the fourth century CE and is attributed to Asaṅga and his more famous brother Vasubandhu who, as the story goes, was persuaded by Asaṅga to become a fellow Yogācārin. Vasubandhu was originally a Sarvāstivādin, who later defended the Sautrāntika doctrine in his seminal texts *Abhidharmakośa* and its commentary *Abhidharmakośa-Bhāṣya*, before becoming a leading exponent of the Yogācāra doctrine in his later works *Viṃśatikākārikā*, its commentary *Viṃśatikāvṛtti*, *Triṃśikā*, and the *Trisvabhāvanirdeśa*.

Yogācāra originally evolved as an attempt to address the weaknesses of the Sautrāntika doctrine raised by the Madhyamakas, who were well established as a Mahāyāna school by then, as well as the Hindus. But the Yogācāra school also represents one way of trying to make sense of the Mahāyāna teaching of emptiness and thus is seen as an attempt to reconcile the Abhidharma and Madhyamaka teachings. It is thus that Yogācāra denies the existence of external objects, which makes it antithetical to its realist Abhidharma roots. This school came to be known as the Mahāyāna-Yogācāra. In the fifth century CE, Dignāga broke away from this Madhyamaka orientation and became the founder of the Yogācāra-Sautrāntika school, or what is known as the Buddhist logic school (Siderits 2007). This school remains firmly within the Abhidharma tradition, as is evidenced by their introduction of the notions of *ālayavijñāna* (storehouse consciousness) and *svasaṃvedana* (reflexive awareness) as a solution to the Abhidharma problematic. Indeed, as we shall see in Chapter 3, these two notions play an important part in describing the mature Abhidharma account of conscious experiences.

1.3 Seminal Texts and Key Philosophers

The best-known Mahāsāṅghika doctrine called the "supermundane doctrine" (*lokottaravada*) is not surprisingly about the "supermundane nature of the Buddha."

All Buddhist schools agree that once a person has become a Buddha (*bodhisattva*), he is radically transformed; the *lokottaravadins* assert that while the actions of the Buddha may appear to be the same as those of ordinary people, they are in reality extraordinary. The Buddha has 112 marks of a superior person, has miraculous powers, can live for eons if he wishes, has a golden hue, etc. The Buddha appears to be like the rest of us in that he is eating, drinking, talking, and walking but in reality, he is in constant meditation, not affected by the actions and doings in this world, and in this sense, he is beyond *karma*. A single Sanskrit text, *Mahāvastu*, of this doctrine survives, while another, known as *Lokanuvartana Sūtra* (the *sūtra* in conformity with the world), exists in Chinese and Tibetan. In this *sūtra* the doctrine of universal emptiness, which became characteristic of later Mahāyāna schools, is stated perhaps for the first time: all things, including all *dharmas*, are lacking in fundamental primary existence or intrinsic nature.

The Sarvāstivāda and Theravāda schools, which emanated from the Sthavira tradition, regard their respective versions of the canon to comprise seven texts each. The Sarvāstivādin *Abhidharma-piṭaka* (Abhidharma canon) consists of the *Saṅgītiparyāya* (discourse on the collective recitation), the *Dharmaskandha* (compendium of *dharmas*), the *Prajñaptiśāstra* (manual of concepts), the *Vijñānakāya* (compendium of consciousness), the *Dhātukāya* (compendium of elements), the *Prakaraṇapāda* (literary exposition), and the *Jñānaprasthāna* (the foundation of knowledge). The Theravādin *Abhidhamma-piṭaka* (Abhidhamma canon) comprises the *Dhammasaṅgaṇi* (enumeration of *dharmas*), the *Vibhaṅga* (analysis), the *Dhātukathā* (discourse on elements), the *Puggalapaññatti* (designation of persons), the *Kathāvatthu* (points of discussion), the *Yamaka* (pairs), and the *Paṭṭhāna* (causal conditions) (Ronkin 2018).

Like in the Hindu traditions, later generations of Buddhist philosophers also composed commentaries on the canonical Abhidharma texts. The most well-known later text of the Theravāda Abhidharma system is Buddhaghosa's *Visuddhimagga* (the Path of Purification) written in the fifth century CE. The Sarvāstivāda tradition is mainly preserved in Chinese translation of the *Mahāvibhāṣā* dated to the second century CE. The *Mahāvibhāṣā* documents several centuries of scholarly activity representing multiple Sarvāstivāda branches, including the most influential Vaibhāṣikas, the Sarvāstivādins of Kashmir. The Vaibhāṣikas have been of major importance in the development of Hinayana Buddhism in the later Abhidharma schools, the Sautrāntika and the early Yogācāra, as well as for the origin of the Mahāyāna tradition. Vasubandhu's *Abhidharmakośa* (treasury of Abhidharma) and *Abhidharmakośa-Bhāṣya*, its auto-commentary, are the most well-known texts of the Sarvāstivādin tradition. They are generally understood as presenting the Sarvāstivāda-Sautrāntika debate. On one reading, the text represents the Sarvāstivāda view and Vasubandhu's own commentary, the Sautrāntika critique. This reading is, however, not universally accepted. Buddhist scholars struggle to disentangle the intertwining of Sarvāstivāda and Sautrāntika views in the text and the auto-commentary to determine Vasubandhu's own position. What is clear though, is that the Sautrāntika view does not stand alone. It is inspired by the Sarvāstivāda view that precedes it and also benefits from the Yogācāra view that follows it. These antecedent and consequent relationships need to be properly fleshed out to appreciate the mature Abhidharma view of mind, mental states, and conscious experiences. The Sarvāstivāda-Vaibhāṣika masters attempted to refute Vasubandhu's Sautrāntika view in the *Nyāyānusāra* (conformance to correct principle) authored by Saṅghabhadra, a contemporary of Vasubandhu. This comprehensive treatise re-establishes the orthodox Sarvāstivāda view and is considered one of the final Sarvāstivāda works to have survived. Another well-known and perhaps the most influential Abhidharma text, *Milindapanha* (questions of king Milinda) was composed in about the first century CE, probably in Sanskrit in the northern part of the Indian subcontinent, post the Greek invasion. The Greek king Menander I supposedly converted to Buddhism after discussions with a Sarvāstivāda Buddhist monk. This text is the record of dialogues between the Buddhist monk Nāgasensa and the Greek king. The extant copy is in Pāli from Sri Lanka, the original having been lost in the land of its origin; some even claim it is a Theravāda text.

Arguably, the most influential scholastic family in the Abhidharma tradition is that of Vasubandhu, the family name given to the three sons of a Brahmin at the court of Purushpura (now Peshawar in Pakistan): the oldest was Asaṅga, the youngest Virincivatsa (believed to have attained *arhat-ship*, or liberation), and the middle son is known only as Vasubandhu. Although born as Hindu Brahmins, all three became monks in the Sarvāstivādin order. Asaṅga was the first to be impressed by Yogācāra views, but initially could not grasp the doctrine of emptiness, no matter how hard he tried, and was frustrated. Finally, though, he managed to come to grips with it, on various accounts, by the supernormal powers gained through meditation, or by his association with Maitreya, the supposed founder of Yogācāra, who taught him this doctrine. Vasubandhu, studied in the Sarvāstivāda tradition, defended the Sautrāntika doctrine, and later in his life became a Yogācārin because of the somewhat deceptive, though certainly well-meaning influence of Asaṅga. Part of the story is that Asaṅga was afraid that Vasubandhu, who had extraordinary intelligence and spiritual prowess, might defeat Mahāyāna through his criticisms. He used the subterfuge of his illness to call Vasubandhu home and then managed to persuade him to take Yogācāra seriously and use his intellectual abilities to assist, rather than hinder, the spread of Yogācāra teachings in the Indian subcontinent. Though Asaṅga is known as the author, or at least the compiler, of the monumental *Yogācārabhūmi*, the seminal texts of the Yogācāra tradition, Vasubandhu's *Viṃśatikā* (twenty verses), *Triṃśika* (thirty verses), and the *Trisvabhāvanirdeśa* (doctrine of three natures) have been extremely influential.

1.4 Distinctive Abhidharma Theses

The Abhidharma is distinctive in its efforts to provide the ontological and epistemological counterpart to the Buddhist practice of meditation as a necessary element of the path to enlightenment. The Abhidharma offers not only prescriptive guidance for achieving enlightenment and escape from the cycle of rebirths, but it is also a descriptive statement of the way the world is and how we can know it. Its focus is on Buddhist metaphysics and epistemology rather than on ethics and the Path. In what follows, I present the descriptive theses of the Sanskrit Abhidharma doctrine, variants of which are defended by individual Pāli Abhidhamma versions. This preliminary discussion helps to show the similarities and differences between the Abhidharma and Abhidhamma philosophies.

The stated aim of the Abhidharma is to offer an account of conscious experience in terms of an exhaustive list of its ultimate building blocks: mental and physical events (*dharmas*). That said, the characteristic Abhidharma activity is to offer a taxonomy of *dharmas* in multiple categories (*mātikā*). Apart from the discussion and justification of these intricate lists, the Abhidharma texts also include explicatory discussions of the Buddhist doctrine presented in the *Nikāyas*. These discussions go beyond mere explication and precisification of the theses in the *Nikāyas* to offer reasoned arguments of their defense. The Abhidharma schools are concerned with the observational adequacy of the *dharma* ontology and thus argue among themselves about the exact number and classification of the *dharmas*: Theravādins list eighty-two categories; the Sarvāstivādins seventy-five. It is important to note that these categories are types, not individual tokens of *dharmas*. The descriptive adequacy of the *dharma* scheme is not a topic of much discussion in the Abhidharma texts, but there are glimpses of such discussion in their attempt to account for the phenomenology of conscious experiences without a self. This book is not going to be concerned with the taxonomic debates among Ābhidharmikas, but I will present a partial list for purposes of explication in Chapter 3. My focus in this book is on the distinctive Abhidharma explication of Buddhist doctrines and their attempt to reconstruct the world and most importantly our conscious experience entirely and solely on the basis of their minimalist *dharma* ontology without a self.

1.4.1 No-Self

The Abhidharma schools offer a revisionary metaphysics that reconstructs our ordinary ways of thinking and conceptual schemes, in which the self, minimally conceived of as the referent of "I," occupies prime position. Instead, they provide an intellectually and morally preferred picture of the world that lacks a self.

Anātmavāda, the "no-self" doctrine, is variously interpreted within the classical Indian Buddhist traditions and by their Hindu critics and continues to be a matter of debate among contemporary Buddhist philosophers. It is commonly agreed that *anātmavāda* is not merely aimed at rejecting the Hindu theory of self, according to which the self is an immaterial, eternal, and conscious entity but also at rejecting any common-sense view of the self as a persisting entity. But beyond this there is not much agreement. There are differing views about the ontological status of persons, that is, whether persons are conventionally or ultimately real. There is also disagreement about the implications of the doctrine that the self is a conceptual construction: some aver that this entails that the self is merely an illusion (Siderits 1997); others disagree (Ganeri 2012a; Thompson 2014).

The centrality of the no-self doctrine in Sūtrānta literature is explained on the basis of its pragmatic role in the path to enlightenment. The ordinary notion of self is the result of a habitual tendency to construct an identity from a stream of physical and mental aggregates (*skandhas*). They are: corporeality or form (*rupa*), sensation (*vedanā*), perception (*samjñā*), mental formations or dispositions (*samskāra*), and consciousness (*vijñāna*).[7] In the Abhidharma texts, arguably the denial of the self is a denial of the subject of experiences and agent of actions. The most succinct statement of this view is found in the *Visuddhimagga* (16:5f), a Theravāda Abhidhamma text, which puts it thus:

> Misery doth only exist, none miserable.
> No doer is there; naught save the deed is found.
> Nirvana is, but not the man who seeks it.
> The Path exists, but not the traveller on it.
>
> (trans. Warren 1896, p. 146)

A more detailed argument for the precisification of the no-self view as the denial of a subject of experience and agent of actions is developed in Vasubandhu's "Treatise on the Negation of the Person" (*Pudgala-pratiṣedha-prakaraṇa*, the ninth chapter of *Abhidharmakośa-Bhāṣya*). This Chapter 9 is a detailed Buddhist critique of the Hindu conception of self and also of the "Personalist" (Pudgalavāda) view in Buddhism. Vasubandhu addresses questions raised by the opponents: Is there an owner of conscious cognitions? Who cognizes? Whose is the memory? Who is the agent of action? Who is the bearer of the fruit of the actions (*karman*)? Vasubandhu's response to these questions is simply to say that there is no owner of experiences; perceptions arise on account of their appropriate causes—that is, sense-faculty, object, and attention. Vasubandhu claims that ownership is just a matter of causal relations between two streams. A detailed interpretation and

---

[7] *Samyutta Nikāya* IV, 102; *Majjhima Nikāya* I, 130.

defense of the no-self view in Vasubandhu's *Abhidharmakośa-Bhāṣya* is given in the next chapter.

The most important critique of the no-self doctrine is that there cannot be a conscious state without a subject who is conscious of that state. In other words, if conscious states are characterized by "what it is like to be in that state" then there must be someone or at least something for "which it is like to be in that state." As the ancient Hindu philosophers and contemporary philosophers put it, the subjective character of consciousness cannot be explained without a subject of conscious experiences. The Buddhist no-self view, thus, is incoherent. This and other concerns will be addressed in detail in Chapters 3–7 of this book which present a larger defense of the Abhidharma Buddhist no-self view.

1.4.2 Two Truths

The *Two Truths* doctrine in the Sūtrānta texts is, as interpreted by the Sarvāstivāda tradition, grounded in the two types of existents: primary existents (*dravyasat*) and secondary existents (*prajñāptisat*). Thus, what is originally an epistemological question (what is the right way to describe the world?) is transformed by the Sarvāstivādins into an ontological one (what is there [ultimately]?) (Westerhoff 2010). It is important, however, to note that this ontological emphasis and hierarchy is not universally shared by all Abhidharma schools; the Theravādins, for example, do not endorse it (Ronkin 2005). Having the "two kinds of existents" in their ontology is especially handy for the realist Sarvāstivādin school since it provides the foundation for the promised Abhidharma explanation of the phenomenology of conscious experiences. For the Sarvāstivādin, primary existents (*dharmas*) are to be understood, similarly to Locke's simple ideas, as analytical and mereological simples but with an essential difference: unlike simple ideas, which are characterized as minimal mental units, primary existents comprise minimal units of mental as well as physical content. Secondary existents, in contrast, are defined as those that disappear under analysis (Cox 1995). Westerhoff (2010) considers mental *dharmas* to be partless atoms or partless moments of consciousness that cannot be broken down further and therefore withstand analysis. This is right with the proviso that these Abhidharmic primary existents are not confused with atoms in the *Nyāya-Vaiśeṣikas* and the *Jaina* ontologies wherein atoms are eternal. Primary existents are ultimate in that they are minimal mental and physical units that "are necessary for making sense of the world and conscious experience" (P. M. Williams 1981, p. 239). That they are necessary is not meant to imply that they are independent. Like everything else in the Buddhist universe, primary existents are not causally independent, but, unlike the secondary existents, they do not depend on language or conception for their existence, nor do they depend on their parts. And it is important to note that, in the Abhidharma traditions, *dharmas* are the only primary existents; conscious experiences and mental and physical aggregates are all secondary existents. This implication seems problematic and will be discussed in detail in Chapter 3 (see section 3.3).

1.4.3 Momentariness

A striking innovation by the Abhidharma philosophers is the precisification of the *Sūtrānta* doctrine of impermanence. Their distinctive contribution is that they reduce the time scale of sequential mental and physical processes and regard them as discrete momentary events (Ronkin 2005). The Ābhidharmikas of the Sarvāstivāda tradition believe that the discrete momentary events (*dharmas*) exist only for an instant or moment, where a moment is the limit of time. There are various opinions regarding such a limit. In the *Abhidharmakośa-Bhāṣya*, Vasubandhu uses the term *kṣaṇa* for "instant" and says that it is "the time it takes for a *dharma* to arise; or rather it is the time that it takes for a *dharma* to progress from one atom to another" (Pruden 1988, p. 474), whereas some Theravāda philosophers say that billions of mind-moments elapse in the time it takes for lightning to flash or an eye to blink. Theravādins use the term *khaṇa* (Pāli for *kṣaṇa*)[8] for "moment"; for example, *cittakkhaṇa* (mind-moment) refers to the instant taken by one mental event. However, a moment is further sub-divided into sub-moments. A *dharma*, for example, a mental event that lasts for a *cittakkhaṇa* occurs in the first sub-moment, endures in the second sub-moment, and perishes in the third. A major difference between the Theravāda and the Sarvāstivāda traditions is that the former claims that only mental phenomena are momentary while physical phenomena last for about seventeen moments each, while for the latter all phenomena are momentary.

The *Two Truths* doctrine morphed into the two existents in the Sarvāstivāda Abhidharma schools and offered a useful tool for the explanation of conscious experience. However, the morphing of impermanence into momentariness hindered, rather than facilitated, their explanations of conscious experience. This is because the pan-Buddhist no-self doctrine in combination with momentariness makes it harder for the Abhidharma philosopher to explain the phenomenological features of experience. The Abhidharma account is that our perceptual experience of the temporally extended, uninterrupted, flow of phenomena is ultimately constituted by a rapidly occurring sequence of causally connected events, each with its own particular discrete object. It is much in the same way that a rapidly projected sequence of juxtaposed discrete images is perceived as a movie. This analogy gives us the rough idea, but when we look closer, there are a

---

[8] Theravada texts are written in Pāli so it appropriate to use Pāli equivalents for Sanskrit terms.

host of problems spawned by the doctrine of momentariness. The fact that Abhidharma-moments, and ipso facto *dharmas*, do not possess any temporal thickness implies that our perception of temporally and spatially extended objects is illusory. This concern is strengthened by evidence from the "hard" sciences, such as neuroscience and neurophysiology, according to which instantaneous experiences are impossible because of constraints on thresholds for stimulus detection (conscious sensation) and conscious perception. This means that ordinary perception of motion, continuity, and change are also relegated to the realm of illusion by the Abhidharma momentariness doctrine. Even more importantly, the doctrine itself comes to be at odds with their philosophical account of causation, according to which causation is a relation requiring the existence of its relata.[9] But, like everything else in the Abhidharma Buddhist universe, present *dharmas* cause and are caused by non-present and non-existent *dharmas*; a problem first perceived by the Sautrāntikas themselves.

The Abhidharma philosophers grappled with these problems over the centuries. Some of their novel concepts—intrinsic nature (*svabhāva*); storehouse consciousness (*ālaya-vijñāna*); ego-consciousness (*kliṣṭa-manas*); and new ways of thinking about the very concept of *dharma* and that of causation—were formulated precisely to address these. The Sarvāstivādins went so far as to claim that "being past" and "being future" are modes of existence of *dharmas*, which though not actually existent, are not absolutely non-existent either. The Theravāda tradition rejected this solution as it cannot be squared up with the doctrine of momentariness. Rather, the Theravādins chose to focus on the concept of intrinsic nature in combination with their theory of momentariness to explain causation. A *dhamma* (Pāli for *dharma*) has an intrinsic nature only in the endurance moment: in the moment of origination, it is yet to obtain intrinsic nature; in the moment it ceases, it is without intrinsic nature. Thus, it exists as an ultimate reality only at the present moment. This solution, on the face of it, is no more satisfactory than that of the Sarvāstivādins. Chapter 3 will deal with each of the challenges posed to the Abhidharma account of conscious experience because of their commitment to momentariness. It will also explore possible solutions with the help of some innovations of the Sautrāntikas and Yogācāra-Sautrāntika to formulate an explanation of various facets of conscious experiences on behalf of the Abhidharma.

1.4.4 Dependent Origination

Dependent or conditioned origination (*Pratītyasamutpāda*, literally, *this* being *that* arises) is one of the most important and influential Buddhist doctrines. The underlying principle is that individual existence in the cycle of birth and

---

[9] The problems mentioned here are also faced by presentists in contemporary Western philosophy.

rebirth unfolds as a series of causes and effects. The Buddha is said to have "discovered" this doctrine in his meditative experience under the Bodhi tree. The doctrine is formulated using the well-known twelve links formula in the later *Nikāyas*: ignorance (*avidyā*), karmic dispositions or formations (*saṃskāra*), consciousness (*vijñāna*), mind and body (*nāmarūpa*), the six senses (*saḍāyatana*), sense contact (*sparśa*), feeling (*vedana*), craving (*tṛṣṇā*), attachment (*upādāna*), becoming (*bhava*), birth (*jāti*), and old age and death (*jarāmaraṇa*). Although the doctrine was standardly explained using these twelve links, by the time the Abhidharma schools emerged, questions were being raised regarding the exact causal relationships between them: for example, it is by no means obvious that ignorance is directly causally related to karmic dispositions. Furthermore, some links are morally neutral, for example, the six senses and the sense contact, whereas others are morally loaded, for example, craving and attachment (as the root causes of suffering). How do we move from morally neutral to morally loaded links? Are these links a description of causal processes in one life, or over lifetimes? Opinions on these and other questions led to the divisions among the Abhidharma schools.

The Sarvāstivāda interpretation of the doctrine suggests that the twelve-link formula of dependent origination is spread over three lives: ignorance and *karmic* dispositions belong to the past life, the next five to the present life, and the last five to the future life. Here, the Theravādins agree. But this conception of the three phases of past, present, and future requires moments to be extended in some sense, which does not sit well with the doctrine of momentariness. The later Sautrāntika and Yogācāra schools assign these links in a very different way: over two lifetimes rather than three. Since they interpret the doctrine of momentariness literally, they can only talk about two phases: what is and what will be; the present *is* and the future *will be* (caused inevitably by the present in accordance with dependent origination).

The doctrine of dependent origination, as spelt out in the twelve-link formula, explains causal conditionality only at the level of conventional reality. Persons, lifetimes, conscious states like desire, craving, and sense organs, etc., however, are complex constructions resulting from the aggregation of *dharmas*. Therefore, dependent origination must have a counterpart at the ultimate level: one that explains the causal conditioning of the *dharmas*. The Theravādins explicate this by what they call the *Patthananaya* (method of causal relations) that is based on the three axioms:

1. Nothing arises without appropriate causes and conditions.
2. Nothing arises from a single cause.
3. Nothing arises as a single solitary phenomenon.

Patthananaya also lists all possible causal relations between *dharmas*. There are twenty-four such conditional relations that describe the causal web of interacting *dharmas*. These include causal influences among mental and physical *dharmas* as well as the temporal dimensions of their interactions.

The Sarvāstivāda and the Theravāda philosophers had different doctrinal positions on causality at the *dharma* level. However, given their commitment to the three phases of existence of *dharmas*, they were open to the challenge that their theory of momentariness compromises the very notion of causation, a challenge forcefully thrown at them by the Sautrāntikas. For, if causes, conditions, and their results are all present momentary *dharmas*, how can a *dharma* that is no longer present have an effect? Again, how can a *dharma*, as the Theravādin says, that undergoes distinct stages of origination, endurance, and cessation in a brief moment have causal efficacy?

Some Sarvāstivādins responded by endowing *dharmas* with a two-fold nature: (i) their intrinsic nature (*svabhāva*), that is, what they are, and (ii) their causal power (*kāritra*), that is, their activities and their capacities (*sāmarthya*) to lead to effects when the appropriate circumstances obtain. The intrinsic natures of *dharmas* simply state what *dharmas* are in themselves. The activities and capabilities, on the other hand, are presented in causal terms, for example, giving rise to perceptions, producing subsequent *dharmas*, etc. There are many Abhidharma debates on the relationship between the intrinsic natures and the causal activities/capabilities, but the overwhelming support is behind a causal theory that makes no separation at all between what something *is* and what it *does*. Surprisingly, on this matter, the Theravādins agree with the Sarvāstivādins. Their account of causation reconceptualizes the notion of *dharma* where its intrinsic nature or essence *is* what it *does* (Gethin 1992).

This position was accepted by the later Yogācāra philosopher Dharmakīrti according to whom *dharmas* are identified with appropriate causal powers. The view is that it is an essential property of *dharma* x that it will produce y under the appropriate conditions. In other words, it is necessary that y is caused by x. It must be kept in mind, however, that while Dharmakīrti strongly advocates an "essential connection" (*svabhāvapratibandha*) between cause and effect, a connection that also guarantees that there is a "nexus where [the effect] will not be without [the cause]," he is not thinking about the necessity (essential connection) as a metaphysical necessity, rather only as an epistemic necessity (Tillemans 2021).

1.4.5 Epistemology

The Abhidharma philosophers are well aware of the Buddhist thesis that reality is cloaked under the guise of conceptual imagination and language. Abhidharma inquiries extended into the field of epistemology to the reality behind ordinary phenomena to see what there really is. And they offer a highly complex description of the processes of consciousness. For Abhidharma, as in Buddhist epistemology in general, sensory perception is the paradigm of perceptual, conscious experience. The various Abhidharma schools agree with the definition of consciousness as being intentional or "of something." For example, the Theravādins and the Sarvāstivādins both propose that there is direct contact between perceptual consciousness and its objects. To this extent both subscribe to what we may call phenomenalist realism (Dreyfus 1997).

Different Abhidharma schools, however, disagree about the nature of perceptual experience, the role of the sense-faculties, and the status of the object of perception. For example, the Sarvāstivādins and the Sautrāntikas differ in their explanations of the relation of perception to its object. The Sarvāstivādins are direct realists in that they hold that perception directly apprehends external reality; there is no need for mediating representations, we directly perceive objects which are a collection of *dharmas*. The external reality, though, does not contain (medium-sized) physical objects, but only their sensible qualities, the *dharmas*. This view is consistent with phenomenalist realism. The Sautrāntika, on the other hand, argue that it is only the present *dharmas* that exist and that only for an infinitesimal moment. This makes it difficult to explain how perception can directly apprehend its object. The Sautrāntika, however, believe that there is a time-gap between the sense-object contact and the arising of sensory awareness and because everything exists only momentarily, the object of the initial contact no longer exists when the conscious perception arises. Therefore, sensory awareness is only of the representation of the object. Thus, they instead turn to what may be characterized as representational realism: objects are apprehended by perception indirectly through the mediation of aspects (*ākāra*) that are representative of the objects (Ronkin 2018). Dreyfus explains that according to the Sautrāntika and Yogācāra traditions:

> The object does not appear directly or nakedly to consciousness but through the phenomenal form (*ākāra* literally "aspect") it gives rise to in the cognitive process, its manifestation within the field of consciousness. Awareness of the object is then the consciousness itself perceiving the phenomenal form or the manifestation of the object. The implication of this view is that consciousness is intrinsically self-aware.   (2011b, p. 120)

The "intrinsic self-awareness" of cognition is further explicated by later Yogācāra-Sautrāntika philosophers, Dignāga and Dharmakīrti, through the doctrine of reflexive awareness of mental states (*svasaṃvedana*).

1.5 Buddhist Meditation: Abhidharma Theoretical Framework

Buddhism is best not thought of as a religion, or even a systematic ethical theory. Charles Hallisey (1996) argues that it is misleading to interpret Buddhist ethics as a systematic theory that fits into Western ethical frameworks. Rather, Buddhism is best thought of as a way of life with a rich philosophy supporting it. Buddhism posits mental transformation as the key to bring an end to suffering and to achieve enlightenment. Meditation plays a major role in this transformation, but it is hard to pinpoint what role that actually is. One function of meditative practices is to calm down the mind so that it is not agitated by emotional disturbances and focus attention on things to investigate how they really are. The idea is that an emotionally unbiased and attentively focused investigation will lead us to discover "things as they really are." But it is questionable whether meditation can claim the status of an empirical investigative method. According to the Abhidharma tradition, meditation is not conceived as an independent investigative method leading to new discoveries about the mind and the world. Rather, the idea is that meditative practice is the key to turn principles that are first proven through scriptural study and rational inquiry—for example, impermanence, not-self, and emptiness—into objects of experience. Tom Tillemans (2013) calls this as a "continuity thesis" claiming that meditative understanding is continuous with and dependent upon preceding philosophical analysis; it has no independent epistemic value of its own. Meditation does not provide independent warrant for the reality of its objects (Kellner 2019).

The Abhidharma tradition lists the stages and the elements of the Path of Meditation in great detail. The Theravāda version of the Path of Meditation can be found in Buddhaghosa's *Visuddhimagga*, while the Sarvāstivāda version is given in *Abhidharmakośa*. These two traditions developed independently, and they disagree a lot when it comes to the details of the meditation practices. But they both share the fundamental Buddhist insight that meditation, knowledge of the texts, and analytical reasoning are essential elements of the Path of Enlightenment. The starting point for all meditation practices is the focusing of the mind. The Theravāda tradition draws a distinction between the initial attention-focusing meditation (*samatha*) which is regarded as a preparation for insight meditation (*vipassanā*). The *Visuddhimagga* lists as many as forty different objects as possible foci of concentration; breath appears to be the most popular choice. The *samatha* practice aims at getting rid of the five hindrances: sensual desire, ill-will, tiredness, excitement and depression, and doubt. The meditator who is able to free herself from the five hindrances can enter the first stage of deep meditation (*dhyāna*) as described under the four stages (*jhānas*) of right concentration. The Theravādins claim that ability in *samatha* and deep meditation is necessary before commencing insight meditation, though it is not a requirement to achieve the fourth stage of deep meditation. In chapters 18–22 of the *Visuddhimagga*, the model for the path of insight meditation is listed in terms of seven purifications, which beginning with the *samatha* finally lead the meditator to deep meditation where they ostensibly experience how things really are. The *Visuddhimagga* (20:104) describes the meditators' experience in the following manner:

[T]he world is no longer experienced as consisting of things that are lasting and solid but rather as something that vanishes almost as soon as it appears—like dew drops at sunrise, like a bubble on water, like a line drawn on water, like a mustard-seed placed on the point of an awl, like a flash of lightning; things in themselves lack substance and always elude one's grasp—like a mirage, a conjuring trick, a dream, a fairy city, foam or the trunk of a banana tree.

(trans. Gethin 1998, p. 190)

It is interesting to note that some of the images mentioned in this quote are mined by Buddhaghosa from the early *Nikāyas*. The detailed description of these purifications makes clear that part of the meditation involves a deconstruction of complex entities, for example, the self, the stream of consciousness, and ordinary objects. This enables the meditator to clearly see that everything that exists, including herself, is impermanent, is suffering, and is not-self. The law of *karma* and the doctrine of dependent origination are all seen and understood by the noble person (*arya*) who sees the fact of momentariness. This state is one step removed from the final purification which entails irrevocable eradication of all the hindrances and defilements acquired on account of past *karma*. Thus, one becomes the enlightened (*arhant*).

The Sarvāstivāda Abhidharma tradition focuses on mindfulness (*smṛti*) meditation rather than the *samatha* and *vipassanā*. The procedure of mindfulness meditation laid out in the *Abhidharmakośa* differentiates six steps: counting, following, fixing, observing, modifying, and purifying (Pruden 1988).[10] The first four steps involve fixating and analyzing breathing, while the last two steps are explicitly evaluative. Each step is spelt out with its precise mechanism of execution: first, attention is applied to counting breaths (strictly to ten); second, attention is applied to following the progress of wind which enters and leaves the body (strictly following its path in and out, but only to a distance of a hand and cubit); third, fixing the attention on two points (for example, tip of the nose and toes) and following the breath held in the body to judge the character of the breath (for example, the feeling associated with it); fourth, observing that breaths are not only wind but also involve other physical elements and their constituent *dharmas* and mental states and their constituent *dharmas*—thus discovering the five *skandhas* (psycho-physical elements and their constituent *dharmas*); fifth, modifying the focus of attention so that it moves from wind to "better" *dharmas*— better in this context implies appreciating the nature of the *dharmas*; and, finally

---

[10] It is interesting to note that some of these steps are ignored in the standard definition of mindfulness in contemporary literature; there is no talk of modifying or purifying, rather the emphasis is on fixedness, openness, and acceptance. Also, the fact that observing and fixing have technical connotations is missed in standard interpretations and teaching methodologies of mindfulness meditation.

the sixth, purifying, in which there is amalgamation of the Path of Seeing and the Path of Meditation.

Mindfulness meditation is aimed at curbing thoughts, which proliferate naturally because of the variety of external objects available. This aim is achieved by controlling the mind through focused attention on breathing to eliminate mind wandering, which ultimately eliminates desire. The progression of this control through the first five steps results in focusing on the *dharmas*, which ultimately rids the mind of unwholesome habits and tendencies anchored in misconceptions of permanence. The sixth step, purification, results in cultivating special powers that enable *seeing truly*, for the first time, the true nature of *dharmas*: this is wisdom (*prajñā*). Oddly, however, this wisdom is equated with sense-faculties, for example, the eye, as in "seeing truly." The reason proffered is that the object of the eye is immediately perceived, it is real, and that it does not refer to knowledge arrived at through imagination or conceptual construction. That is, seeing *dharmas* truly for the first time amounts to non-conceptual awareness of *dharmas* without any conceptual cloak. This *prajñā* is the true teaching of Abhidharma and is equated with the achievement of the highest understanding or *Bodhi* achieved through meditative cultivation preceded by scriptural knowledge and rational inquiry. This state puts the meditator surely on the path to deep meditation to enlightenment, becoming a Buddha.

This ends the preliminary discussion of the distinctive Abhidharma theses. The brief discussion in this chapter should give the reader a sense of how the Abhidharma ontology of *dharmas* ties together Buddhist metaphysics, epistemology, and soteriology.

1.6 Conclusion

This chapter was aimed at placing the Abhidharma tradition within the broad corpus of Buddhist thought. The distinctive Abhidharma theses are derived from the *Sūtrānta* literature. In this chapter, I have shown that the various Buddhist traditions, their respective schools, and thinkers offer their own precisifications and versions of the *Nikāyas*. This chapter should leave the reader in no doubt that this book is not about "the" Buddhist no-self view, for there is no such thing. Rather this book develops "a" Buddhist no-self view, specifically Vasubandhu's no-self view. In the next chapter, I begin by placing this view in the contemporary landscape of self/no-self debate.

2

Self/No-Self in Abhidharma Philosophy

2.1 Introduction

Buddhist conceptions of no-self are best understood against a background analytical framework within which we place the different conceptions of self. The diversity of views in contemporary and classical sources makes the task of formulating an integrated conception of self impossible. It is difficult, if not fruitless, trying to combine these diverse and often competing positions. The best we can do, is to settle for a pluralism about the concept of self. Pluralism might not be palatable to someone who wishes to offer a unified theory of self, but, fortunately, that is not my aim in this chapter or in this book. My first aim in this chapter is to locate Vasubandhu's no-self view in the contemporary landscape of the self/no-self debate. I will argue that pluralism about the concept of self, combined with eliminativism about the ontology of selves, provides a way of locating Vasubandhu's and other Buddhists' no-self views in an analytical framework. These views can thus be understood as showing that for any given conception of self, there is nothing in the world that fits it. Vasubandhu's version of the Abhidharma no-self theory specifically targets the background Hindu conception of self as eternal conscious substance (the subject of experiences and the agent of actions) but is also concerned with the views about persons held by other Buddhists. After presenting a framework for the Buddhist no-self views in section 2.2, in section 2.3 I shall present Vasubandhu's argument for this no-self view. This argument reveals Vasubandhu's strategy which consists in showing that there is no need to posit a self because it is causally impotent. It is the different components of the "mental" that do the work usually assigned to the self. Vasubandhu, unlike many contemporary Buddhist philosophers, is not suggesting that the work of the self can be transferred to conventional persons or any other self-like entities or processes. The second aim of this chapter is to show that Vasubandhu does not posit persisting persons to do the work of the self.

Vasubandhu's no-self and no-person view is, without doubt, deeply counterintuitive. As a consequence, ancient and contemporary Buddhist philosophers acquiesce in recovering some sort of conventional person to do the work of the self in a no-self universe. Vasubandhu, however, does not fall into this trap. Though he acknowledges the distinction between ultimate and conventional reality, he denies that merely conventional entities, persons in this case, can do any real

Selfless Minds: A Contemporary Perspective on Vasubandhu's Metaphysics. Monima Chadha, Oxford University Press.
© Monima Chadha 2023. DOI: 10.1093/oso/9780192844095.003.0003

causal work. In section 2.4, I analyze two influential attempts by contemporary philosophers, Sidertis (1997) and Ganeri (2007), to introduce conventional persons to carry the burden of the self in the Buddhist no-self universe and show why they are flawed. To reconstruct a person from the scraps of the no-self view is, I think, to misunderstand the strategy employed by Vasubandhu. To be true to Vasubandhu's spirit and argumentative strategy, rather than reconstructing persons to do the work of self, we should aim to explain conscious experience and thought about the world in a self-less universe. That is the one of the main aims of this book.

2.2 A Framework for Buddhist No-Self Views

In the intellectual milieu of ancient India, where Brahmanical views dominated the philosophical landscape, the Buddha put forward a revisionary metaphysics lacking a "self" to provide an intellectually and morally preferred picture of the world. This view is deeply counterintuitive, and Buddhists are acutely aware of that fact. To evaluate the merits of the preferred Buddhist worldview, the first task is to understand the target of the no-self doctrine. This is important in the contemporary context as interest in the idea of self (and no-self) is not just restricted to analytic philosophers and phenomenologists, but is also displayed by a variety of scholars in other disciplines including psychology, neuroscience, developmental psychology, psychiatry, anthropology, cultural studies, and so on. As a result of this growing interest, there are many different conceptions and notions of self in the contemporary literature. Correspondingly, there are many different versions of no-self views championed by contemporary Buddhist and non-Buddhist philosophers. I am not going to attempt a taxonomy of the different notions of self in the literature, for no such taxonomy is immune to revision. Furthermore, such a taxonomy would raise additional questions about the relations between different notions, some of which are complementary and others conflicting.[1] Nor will I make the assumption, as some in the literature do, that the target of all Buddhist no-self accounts is the Brahmanical or Hindu view of self as a substantial, independent, and unchanging self existing apart from mental and physical states (Thompson 2014). Rather, I will argue that Buddhist schools and philosophers present no-self theories targeting different conceptions of self. There are three views one might adopt regarding the concept of the self.[2] We might be:

---

[1] Many taxonomies have been offered in the literature; see Ganeri (2012a), Zahavi (2005), Strawson (1999), and Neisser (1988).

[2] I am indebted to Tim Bayne for suggesting these three ways of thinking about the concept and ontology of self.

Monists: there is a single concept of "self."
Pluralists: multiple concepts are associated with "self."
Eliminativists: there is no coherent notion of "self."

Arguably, contemporary and ancient Buddhists endorse pluralism: multiple precisifications of "self" give rise to various versions of "no-self." But there are exceptions. Ganeri (2017) puts forward a monist account of self. In responding to Johansson's (1985) claim that *citta* can be regarded as "core self," Ganeri writes: "The 'core self,' *citta*, is a surrogate self... and cannot properly be called 'self' if, as the thinker-rule maintains, it is fundamental to the functional role of that [the self] concept that it is what provides experience with agency" (2017, p. 331). Thompson (2014), on the other hand, embraces pluralism. Although, he labels his Madhyamaka Buddhist inspired view as the "enactive view" of the self, the systematic development of the view shows multiple conceptions of self at play. The process of "I-making" or self-construction happens at the biological, psychological, and social levels, which results in three distinct conceptions of self: a bodily conception, a psychological conception, and a social conception. It is hard to pin eliminativism about the concept of self on any contemporary Buddhist philosopher. The best contemporary advocate of this view is Olson, who says:

> People often speak as if there were a serious philosophical problem about selves...I doubt seriously that there is any such problem. Not because the self is unproblematic, or because there are unproblematically no such things as selves. My trouble is that a problem has to be about something: even if there are no selves, there must at least be some problematic idea or concept of a self, if there is to be a problem of the self. As far as I can see there is no such idea. What is a self? For every answer to this question, there is another answer not only incompatible with it, but wholly unrelated. There is virtually no agreement about the characteristic features of selves: depending on whom you believe, selves may be concrete or abstract, material or immaterial, permanent or ephemeral, naturally occurring or human constructions, essentially subjective or publicly observable, the same or not the same things as people. There are not even any agreed paradigm cases of selves, things we could point to or describe and say, "A self is one of those." But no concept could be so problematic that no one could agree about anything to do with it. For lack of a subject matter, there is no problem of the self. (1998, p. 645)

Eliminativism, as Olson explains in the above quote, is the result of looking for a monist conception of self: a coherent set of characteristic features that are individually necessary and jointly sufficient for the concept of self. The lack of subject matter is the result of failing to find the one central, true, or privileged concept of self. In addition, the quote above suggests that monism about the concept of self is difficult, if not impossible, to defend. There is, in fact, no particular conception of self that would be the uncontroversial winner of the title "self'" in any discussion in philosophy or other disciplines concerned with notions of selfhood. Olson is right, the monist concept of self is fraught with problems. Once we abandon the monist concept and are willing to embrace pluralism about the nature of self, the problems of the self reappear. Furthermore, there are other independent reasons to favor pluralism about the concept of self. First, there are several constraints on the concept of self, and it is not clear that they can or should operate together. To give the reader a flavor of the constraints and their competing requirements, I consider some next. I do not mean to suggest that these constraints are exhaustive or that they are ranked in any order. It is simply a list to motivate the case for pluralism about the concept of self.

First, consider introspection. What is the data furnished by introspection? And how seriously should we take that data? According to Blackburn's philosophical dictionary, there is no such data: the self is "the elusive 'I' that shows an alarming tendency to disappear when we try to introspect it" (1994, p. 344). The opposition insists that the self is something inner that I take myself to be, but that it is private and ineffable. If it is so private and ineffable then the data is not going to be of much use in a philosophical debate about the self. So, introspection delivers no useful answer to the question: what, if anything, is the concept of self?

Perhaps we should turn to linguistic considerations. What kind of self do our linguistic practices require? What is the self conceived of as "the referent of I"? It is often taken as platitudinous to say that "I" refers to oneself as oneself; when I use "I," I cannot fail to refer to myself. Furthermore, there is no possibility of misidentifying myself. But what is this "I"? Kant calls the self the "poorest of all representations" (Kant 1998 [1787], B408). Descriptively, the self-concept picked out by "I" is exceedingly thin and we cannot draw any metaphysical conclusions from it (Nichols 2014). Furthermore, there is the possibility of thinking I-thoughts under amnesia (Perry 1977). A total amnesic can think, "I have a headache," even though he has no distinctive descriptive content associated with "I." Some clinical evidence can be found for this from cases of patients with Alzheimer's disease using the first-person indexical frequently and appropriately, even in late stages of the disease (Tappen et al. 1999). This leaves it quite open as to what the self really is to which the "I" refers, but it is not entirely empty of categorical information. Nichols (2008) offers the following example: the thought that "I am a curtain" seems somehow defective. Such information is, however, too limited to lead us to a concept of self.

Perhaps we should turn to metaphysical considerations. What kind of self does metaphysics require? There are a variety of views in the philosophical literature. Peter Strawson (1959) suggests that selves are the owners of mental and physical states, the one and the same thing to which we can ascribe M and P predicates. He calls them "persons" (Strawson 1959, p. 41). Galen Strawson (2000) makes a thinner claim: wherever there is an experience, there must be a subject. Experience in its nature is an experiencing by a subject. Thus, he defends the claim that selves are objects, minimally a mental thing distinct from other things, a "conscious feeler and thinker," a unified thing, and a thing that in its nature need not, and does not, last long, being there for what he calls a "hiatus-free" period of experience. This "most fundamental way of conceiving of the subject" is that of a minimal subject of experience, which is identical with the experience itself and lasts as long as the experience lasts (Strawson 2000). Ganeri stakes out a different position inspired by his Buddhaghosa. The concept of self is that of a "detached author, the simple origin of willed directives" (Ganeri 2017, p. 3). The self as the "author" is an agent that is detached from action and experience.

How do we decide between these competing metaphysical conceptions? Is acting more central than experiencing or thinking? Are they complementary notions? Even if they are, the kind of self-conception that Galen Strawson and Jonardon Ganeri are putting forth does not necessarily commit us to a permanent substratum self, nor is there any talk of the self being physical. But for that very reason, they both seem suspiciously thin to satisfy ordinary ways of thinking about the self. Peter Strawson's notion probably has more chance of fitting in with the ordinary conceptions of the self, but then it is way too thick and thus much more constrained than what is required to satisfy linguistic considerations, which incidentally are also very important to him. In addition, the thick conception of a self-same persisting thing is brought under stress by thought experiments and actual situations. These show that psychological and bodily predicates or properties cannot always be ascribed to the same thing. We learn this from the well-known thought experiments discussed by Williams (1970) and Parfit (1984). Actual cases involving patients suffering from late-stage dementia and Alzheimer's disease mentioned above also suggest the same (Tappen et al. 1999).

Next, we turn to religious, moral, and prudential considerations. What kind of self do these considerations motivate? Religious considerations point towards a self as a persisting (even beyond death) thinking thing (St. Augustine 2003 [1467]). Moral considerations suggest a deep self, thought of in terms of psychological traits that one identifies with and values (Sripada 2015). Practical considerations like social treatment and compensation do not track a single notion of self. Shoemaker (2007, 2011) argues that our practical concerns are commonly thought to track a psychological notion of self, but sometimes these concerns can track biological continuity as well. He offers the case of a person who has total psychological discontinuity because of a traumatic brain injury; we still continue to treat her as the owner of her property, and also as a spouse of the pre-transformation person's spouse, parent of her daughter, and so forth.

We can choose to put aside these philosophical considerations and, as a last resort, turn to common sense. What do ordinary people think about when they are thinking of the self? But here too, there is no canonical conception of self.

Empirical research indicates that people really do have at least two different ways of thinking about personal identity, one in terms of psychological traits and another that conforms more closely to a biological criterion (Tierney et al. 2014). There is also some evidence in favor of a primitivist conception, especially in cases where we are thinking about future pain (Williams 1970). Changes in psychological traits and biological traits do not have any effect on anxiety about future torture. Tierney et al. (2014) conclude that folk views regarding the self are best characterized by adopting pluralism.

Prima facie there is no reason to reject any of these considerations, nor is there reason to rank some as more fundamental than the others. While some of these considerations clearly point towards plural conceptions of self, there are others that point to a more specific conception, but they do not offer any reason to rule out other conceptions of self that will respond to different considerations. The upshot of this discussion is that there is a variety of considerations that constrain the concept of self, and these competing constraints do not provide us with a unified concept. Monism about the concept of self is therefore not tenable. Olson's eliminativism leaves us without any understanding as to what to make of our ordinary thought and talk about the self and other considerations that invoke the self.[3] The best option for us then is to favor pluralism about the concept of self.

Presumption in favor of pluralism about the concept of self is also warranted by the fact that pluralism not only fits with what people say but also captures folk practices. And on many views of metaphysics, folk conceptions define domains (e.g., Lewis 1972; Jackson 1998; Strawson 1959). Frank Jackson defends this view by noting that until we have defined the subject matter, we cannot make progress on metaphysical questions. Jackson writes:

> What...are the interesting philosophical questions that we are seeking to address when we debate the existence of free action and its compatibility with determinism...? What we are seeking to address is whether free action according to our ordinary conception or something close to our ordinary conceptions, exists and is compatible with determinism.   (1998, p. 31)

I think that the folk concept of self, at the highest level of abstraction, is whatever it is in virtue of which one persists over a lifetime (and possibly beyond). But what does that tell us about someone's concept of self? Not much more than

---

[3] Olson's approach is to eliminate the self and turn his attention to persons instead. Compared to self, Olson thinks, person is a model of clarity and accord (Olson 1998). But is that really the case? In her anthology focused on the history of the concept of person, Antonia LoLordo identifies at least five important concepts that capture different uses of "person": as a particular, as a role (initially as part in a play, later as legal, political, or social role), as a morally significant individual, as a rational being, as a self (LoLordo 2019). There seems to be no single concept of person that is compatible with all of these conceptions. "Persons," it seems, are not much better off than "selves" after all.

whatever it is, it is independent of psychological and physical traits because they do not persist over a lifetime and certainly not beyond. An independent substantial self certainly presents itself as a plausible candidate for the concept of self. This concept is the target of many Buddhist no-self views, especially Vasubandhu's which is of interest to us here. But the plausibility of this candidate as a "good enough deserver" of the name "self" does not mean that other candidates for the concept self are ruled out; many contenders remain. It should be no surprise then that pluralism about the concept of self is rampant in contemporary philosophy. Galen Strawson (1999) tops the list with twenty-one concepts, Jonardon Ganeri (2012a) offers eleven, Alex Watson (2014) offers three, Dan Zahavi (2003) offers three, Shaun Nichols (2014) offers two, and so on.

One might be concerned that pluralism is not theoretically satisfactory. We might be faced with the problem of too many selves in one home/body. But note that pluralism about concepts does not lead to overcrowding, because pluralism about concepts does not commit us to a pluralism about ontology of selves. Pluralism about the concept of self leaves open various views of the ontology of selves: monism, pluralism, and eliminativism. Ontologically speaking, given pluralism about the concept of self, monism about the ontology of self is rather unlikely. Pluralism about the ontology of selves is threatened by incoherence from several quarters. Olson raised the problem of too many thinkers in one body (2007) and also the epistemic problem raised by the too-many-thinkers worry: how do you know which one is you? (2009). Furthermore, numerical identity is a one-to-one relation, one cannot be identical with more than one thing in the future. All of these are genuine concerns, but they arise only for someone who proposes pluralism about the ontology of selves. I think we should resist such a view.[4] My suggestion is that the best way to represent the variety of no-self views in the Buddhist literature is to be pluralist about the concept of self but eliminativist about the ontology of selves.

Following this suggestion, we can place various Buddhist views in this framework. It will be best to start with the Buddha's view. In his second sermon, the "Discourse on the Definition of No-Self," the Buddha uses the doctrine of the five *skandhas* (aggregates, i.e., material form, consciousness, perception, disposition, and feeling) individually and as a group, to show that nothing among the aggregates could count as a self. The aggregates are not permanent, they lead to suffering, and they are not controlled by the self. Buddha's conception of self thus requires that if something were to be a self, it (i) would not lead to suffering, (ii) would be in control of the aggregates, and (iii) would be permanent (Williams, 2000).

Although Williams ascribes this view to the Buddha, we cannot talk about it, or indeed any other Buddhist view, as the Buddhist view. Buddhism is a plural tradition. It contains many schools of thought and within every school many

---

[4] For a recent defense of ontological pluralism about selves, see Tierney (2020).

philosophers, each of whom champions their own particular version of the no-self view and their own particular argument for it. Despite this plurality, there are some commonalities in their target conception of self. The self that they deny is the permanent inner core that does the experiencing and the acting. It is important to note that this concept of self captures the core of the common-sense or folk view of the self. This is because Buddhists are not only interested in targeting the Hindu philosophers' concept of self as an eternal substance but also have the common-sense concept of self in their sights. In the *Abhidharmakośa-Bhāṣya*, Vasubandhu's target conception of self is that of a permanent substance existing independently of the mental and physical states. But he also targets the more common-sense notion of a person in the same chapter. You can think of self as an independent substance (as the Hindus do) or unitary persons that depend on physical and mental aggregates (as some fellow Buddhist Pudgalavādins do), but both notions are causally impotent and thus unreal. This makes clear that Vasubandhu himself is a pluralist about the conception of self and an eliminativist about the ontology of any candidate self.

Before we move to a detailed discussion of Vasubandhu's no-self view, it might be useful to give the reader a flavor of pluralism within the Buddhist tradition by mentioning other Buddhist no-self views. I offer two examples, one from the Abhidhamma tradition and the other from the Madhyamaka tradition. In the *Visuddhimagga*, Buddhaghosa's target conception of self is that of an "author of actions and experiences." To counteract such a proposal about the self, Buddhaghosa proposes that we find no internalized central controller. Rather the human being is like a mechanical doll, whose movements seem as if they are produced by an inner directing self. But these appearances are misleading. There is no such self inside that does the bending and the stretching, the eating, the putting on of robes, etc. In the *Mūlamadhyamakakārikā*, Nāgārjuna targets the conception of self as distinct from both our body and our psychological states, as essentially unchanging, as a unifier of our diverse beliefs, desires, and sensory impressions, and as an agent that makes the decisions that shape our lives. To counteract such a proposal about the self, Nāgārjuna suggests that we do ascribe mental and sensory states to a single self but our ascriptive practices do not commit us to the existence of the self at the ontological level. All there is, is a complex causal network of psycho-physical aggregates which are interconnected in a complex web. Let us now explore Vasubandhu's target conception of self and person and his argument for the no-self and no-person view.

2.3 Self and No-Self in Vasubandhu's Philosophy

Vasubandhu begins Chapter 9, *Refutation of the Theory of Self*, of the *Abhidharmakośa-Bhāṣya* with the question: How do we know that the term "self" refers to a series of aggregates (*skandhas*) of mental and physical atoms (*dharmas*) and not to something else? He responds by saying that we know this because no proof establishes the existence of a self apart from the aggregates. According to Vasubandhu, there are only two instruments (*pramāṇas*) of valid cognition or knowledge (*pramā*): perception and inference. We can know the objects of the five senses and the objects of mental consciousness by direct perception. And we can know about the existence of sense-faculties on the basis of inference. Sense-faculties can be inferred as a *cause* from the fact that even though some of the causes of perception—external objects, light, attention, etc.—are present, the blind and the deaf cannot perceive the objects because their sense-faculties are faulty. Thus, we can infer the existence of the sense-faculties—eye, ear, etc.—as a cause whose presence together with the other factors brings about a sense perception. But it is not like this for the self. We cannot perceive the self, nor are there any considerations that would lead us to infer or postulate a self; so, we can conclude there is no self (Pruden 1988). Vasubandhu's initial argument against the existence of the self is that there is no self because there is no perceptual or inferential evidence for one.

Before I look at Vasubandhu's argument in detail, I want to comment briefly on the structure of the argument in the *Abhidharmakośa-Bhāṣya*. Kapstein (2001) and, more recently, Kellner and Taber (2014) suggest that Vasubandhu's argument is basically an epistemological argument. According to Kellner and Taber (2014), the argument against the existence of the self in the *Abhidharmakośa-Bhāṣya* is example of an argument from ignorance, a general argumentative strategy used by Vasubandhu in the *Viṃśika* to refute the existence of external objects. The argument from ignorance may seem like a bad strategy. Arguments from ignorance seem to have the following fallacious form: since *P* is not known or proved to be true, *P* is false. But from the fact that the general form of an argument is fallacious or invalid, it does not necessarily follow that every instantiation of the invalid form is necessarily invalid. Arguments instantiating fallacious forms can be sound because of other features, for example the semantic meanings of the terms, contextual features, etc. Kellner and Taber (2014) emphasize that some arguments from ignorance are successful when they function as arguments to the best explanation, especially in contexts where there are agreed-upon standards of verification. For example, the medical community agrees that the most accurate and sensitive test for typhoid is testing the bone marrow for salmonella-typhi bacteria. If it turns out that it cannot be proven that one has typhoid (because of the absence of this bacterium in one's bone marrow), then it is false that one has typhoid. No matter how suggestive the symptoms are, if the specific bacteria does not show up in the bone marrow within a specific time period, then one does not have typhoid. So, then, the question is: Is Vasubandhu's argument from ignorance successful in refuting the existence of self? Arguments from ignorance cannot work with the single premise that *P* is not known or proved to be true, to the conclusion that *P* is false. In an extended study of arguments from ignorance, Walton (1995) adds a second premise: if *P* were true, it would have been known that

P. Kellner and Taber (2014) point out that Dharmakīrti, a leading philosopher of the later Abhidharma Buddhist tradition, introduces restrictions on the argument from ignorance to the effect that non-apprehension of a thing proves the non-existence of a thing only when the thing in question would have to be apprehended, were it to exist. Dharmakīrti's restriction adds exactly this second premise. Without this premise, Vasubandhu's argument from ignorance against a self can only have a presumptive status, its conclusion can be presumed to be true given that it is reasonable to assume that there is no counter-evidence. For a start then Vasubandhu's initial argument establishes that there is good reason to presume that the self does not exist. Vasubandhu then shows that there is no counter-evidence against this presumption by launching an attack against the postulation of selves by the Naiyāyikas and postulation of persons by the Pudgalavādins (Personalists).

The Nyāya concept of self is that of a permanent conscious substance that is independent of the aggregates and is the locus of conscious properties, like desire, aversion, pleasure, pain, etc. The Pudgalavādin concept of a person is that of a permanently existing thing that depends on the psycho-physical aggregates. Vasubandhu's strategy is to use the *Causal Efficacy Principle* (which I return to below) to show that selves and persons lack specifiable cause-and-effect relations and thus are causally impotent. Furthermore, although selves and persons are posited to causally explain ordinary notions, subjectivity, agency, moral responsibility, memory, etc., they are explanatorily redundant. Rather, Vasubandhu explains that the real causal work is done by psychological atoms (*dharmas*) like attention, intention, etc., and aggregates thereof (*skandhas*). Thus, selves and persons as persisting subjects, agents, knowers, and bearers of responsibility are causally irrelevant and so ultimately non-existent. Vasubandhu's central argument against the self can be reconstructed thus:

S1.   The self is presupposed to be a persisting conscious substance that exists independently of the psycho-physical aggregates. (Nyāya premise)

S2.   Everything that is real or substantial (*dravya*) is causally efficacious, having specifiable cause-and-effect relations with other entities. (Vasubandhu's claim [Gold 2021])

S3.   The self (as presupposed by the Naiyāyikas) is causally inefficacious since it does not have specifiable effects. (Vasubandhu's claim[5] [trans. Pruden 1988, pp. 1338–55])

SC.   Hence, there is no need to posit a self (as presupposed by Naiyāyikas).

Vasubandhu's hypothetical Nyāya opponent objects to S3 by claiming that such a self is implicated as the owner of experiences and the agent of actions. The

---

[5] *Abhidharmakośa-Bhāṣya*, Chapter 9.

Naiyāyikas ask: How can we make sense of agents of physical actions and that of the subject of experience and knowledge without there being a self? The list goes on: cognition, happiness, and pain are qualities had by a substratum. What is the substratum of these qualities; who is the referent of the notion "I"; who is the one who is happy or unhappy; and, finally, who is the agent of *karma* and the enjoyer of the results of *karma*? None of these questions, Vasubandhu argues, forces us to accept the existence of selves over and above the collections of psycho-physical atoms or aggregates. Each of these claims about the agents of action, subjects of experience, knowers, and bearers of moral responsibility, etc., can be reinterpreted so that it refers only to a causal series of psycho-physical elements (*dharmas*). For example, the Naiyāyikas ask, if there is no owner of experiences, whose is the memory? Vasubandhu's response is simply to say that there is no owner of memories just as there is no owner of cognitions more generally. Perceptions arise on account of their appropriate causes—that is, sense-faculty, object, and attention. Vasubandhu claims that ownership is just a matter of causal relations between two streams. The discussion with the hypothetical Nyāya philosopher as the objector in the text goes thus:

Objector: If a self does not exist, whose is the memory? "Whose" designates the owner.

Response: Explain by example how you understand that someone is the owner of the memory?

Objector: As Caitra is the owner of the cow.

Response: In what sense is Caitra the owner of the cow?

Objector: In that he directs and employs the cow as he pleases...

Response: One says that the "Caitra" series owns the "cow" series because the Caitra series is the cause of the geographic displacement and the various changes of the cow-series. There is not there any one, real entity "Caitra," nor another entity "cow" and there is not, for the Caitra series, any quality of owner or master outside the quality of being the cause of the movement, etc. of the cow-series.

Conclusion: There is no being-an-owner (of memory or cognition) above and beyond being-a-cause.

...

Objector: Who cognizes? Of whom there is consciousness?

Response: What's special here is the appropriate cause, i.e. sense faculty, object and, attention.

...

Conclusion: It is said that "consciousness cognizes" by being similar [to the object it represents] in nature without having done anything.[6] (trans. Kapstein 2001, pp. 368–9)

Next, Vasubandhu addresses the question: Is there an agent of actions? Who walks? His response is simply to say there is no agent of actions; action arises on account of its appropriate causes—walking is just the aggregates coming into being elsewhere on account of its causes.

Objector: And how does Devadatta walk?

Response: The instantaneous conditions in an unbroken continuum—which is regarded by childish persons, who grasp it as a unified lump of existence as the so-called "Devadatta"—are the cause of its own coming into being elsewhere, which is spoken of as "Devadatta walks." For "walking" is that very coming-into-being-elsewhere … an agentive term [is used to express] the cause. E.g., [in the phrase] "the bell cries," "a lamp-light moves."

Objector: Now, how does a lamp-light move?

Response: "Lamp-light" designates the continuum of a flame [similarly, Devadatta designates the continuum of aggregates]; it is said to move to a place whenever it comes into being elsewhere.[7] (trans. Kapstein 2001, pp. 368–9)

The need to postulate an agent for bodily actions like eating, bathing, walking, etc., is explained in the following manner. We do not need a self as the agent of an action of the body since we cannot infer it as a cause. Nor is there a need to postulate a self as the enjoyer of *karmic* fruits. The discussion continues:

Objector: There being no self, who is the doer of these deeds? And who is the enjoyer of their fruit?

Response: What is the meaning of "doer"?

Objector: The doer is the one who does, the enjoyer is the one who enjoys.

Response: Synonyms have been offered, not meaning.

Objector: The grammarians say this is the mark of the "doer": "the doer is autonomous."

Response: Now whose autonomy is there with respect to what effects?

---

[6] *Abhidharmakośa-Bhāṣya*, Chapter 9.   [7] *Abhidharmakośa-Bhāṣya*, Chapter 9.

Objector: In the world, Devadatta is seen with the respect to bathing, sitting, locomotion, etc.

Response: But what is it that you term "Devadatta"? If the self, then that remains to be proven. Then the five bundles? In that case, those are the doer. Moreover, this action is threefold: action of body, speech, mind. There, with respect to the actions of body [speech], they are undertaken depending upon the mind. And those of mind are undertaken depending upon a proper cause with respect to body [and speech]. That being so in that case, nothing at all has autonomy. For all things coming about depending on conditions...Therefore, no doer characterized [as autonomous] is apprehended. That which is the dominant cause of something is called its doer. But the self is not found to be a cause, with respect to anything. Therefore, there cannot thus be a self. For from recollection there is interest; from interest consideration; from consideration willful effort; from willful effort vital energy; and from that, action. So, what does the self do here?[8] (trans. Kapstein 2001, p. 373)

As is evident from these passages, Vasubandhu's strategy is to respond to each of these concerns by giving an alternative explanation of phenomena at issue by appeal to nothing but the psycho-physical aggregates and the relations of cause and effect combined with conventional practices or the way we talk about these phenomena. A self contributes nothing to the arising of an action. For example, in the case of the desire to eat, say a mango, the desire arises from a memory of enjoying a mango in the past. From this desire arises a consideration as to how it can be satisfied, and from that consideration arises an intention to move the body for the sake of satisfying the desire, which movement, say of the hand to acquire and cut a mango, then finally leads to the action of eating the mango. There is no need to invoke a self as the owner of the experiences or the agent of actions at any point in this explanation. For the Abhidharma Buddhist, the self is an ontological dangler without a causal role or explanation. Vasubandhu says that by the very fact that we cannot apprehend the capacity of the self, any more than the capacity of the various chants uttered by a quack doctor, for example *Phut! Svaha!*, when it is established that the effect has been brought about by the use of certain herbs, we must conclude that the hypothesis of the self is problematic (Pruden 1988). The point of these explanations is not just that there is a better alternative explanation of the phenomena, but that these alternative explanations show that there is no need to postulate or infer a self to explain them.

Vasubandhu's argument against persons begins by raising a dilemma for the Personalists. Is the person caused or uncaused? As Buddhists, Personalists must

---

[8]   *Abhidharmakośa-Bhāṣya*, Chapter 9.

reject the second horn of the dilemma. Everything in the Buddhist universe obeys the law of dependent origination. Persons cannot be uncaused or unconditioned. That cannot be a Buddhist view. If persons are unconditioned (that is to say, without a cause) they are useless (Pruden 1988). So, the Personalists must specify the cause of persons. In response, the Personalists offer the analogy of fuel and fire. Persons "depend on" the aggregates exactly in the way that the fire depends on the fuel but is neither the same nor different from it. Persons are not identical with the aggregates because persons persist over time whereas aggregates change. Nor are persons different from (understood as causally independent of) the aggregates, since they would then have to be uncaused, as nothing other than the aggregates exists. The only option, Vasubandhu insists, is to say that persons are not real, they exist in name only, they are mere conceptual constructions. The argument can be reconstructed thus:

P1.   The person is presupposed to be a persisting being that exists "depending on" the psycho-physical aggregates. (Pudgalavādin premise)

P2.   Everything that is real or substantial (*dravya*) is causally efficacious, having specifiable cause-and-effect relations with other entities. (Vasubandhu's claim [Gold 2021])

P3.   The person (as presupposed by the Pudgalavādin) is causally inefficacious since it does not have specifiable effects. (Vasubandhu's claim[9] [trans Pruden, pp. 1314–38])

PC.   Hence, there is no person (as presupposed by the Pudgalavādin).

Vasubandhu's opponents object to P3 by claiming that orthodox Buddhist positions in the scriptures imply that persons are causally efficacious. The Pudgalavādins ask, if there is no person, how can the omniscience of the Buddha be explained? How can we make sense of the talk of a "bearer of the burden"? Again, if there is no person, how can we make sense of claims that assert transmigration? And what are we to make of Buddha's claims that he remembered being this or that person in a previous existence? None of these statements, Vasubandhu argues, is to be taken as referring to or implying that there are persons. Each of these can be reinterpreted to refer only to aggregates (*skandhas*). In the discussion, the hypothetical Pudgalavādin opponent quotes the "*sūtra* of the burden-bearer" (*Bhārahārasūtra*) and asks if the aggregates were the person, why did [the Buddha] say the following:

---

[9] *Abhidharmakośa-Bhāṣya*, Chapter 9.

Objector: O monks, I will teach the burden, the taking up of the burden, the casting off of the burden, and the bearer of the burden.

Response: Why shouldn't this have been said?

Objector: Because the burden itself is not rightly the burden bearer.

Response: Why so?

Objector: Because this is not seen.

Response: Neither is it rightly ineffable.

Objector: Why so?

Response: Because this is not seen. It is then implied that the one who takes up the burden is not subsumed by the aggregates. The Fortunate Lord taught the meaning of the burden-bearer:

The one who is that long-living one, with such-and-such a name...up to...with such-and-such a longevity, with such-and-such an end to life.

What he has made known thus, should not be known otherwise, i.e., as "permanent" or "ineffable." The aggregates are painful in nature, thus they receive the name "burden"; the later aggregates are caused by the former aggregates, thus the later ones receive the name the "bearer of the burden."[10] (trans. Kapstein 2001, pp. 360–1)

For example, Vasubandhu's opponents the Personalists ask if only *skandhas* exist, how can we explain the words of the Buddha (Blessed one), who remembers, in the past life, I was the teacher Sunetra? Vasubandhu replies thus:

Response: Why shouldn't that have been said?

Objector: Owing to the difference in the aggregates.

Response: But if this were the person it would be eternal! Hence, "I indeed was Sunetra" denotes being one continuum of aggregates. In saying that, "I was the teacher Sunetra" he [Buddha] teaches us that the *skandhas* that constitute his present self formed part of the same series of *skandhas* that constituted Sunetra. In the same way, one says: "This burning fire has moved here."[11] (trans. Kapstein 2001, p. 366)

I will not evaluate the success of Vasubandhu's argument at this stage. I am well aware of the many concerns that might arise in the mind of the reader. One could be concerned about the outright dismissal of the suspected incoherence of the denial of the need for an owner of experiences, agent of actions, the bearer of karmic responsibility, etc. Or, one could be concerned about the adequacy of the

[10] *Abhidharmakośa-Bhāṣya*, Chapter 9.   [11] *Abhidharmakośa-Bhāṣya*, Chapter 9.

explanation of memory, intentional action, and moral responsibility, etc. These concerns are addressed in later parts of the book. For now, we will assume that there is good reason to think that Vasubandhu is right.

There are two important lessons to draw from the discussion in this section. First, Vasubandhu's strategy to argue against the existence of selves and persons is to show that they are causally irrelevant. This suggests that he is not willing to grant that persons are any more real than selves. Second, Vasubandhu's no-self view denies that there is an agent of action and owner/experiencer of perceptions, pleasures, and pains. Both points do not receive much attention in the contemporary literature on Buddhist philosophy. Regarding the first point, it is obvious that Vasubandhu would like us to be wary of talk about persons, but philosophers like Siderits (2015), Ganeri (2007, 2017), and Garfield (2015) are not worried by this point. I think, they should be. Since persons are causally inefficacious by Vasubandhu's standards, they cannot stand-in for selves and thus should not be expected to soften the blow of the revisionary no-self metaphysics. No doubt, our ordinary notions of memory, subjectivity, agency, responsibility, and, in the Indian context, the notions of *karma* and rebirth, require an explanation in light of the Buddhist no-self doctrine. It is a mistake to place this explanatory burden on the notion of persons since being causally inefficacious they cannot carry the burden of causal explanation. In this respect, they are just as useless as selves. Vasubandhu's strategy is to shift (cleverly) the explanatory burden away from the self and person to a mind (or minds) conceived of as a series of causally connected mental *dharmas*. This theme will be explored in Chapters 3–7. Regarding the second point, Vasubandhu would like us to embrace the view that we need not postulate agents for action and owners for experiences. Although there is much discussion of the no-agent view in the contemporary literature (Ganeri 2017; Dreyfus forthcoming), there is almost nothing on the no-ownership view. I suspect part of the reason for this shortcoming is that contemporary Buddhist philosophers think that such a view is incoherent, and therefore do not want to saddle Vasubandhu with it. I think that the no-ownership view can avoid this charge of incoherence and therefore deserves serious consideration, rather than hasty dismissal. This will be dealt with in detail in Chapter 7. My aim in this chapter is not to defend Vasubandhu's Abhidharma no-self view, but only to present it as the backdrop for a larger defense of the Abhidharma no-self view.

2.4 Contemporary Reconstructions of Persons in Buddhist Philosophy

The Abhidharma no-self account, particularly Vasubandhu's account that I have presented here, is not only counterintuitive, but also, some might say, indefensible. To defend it, some contemporary scholars reconstruct the account by introducing conventionally real persons to carry some of the burdens of the self. In this section, I analyze two such attempts by philosophers who argue that it is indeed possible to retrieve a useful notion of person from Vasubandhu's Abhidharma account. The question, then, is whether persons so introduced can do the work of the self. The Personalists obviously think so. Importantly for them, persons are carriers of *karma* (moral responsibility) in this life and future lives and the entities that attain *nirvāṇa*. According to the Personalists, persons are persisting entities since it is assumed that there is identity between the agent of the action and the experiencer of the fruits of action. Persons in this sense are agents of actions and owners/experiencers of the results of the actions. But, what are persons in Vasubandhu's accounts? We have seen that Vasubandhu argues that there is no need to posit agents and owners of experiences, so we do not need persons for that role. For him, "person" is a mere convenient designator for a complex series of aggregates.

Contemporary Buddhist philosophers, for example Ganeri (2007) and Siderits (2015), hold that persons as conceptual constructs are conventionally real, impermanent, impersonal psycho-physical atoms and causal relations. These contemporary reconstructions of the Buddhist no-self view misrepresent Vasubandhu's Abhidharma-Buddhist view. Let me explain how. These reconstructions draw on Vasubandhu's distinction between ultimate and conventional reality:

> That which does not have a cognition when it has been broken is real in a concealing way (*saṃvṛti sat*); an example is a pot. And that of which one does not have a cognition when other *dharmas* have been excluded from it by the mind is also conventionally real; an example is water. That which is otherwise is ultimately real (*paramārtha sat*).[12]   (trans. Ganeri 2007, p. 170)

Vasubandhu's examples are not very helpful. It might be useful to have a contrastive example of things that exist ultimately. The physical form of the pot is not ultimately real because it ceases to exist when the pot is broken, but the physical form of the ultimate constituent physical *dharmas* is ultimately real. Ganeri claims that this definition of conventional reality suggests that what is at issue is not so much the existence of social practices or conventional fabrications as opposed to metaphysically reality, but what we might call "stability under analysis" (2007, p. 171). To develop his claim, he uses the example of an impressionist painting that ceases to represent anything when investigated too closely. The idea is that persons are conventionally real in the sense that they slip out of cognitive focus when we "zoom in" and divide the person into the aggregates. But persons, Ganeri insists, should not be considered as subjective illusions; they are objectively

---

[12] *Abhidharmakośa-Bhāṣya*, 6.4.

real. Person-involving conceptual schemes are subject-specific or interest-specific; they *are* positional observations, but not subjective illusions for that reason (Ganeri 2007). Persons, in this sense, are not natural kinds. This does not imply that persons are not real, but they are artificial kinds. Person-involving conceptual schemes are artificially constructed; persons are real in the sense in which pots and heaps are real. Ganeri says:

> Vasubandhu does not seem to mean that persons are merely conceptual, that they are internal or subjective fictions. He seems to mean that reference to them is supported by a concept-mediated, fluid and aggregative model of classification, that the delimitation of the psychophysical raw materials out of which persons are made into individual streams is not simply a matter of cutting nature at its own hard natural joints. In fact, Vasubandhu does not say either that persons are "ultimately real" (*dravyasat*), or that they are not ultimately real; and his silence is well-motivated.   (2007, p. 167)

As we saw, in section 2.3, Vasubandhu clearly implies that persons are not ultimately real, since they are not causally efficacious. That is what the debate with the Personalists is about. Vasubandhu rejects the ultimate reality of persons; persons are "mere names," mere illusions of conception. Ganeri does talk about the Personalists' view, but he does not discuss Vasubandhu's refutation of their position. He concedes that, according to the Abhidharma Buddhists, conceptual schemes containing persons are ethically inadequate. He says, "we are not in error when we think of the world in a person-involving way; it is just that we could do better—ethically better—by thinking of it in some other way altogether" (Ganeri 2007, p. 174). But in this sense, person-involving schemes are no better than conceptual schemes containing selves. Person-involving schemes are ways of thinking about the world as organized into persisting persons, divided into me, you, ours, and others. There are no such persisting things or strict divisions and boundaries between persons at the level of reality. And, furthermore, thought and talk about persons is just as misleading as talk about selves, they are the results of ignorance and false conception that augment suffering. I will argue that Abhidharma Buddhists should not endorse such a scheme as objectively real unless they are willing to endorse a scheme containing selves as well.

Another prominent Buddhist scholar and philosopher, Mark Siderits, claims that Vasubandhu, and Abhidharma philosophers more generally acknowledge the reality of some composites in a "loose and popular" sense, even while they maintain that composites are not ultimately real. Siderits explains the Abhidharma position thus:

> The Abhidharma term for this "loose and popular" sense is "conventionally existent" (*saṁvṛti-sat*); things that exist in this way are termed conceptual constructions (they are *prajñapti-sat*). Abhidharma thus posits a two-tier ontology:

ultimately real entities (the *dharmas*) that are genuinely impartite or non-composite; plus the ontological back-benchers, those composite objects to which we express ontological commitment in our everyday speech and thought. The Abhidharma bias against the composite can be seen as an expression of their uncompromising realism about truth: the real is the concrete particular, and aggregation of particulars is the mark of the mental.   (2014, p. 437)

Siderits labels this Abhidharma position as mereological nihilism, the claim that only simples exist ultimately, composite things are not ultimately real. According to Siderits' favored version of Buddhist reductionism, only *dharmas* exist ultimately. However, Siderits agrees that persons are not ultimately real. But he thinks there is a key role for appealing to persons as part of the conventional truth. He writes:

Early Buddhism and Abhidharma have often mistakenly been seen as Eliminativist. The error arises through attending solely to what is said at the ultimate level of truth, and failing to appreciate the relation between the ultimate and conventional levels of truth. Eliminativism is not simply the view that talk of persons may in principle be eliminated. Both Reductionist and Eliminativist maintain that ultimately there are no persons. But the Eliminativist urges in addition that the claim that there are persons be seen as conventionally false as well, since the Eliminativist maintains that our commonsense theory of persons is incoherent, or at least so misleading as to be more troubling and confusing than theoretically useful. By contrast, the Reductionist holds that while unquestioning adherence to the commonsense theory of persons does result in misguided views about how we should live our lives, the theory does have its uses, which fact requires explanation; hence it is conventionally true, though ultimately false, that there are persons.   (1997, p. 465)

The foregoing gives the Buddhist Reductionists the license to use the expression "person" because it is useful for creatures like us to talk about persons. By labelling something as merely conventionally existent, we are claiming that it is not part of our fundamental ontology. It works as a convenient shorthand and thus is to be regarded as a useful fiction. Armed with the *Two Truths*, Siderits thinks, he can explain why the term "I" does not refer to any real entity and also explain our ordinary thought and talk about composites. The Abhidharma reductionist claims that, strictly speaking, chariots do not exist, and that "chariot" is just a convenient designator for *dharmas* arranged chariot-wise. Given the demands of everyday life, it is just easier for us to talk about the existence of ordinary enduring middle-sized objects, like pots and chariots. That ease reflects our interests and cognitive limitations. But it does not reflect how things really are. Siderits notes that "to allow those interests and limitations to colour our representations about how things are can sometimes lead to cognitive error, and erroneous beliefs can lead to harm" (2015, p. 98). Belief in the existence of pots and chariots cannot cause serious harm, but this tendency to posit pots as referents for our linguistic devices can lead us to think there is a single unified concrete particular whereas there are in fact many concrete particulars (*dharmas*) arranged pot-wise. In the case of "I," Buddhists believe that this tendency does serious harm as positing a referent for "I" leads to existential suffering. Siderits supposes that the referent of "I" is a self. This, however, is not true of our ordinary everyday use of "I" which refers to person and self interchangeably. According to Siderits, selves are harmful. Persons, however, are useful fictions. The question then is, what is the basis of Siderits' differential treatment of persons and selves?

I think it is best to examine this question in the light of the Buddhist views about selves and persons more broadly. According to Buddhists, selves are simple and exist independently of the aggregates, whereas persons are composites that exist dependently on the aggregates. In spite of these important differences between Buddhist philosophers' conceptions of selves and persons, they are afforded the same treatment by most classical Buddhist philosophers, except, of course, the Personalists. There are numerous places in the *Sūtras* where the Buddha does speak of "person." Buddhists do not want to say that the Buddha was lying or unwittingly making false statements. Siderits cites this as one of the reasons that the Buddhist philosophers must account for persons. Different schools in the Indian Buddhist tradition have different strategies for making sense of this talk of persons. Both the Abhidharma as well as Madhyamaka traditions hold that persons exist conventionally. There are some differences though. According to the Madhyamakas, the pragmatic usefulness of person-talk is important as a catechetical device for teaching the doctrine to the uninitiated. All talk of persons and other continuing entities is preliminary and merely provisional teaching meant to offer a transition from adhesion to worldly beliefs to the doctrine of universal emptiness (Eltschinger 2014). The Ābhidharmikas, on the other hand, do not think of "person" as a useful pragmatic device or skillful means, but emphasize that it is nothing but a conventional designation, a mere name for the group of aggregates (the collections of *dharmas*). Persons are nothing over and above series of aggregates which in turn are *collections* of *dharmas*.

No Buddhist wants to say that selves are ultimately real. So, what about the conventional existence of selves? Classical Buddhist philosophers readily admit that selves exist conventionally. Madhyamaka philosophers, for example Nāgārjuna, have no trouble speaking about selves as conventionally existent, as long as one does not think that this talk of selves is grounded in the ontologically significant substance–property distinction. It is nothing more than, as Westerhoff (2019) puts it, a shifting coalition of psycho-physical elements. Just like persons. Abhidharma philosophers, including Vasubandhu himself, admit that selves are conventionally real. In a passage not often cited in the contemporary literature, in Chapter 3 of the *Abhidharmakośa-Bhāṣya*, Vasubandhu opens the discussion of dependent origination (*pratītya-samutpāda*) by raising an objection from the opponents who believe in the self (*ātman*). The Buddhist belief in rebirth, according to the opponent, proves the existence of the self. Vasubandhu responds by saying that there is no self that takes up the aggregates at the beginning of life, abandons them at death, and takes on new aggregates in the next life; there is no internal agent of actions that abandons the aggregates at the end of this life and takes up new aggregates in the next one. The opponent then asks, is there any kind of self (*ātman*) that you do not deny? The reply here is revealing: "We do not deny an *ātman* that exists through designation, an *ātman* that is only a name given to the aggregates" (Pruden 1988, p. 399). The point simply is that Vasubandhu thinks that selves exist conventionally, as long as we are clear that the term "self" is just a name given to the aggregates. Just like persons. So, it seems that for these classical Buddhists selves have as much reality (conventionally speaking) as do persons.

Let us now return to the question of useful fictions. As we saw, the Madhyamakas (for example, Nāgārjuna) regard both persons and selves as useful fictions, while the Ābhidharmikas (for example, Vasubandhu) do not regard either as useful fiction. To them persons and selves are mere names, convenient designators that are nothing more than shorthand for the aggregates which are, ultimately, collections of *dharmas*. Again, it seems that for these philosophers either both persons and selves are useful fictions, or neither is. Siderits' position differs from these classical Buddhist philosophers. He wants to say persons but not selves are useful fictions. In some sense, Siderits' version of Buddhist reductionism combines the Abhidharma and Madhyamaka strategy. He says that the right way to think about the Buddhist Reductionist position is to say that the term "person" is both "tolerable (because of translatability), and of some utility given our interests" (1997, p. 457). Ordinary language does not provide a promising approach. Ordinary folk do not distinguish between self and person, perhaps because they have the same job description. In ordinary language, "person" is synonymous with "self," or at any rate there is no clearly marked semantic distinction between the two. It is important to note that the target of the Buddhist no-self theory, in particular its Abhidharma versions, is not just to reject the Hindu view of self in the Indian debate, but to diagnose a deep mistake in our ordinary primitive conceptual scheme (Ganeri 2012b). Ordinary ways of thinking about the self assume that the self, whatever it is, persists within a lifetime and possibly across lifetimes. And since psychological and physical properties do not persist over a lifetime, let alone beyond a lifetime, the self must be conceived of as independent of psychological and physical properties. What about the ordinary concept of person? Mostly, the concept of self and person are used interchangeably in the language, except that we hardly ever use the word "self." We use reflexive pronouns like "myself" and "yourself" to claim identity with the thing that is referred to by the "I" or "you." What is that thing? Self or person? There is no settled common-sense view about the nature of this self/person duality except that it undergirds our identity over time. In other words, our ordinary talk of "I" does not distinguish between self (*ātman*) and person. Thus, it is hard to see how we can use common sense as motivation for justifying that persons are a useful fiction, but selves are not. Given that the notion of useful fiction is tied to folk usage of terms like persons and selves, and that folk usage does not distinguish between the two, either both are useful fictions or neither is. There might be other grounds to push for an asymmetry between selves and persons. In a recent paper Siderits writes:

> Why do most Buddhists think that people should be reductionists and not eliminativists? If eliminating belief in the self is important to the project of overcoming suffering, then why stop at half measures concerning the person? The answer is to be found in something Buddhists say concerning personal identity over a single lifetime... One example given in this text is that of a criminal who does not appropriate earlier and later parts of the series. Predictably this individual fails to take responsibility for his past crime, sees his present punishment as unjustified, and persists in criminal behaviour after release. Clearly, adoption of the personhood concept promotes practices we wish to encourage.
>
> (2019, pp. 315–16)

Siderits is presupposing that persons, conceived of as the bearers of *karma*, are persisting loci of agency and responsibility at least during a lifetime (and possibly across lifetimes). And this notion of person seems to share the very features that lead Abhidharma Buddhists to view selves with suspicion and reject the Personalists' notion of person. In any case, thinking of persisting persons as useful fictions comes with a huge cost.

Furthermore, the standard Buddhist arguments for the non-existence of the self derive from the fact of impermanence or momentariness (Siderits 2011). But the notion of person seems to be caught up precisely in persistence beyond the momentary. Persons are just as ethically problematic as selves because they can be equally responsible for our sense of being the same thing within and across lifetimes. The central Buddhist teaching is to extirpate the false sense of "I" and in that endeavor, the conventional posit of person cannot be a useful fiction; it will be an obstacle.

In addition, Buddhist soteriology aims at escape from existential suffering. The core Buddhist idea is that we suffer because we mistake there to be a persisting being which is the referent of "I" and is the sole locus of meaning and value. The Buddhist insight is that there is no such persisting thing, everything that exists is transitory. If there is no persisting being, there is no locus of value and meaning, irrespective of whether we think it is a simple self (that exists independently of the aggregates) or a composite person (that exists dependently of the aggregates).

This also grounds an argument for compassion. Ultimately, we are collections of physical and mental *dharmas* causally related to future and past *dharmas* within a series and with other series of *dharmas*. This way of looking at the world undermines the basis of "me" and "mine," and "others" that are distinct from me. Thus, there is no basis for discriminating between "my" suffering and that of "others." The aim of the Buddhist teaching is to reduce all suffering, impersonally and selflessly. The concept of self, therefore, must be rejected because it distorts this Buddhist vision. It creates artificial distinctions between "me" and "others" and thereby increases suffering. It seems that the concept of person will do the same, and, therefore, should be rejected for the same reasons. Persons are fictions to be sure, but for the Buddhist they seem to be no more useful than selves.

I have argued that in critical respects, selves and persons are at par for Buddhists. Both selves and persons are causally irrelevant. Therefore, both are conceptual constructs and so ultimately not real. In addition, I have argued that, at least for Abhidharma Buddhists, selves and persons seem to be equally problematic from a soteriological perspective: they are a result of flawed ways of thinking about the world and these ways of thinking create suffering. So, I think, contra Siderits, eliminativism about persons and selves is the right way to think about Vasubandhu's position. For the Buddhist, persons, like selves, should be regarded as dangerous fictions, not useful ones. Eliminativism about persons comes at a cost to our person-related practices and concerns. For example, persons in the absence of selves can play the role of agents for actions and bearers of moral responsibility for the results of the action. Without selves and persons, we cannot hold each other accountable for what we do. The costs of adopting the Abhidharma Buddhist selfless and personless scheme will be discussed later in Chapters 8 and 9.

2.5 Conclusion

In this chapter, I have shown that the best way to think about Buddhist no-self views is to regard them as embracing pluralism about the concept of self and eliminativism about the ontology of selves and person. This gives us a nice way of thinking about Vasubandhu's no-self view among the many other Buddhist views. Vasubandhu, following the Naiyāyikas, thinks that an important way to think about the self is as permanent conscious substance, as the substratum of conscious states. But he leverages the explanatory redundancy as a reason to show that there is no need to postulate an independently existing substratum of conscious states. He uses the *Causal Efficacy Principle* to argue against the postulation of selves and persons. The challenge for Vasubandhu is to explain, or explain away, the phenomenology of ownership and agency without a subject and agent. We return to this in Chapters 6 and 7. These are not, however, the only challenges for Vasubandhu's no-self view. The additional Abhidharma commitment to momentariness and mereological nihilism poses further challenges. These will be explained, in detail, in the next chapter where I will also offer a defense on part of the Abhidharma philosophers against the challenges posed by the commitment to momentariness and mereological nihilism. And, of course, there are the concerns about diachronic and synchronic unity of experiences which were raised by the Hindus in classical India. These will be dealt with in Chapters 5 and 6.

3

The Abhidharma Buddhist Account
of Conscious Experience

3.1 Introduction

A main aim of the Abhidharma Buddhist schools is to provide a systematic and phenomenologically informed account of experience by analyzing conscious experience into its constituent mental and physical factors. Accordingly, Abhidharma writings are replete with attempts to explain phenomenological and other features of our experience of the world in the absence of selves. Any such Buddhist account of experience, however, faces serious challenges because of the cardinal tenets of their revisionary metaphysics: the doctrine of mereological nihilism and the doctrine of impermanence, the latter of which is transformed into the doctrine of momentariness in the Abhidharma period (Ronkin 2018). Although much scholastic attention in the classical and contemporary Abhidharma literatures has been focused on the issues of continuity and causation of mental states, there is not much discussion specifically about the constitution of conscious experiences.

The Abhidharma Buddhists are committed to what appear to be deeply problematic claims. First, the claim that only individual *dharmas* are ultimately real and conscious experiences are collections of *dharmas* seems to lead to the conclusion that conscious experiences are not ultimately real. Second, rich conscious experiences, say listening to a melody, have temporal width and are not made fully available in a moment. The commitment to momentariness thus seemingly conflicts with such experiences. Third, empirical research shows that the temporal extent of a conscious perceptual state must necessarily exceed that of the present moment (e.g., Pockett 2002, 2003). The Abhidharma philosophers regard sensory perception as the paradigm of conscious experience, but apparently their account cannot accommodate perceptual experiences as they require some temporal width.

Some of these concerns have been raised in the contemporary literature. Siderits (1997, 2015) argues that Abhidharma Buddhists promote mereological nihilism, the view that only simple *dharmas* are ultimately real. This leads him to the bracing conclusion that consciousness, or subjectivity, is not ultimately real. It is at best a useful fiction (Siderits 2011). I call this the "Subjectivity Challenge." The conflict between momentariness and conscious experience has also been explored in different contexts in contemporary phenomenology and analytic

Selfless Minds: A Contemporary Perspective on Vasubandhu's Metaphysics. Monima Chadha, Oxford University Press.
© Monima Chadha 2023. DOI: 10.1093/oso/9780192844095.003.0004

metaphysics. I discuss two challenges that result from this conflict. The first, I will call the "Phenomenological Challenge." This primarily concerns the temporal properties of what is represented in conscious experience. The second, I will call the "Metaphysical Challenge," which concerns the temporal properties of conscious representation itself. A version of the Phenomenological Challenge has been raised by Zahavi against the Abhidharma denial of a persisting self as the principle of diachronic unity (2012). Zahavi raises this challenge specifically against Dreyfus' Abhidharma account which endorses synchronic unity but not diachronic unity (Dreyfus 2011b). A version of the Metaphysical Challenge has been raised by Le Poidevin (2011) and McKinnon (2003) concerning temporal properties of conscious representation. The challengers believe that the temporal extent of a conscious state must necessarily exceed that of the present moment. This version of the Metaphysical Challenge is a longstanding issue in the phenomenology of time, but so far it has not been explicitly raised as a concern for the revisionary Abhidharma metaphysics. I will present a reconstruction of this challenge as a problem for Abhidharma philosophers.

There has been little attempt in the literature so far to respond to these challenges on behalf of the Abhidharma philosophers. In this chapter, I shall explore these challenges and offer a resolution of these genuine concerns on behalf of Vasubandhu and Abhidharma philosophers. The plan of the chapter is as follows. In section 3.2, I offer a brief reconstruction of the Abhidharma account of conscious experience. In section 3.3, I discuss the Subjectivity Challenge and argue that although it is possible that Abhidharma philosophers favored mereological nihilism, there is reason to doubt that they would (or should) sustain their commitment to mereological nihilism in light of the implications drawn out by Siderits. In sections 3.4 and 3.5, I discuss, respectively, the Phenomenological Challenge and the Metaphysical Challenge, and show that the Abhidharma view of consciousness is vulnerable to these challenges. The final section 3.6 will discuss how the Ābhidharmikas might address these challenges that arise due to their commitment to momentariness. A satisfactory response on behalf of the Ābhidharmikas will incorporate features of consciousness brought out by the later Sautrāntika-Yogācāra philosophers and some later representatives of the earlier Sarvāstivāda tradition. This is to be expected: Abhidharma is best understood as an evolving tradition. Its most important protagonist, Vasubandhu himself, as mentioned in the introductory chapter, studied in the Sarvāstivāda traditions, founded the Sautrāntika doctrine, and later in his life became a Yogacārin.

3.2 Abhidharma Account of Conscious Experience

The Buddhist analysis of experience maintains that what we experience as a temporally extended, uninterrupted flow of phenomena is, in fact, a rapidly occurring sequence of causally connected events, each with its particular discrete object. To explicate this, Buddhist philosophers decompose the world and ourselves in it into a causal sequence of evanescent mental and physical states (*nāma-rūpa*). Though there are various construals of this central Buddhist doctrine in the literature, the best way to understand the notion of *nāma-rūpa* is as that of a minded-body (Ganeri 2017). In Abhidharma Buddhism the minded-body is further analyzed into *dharmas*, which are discrete momentary physical and mental factors.

On the Abhidharma picture, mind is not a substance or central processor that produces experiences and thoughts; rather it is an aggregate of many simultaneous series of mental *dharmas*. Phenomenologically speaking, these mental *dharmas* are best thought of as "phenomenologically basic" features that constitute conscious experience (Dreyfus 2011b). This does not, however, mean that the phenomenological features are readily available in ordinary introspection. The claim is that mental *dharmas* are in principle available in first-person experience, though discerning the *dharmas* requires meditation practice. Indeed, some *dharmas* are better thought of as subliminal mental factors that can be brought to the surface only through sustained meditation practice. Metaphysically speaking, it is best to think of *dharmas* as tropes (Ganeri 2001; Goodman 2004). *Dharmas* are neither substances nor universals, they are property-exemplifications, e.g., the whiteness of snow is a particular white. Mental *dharmas* are located in time and physical *dharmas* are located in space and time. Vasubandhu regards objects such as pots and persons as nothing over and above the *dharmas* that make them up, just as trope theorists think of composite physical objects as nothing more than aggregates of tropes. So, for example, Vasubandhu was an aggregate of physical tropes, Vasubandhu's color, Vasubandhu's height, etc., and mental tropes, Vasubandhu's intelligence, Vasubandhu's attention, etc. Vasubandhu's color and intelligence are similar to Asaṅga's intelligence and color; they both are exemplifications of intelligence but there is no property or universal "intelligence" that they both exemplify. According to the Abhidharma view, *dharmas* or property-exemplifications are all there is.

In Buddhist epistemology, sensory perception is the paradigm of conscious experience. According to most Abhidharma schools, sensory perception is always intentional, and is brought about by an interaction among the sense organs (e.g., eye), the corresponding type of consciousness (e.g., visual consciousness), and their appropriate sense objects (e.g., form, color, etc.). On this view, the objects of experience are not unitary and stable particulars, like tables, planets, etc., but complex and ephemeral formations of basic momentary events (*dharmas*) arising within complex causal nexuses. A key thesis of Abhidharma philosophy of mind is that experience is constituted by psychologically primitive processes that normally lie below the level of phenomenal consciousness. All schools agree that there are, at a minimum, five universal factors that accompany every conscious mental state: contact (*sparśa*), attention (*manasikāra*), feeling (*vedanā*), discrimination (*saṃjñā*), and intention (*cetanā*). The role of these mental factors in conscious experience becomes obvious if we take into account that the mere coming together of an object, sense-faculty, and its corresponding consciousness is not sufficient for a conscious experience to arise. The senses always process a steady stream of sensory impressions, some clusters of which become a concrete object of conscious experience only when attention is directed toward specific regions of the perceptual field. Attention, thus, is necessary but not sufficient for conscious experience. Intention, in addition to influencing action, is also necessary as it is responsible for tying together all the concomitant *dharmas* to produce ordinary conscious experience, for example, seeing a mango. A similar analysis can be offered for the role of other universal mental factors, namely contact, discrimination, and feeling, in the constitution of conscious experiences. Concrete objects of conscious experience are created by the interplay of these five mental factors. Ganeri puts it succinctly:

> The great elegance and attraction of the [Abhidharma] theory lies in the fact that simultaneously it recognises the irreducibility of the phenomenal character of experience, it admits the joint contribution of sensation and conceptualisation in the constitution of experience, it acknowledges that experience is, as it were, saturated with affect, that appraisal is built into the fabric of experience, it maintains that every experience has, as a basic ingredient, a capacity or tendency to combine in various ways with various others, and it makes the attention intrinsic to experience.   (2012a, p. 127)

The Abhidharma schools disagree about the number, classification, and role of these features in experience. So, the Abhidharma philosophers take great pains to provide ever new lists and classifications of mental *dharmas* and detailed arguments to justify the proposed revision. However, Abhidharma schools agree on the starting point for grouping the mental factors: they are primarily classified as good (*kusala*), bad (*akusala*), and neutral (*abyākata*). "Good" (*kusala*) is defined as that which is salutary, blameless, and skillful and thus reduces suffering. "Bad" (*akusala*) is just the opposite; it is unhelpful, blameworthy, and unskillful and augments suffering. Some mental factors are wholesome or good in themselves, e.g., compassion, wisdom, etc.; others are unwholesome or bad in themselves, e.g., anger, greed, craving, etc.; and yet others are neutral e.g., equanimity, resolve, etc. The moral valence of a given conscious state or thought, i.e., whether it is good or bad, is determined by the moral valence of mental factors that comprise conscious thought and experience. For example, a thought associated with compassion would be good because compassion is a good factor; a thought associated with equanimity would be indifferent because equanimity is disinterested; a thought associated with greed and ignorance would be bad because greed and ignorance are bad factors.

The overarching aim of the Abhidharma philosophy is to cultivate the wholesome mental factors and eradicate the unwholesome ones. This, in turn, will ensure a prevalence of good thoughts, intentions, and actions and thereby reduce suffering. How does one go about identifying the good and the bad factors? The Abhidharma answer is to turn to the tradition as a repository of moral knowledge delineating the good and bad factors. However, experienced teachers also suggest a turn to moral phenomenology. The idea is to pay attention to how thoughts or actions appear or feel to a person. In developing their moral phenomenology, Buddhists begin by noticing that the pursuit of sense pleasures is typically mixed with hardship and disturbances in the mind because such pursuits involve greed and craving for more of the same. In contrast, by purifying the mind through restraining oneself from indulging in sense pleasures, one "experiences internally an unmixed ease (*sukha*)"[1] (Davis 2016, p. 143).

For example, loving-kindness and compassion, by their very presence in the mind, have a calming influence and result in easing the mind. Good and bad thoughts and actions can both appear joyful and pleasurable, but only bad thoughts cause distress and disturb the mind. In the Abhidharma psychology, good or wholesome (*kusala*) thoughts are never painful or distressing, though they can be neutral. They are felt as neutral when they are experienced through equanimity and disinterest. The thought is that we focus on experientially available distinctions to figure out which mental factors are wholesome or good. Wholesome factors can be differentiated from unwholesome ones in that the former involve a healthy and uplifting state of mind in contrast to the latter that distress and disturb the mind.

The Abhidharma philosophers are not concerned with distinguishing mental states and processes from other mental factors. They are concerned with the action-guiding role of these states, factors, and processes, but it bears emphasis that these actions are set in the context of the guiding principle of reducing suffering in the world. Thus, the primary division among mental factors will be in terms of whether they reduce suffering (good) or increase suffering (bad) or have no effect on suffering (neutral). Ignoring the neutral factors for now, a partial list of good and bad factors is reflected in Table 3.1 to give the reader a sense of the Abhidharma typology.

This brief sketch of the Abhidharma phenomenology and metaphysics shows that it is susceptible to many challenges. The Ābhidharmikas take the phenomenology of experience as the primary data to be explained by the *dharma* metaphysics.

---

[1] *Majjhima Nikāya*, 58.

Table 3.1 Mental factors organized by moral valence

Mental factors with good moral valence	Mental factors with bad moral valence
Right view (*sammādiṭṭhi*)	Wrong view (*micchādiṭṭhi*)
Right thought (*sammāsaṅkappa*)	Wrong thought (micchāsaṅkappa)
Right effort (*sammāvāyāma*)	Wrong effort (*micchāvāyama*)
Right concentration(*sammāsamādhi*)	Wrong concentration (*micchāsamādhi*)
Right mindfulness (*sammāsati*)	
Non-greed (*alobha*)	Greed (*lobha*)
Non-hatred (*adosa*)	Hatred (*dosa*)
Non-delusion (*amoha*)	Delusion (*moha*)
Non-covetousness (*anabhijjhā*)	Covetousness (abhijjhā)
Non-malice (*abyāpāda*)	Malice (*byāpāda*)
Shame (*hiri*)	Shamelessness (*ahirika*)
Fear of wrongdoing (*ottappa*)	Fearlessness (*anottappa*)
Impartiality (*tatramajjhattatā*)	Pride (*māna*)
Compassion (*karuṇā*)	Self-contempt (*omāna*)
Sympathetic joy (*muditā*)	Envy (*issā*)
	Avarice (*macchariya*)
	Remorse (*kukkucca*)

Experiences give us information about objects having a spatial and temporal extension, e.g., seeing a table, hearing a melody, seeing an apple falling, etc. However, the *dharma* metaphysics permits only simple, momentary, point-like existents in the present instant. But how long is a moment? There are different answers given by different Abhidharma schools. Vasubandhu, for example, says sixty-four moments pass in the time it takes a healthy man to snap his fingers.[2] Are there any composites? Yes, there are, but they are only conventionally real, for example, pots, water, etc. Neither the ultimately real objects of experience nor the conscious states representing those objects are spatio-temporally extended, because nothing is. Direct realism gives way to representationalism. This representationalist stance gives the Abhidharma philosophers some additional resources to explain the phenomenology of conscious experiences by an appeal to more than what is *given* to the senses in the present infinitesimal moment. However, this account, inescapably, needs to deal with the concerns discussed below.

3.3 The Subjectivity Challenge

The "chariot analogy" provides what is perhaps the most famous example in Buddhist philosophy. As part of an argument that there is no self, Nāgasena

---

[2] *Abhidharmakośa-Bhāṣya*, 3.85b–c.

convinces King Milinda that the notion of a chariot is merely conventional; the chariot is not ultimately real. Here is part of the exchange:

NĀGASENA: Is it the pole that is the chariot?
MILINDA: I did not say that.
NĀGASENA: Is the axle the chariot?
MILINDA: Certainly not.
NĀGASENA: Is it the wheels, or the framework, or the ropes or the yoke, or the spokes of the wheels, or the goad that is the chariot?
MILINDA: No.
NĀGASENA: Then is it all these parts of it that is the chariot?
MILINDA: No, Sir.[3] (trans. Davids 1969 [1890], pp. 43–4)

At this last step, Milinda concedes immediately without protestation. But that seems altogether too quick. Of course, the reins are not the chariot, and the yoke is not the chariot. Nor do the parts of a chariot dispersed in a field make a real chariot. But when those parts are composed into a chariot that conveys the king from place to place, at that point it seems that the chariot is indeed a real thing, not just a convention.

Presumably there is a missing premise here. One premise that would do the required work is to appeal to the *Two Truths* doctrine which claims that chariots, like pots, are not ultimately real, since they can be deconstructed into parts. Obviously, there is no thing that is both simple and chariot. Siderits promotes this way of thinking about chariots as flowing from Abhidharma views, according to which, "the real is the concrete particular, and aggregation of particulars is the mark of the mental" (2014, p. 437). This applies to the case of the chariot; in particular:

> [A] chariot is actually not a real thing. The parts are real, but the whole that is made up of those parts is not. The whole can be reduced to the parts, it isn't anything over and above the parts. This is the view known as "mereological reductionism." (Siderits 2007, p. 54)

More recently, Siderits calls this view "mereological nihilism" (2015). Mereological nihilism seems incredible since it denies the reality of all partite things. Most of the concepts we use involve partite things: persons, planets, neurons, molecules, mountains, rivers, tables, computers, and so on. According to mereological nihilism, none of these things "really" exist. Abhidharma Buddhists, according to Siderits, embrace a more thoroughgoing nihilism that advocates that there are no

---

[3] *Milinda Pañha*, 25–7.

enduring substances at all (2015). On this reading of the Abhidharma texts, the only things that are ultimately real are individual *dharmas* (elements or tropes). Substances, on this view, are analyzed into bundles of tropes. So, Siderits claims, "there will ultimately be no elementary particles, nor will the dualist or idealist be able to claim that there are at least minds" (2015, p. 97).

Siderits' version of Abhidharma reductionism has a striking conclusion— mereological nihilism—that the only things that are ultimately real are fundamental elementary tropes, the *dharmas*. Composites are, at best, useful fictions. Chariots are not *dharma* and neither are planets, nor organisms, nor even neurons. These are all useful fictions. These particular implications may not worry Abhidharma Buddhists, but there is one implication that will be concerning. It seems conscious experiences are composed of aggregates of *dharmas*. Is consciousness (*citta*) a simple and thus ultimately real? This question is not an easy one to answer since the treatment of consciousness is equivocal in Abhidharma Buddhist literature. *Citta*, which is usually translated as consciousness, sometimes signifies a single conscious *dharma* but is also used to signify what we would call an ordinary conscious experience. Consciousness in this literature is sometimes conceived of as a single *dharma*, or as a conscious experience which is an assembly of *dharmas*, and, even more surprisingly, sometimes as one of the psycho-physical aggregates (*skandhas*). For example, envy (*īrṣyā*) is unwholesome consciousness (*akusalacitta*), which is consciousness accompanied by hatred (one of the unwholesome mental factors). Ordinary conscious experience of envy involves negative feelings (*vedanā*), intention (*cetanā*) to act in a certain way towards the envied object, and so on, but these mental factors (*cetasikas*) are not ordinarily experienced as separate factors; they form the whole experience of feeling envious. Ronkin presents a model of the Abhidharma account of *citta*:

> The archetype of the operation of consciousness is *citta* as experienced in the process of sensory perception that, in Abhidharma (as in Buddhism in general), is deemed the paradigm of sentient experience. *Citta* can never be experienced as bare consciousness in its own origination moment, for consciousness is always intentional, directed to a particular object that is cognized by means of certain mental factors. *Citta*, therefore, always occurs associated with its appropriate *cetasikas* or mental factors that perform diverse functions and that emerge and cease together with it, having the same object (either sensuous or mental) and grounded in the same sense faculty. Any given consciousness moment— also signified by the very term *citta*—is thus a unique assemblage of *citta* and its associated mental factors such as feeling, conceptualization, volition, or attention, to name several of those required in any thought process. Each assemblage is conscious of just one object, arises for a brief instant and then falls away, followed by another *citta* combination that picks up a different object by means of its particular associated mental factors.   (2018)

The key claim here is that a conscious *dharma*, e.g., a sensation arising from contact between a sensory organ and an object, can never be experienced in its own right. Ordinary conscious experience, on this view, is a unique assembly of various mental factors (feeling, intending, categorizing, etc.) that arise and cease together with the sensation. Thus, although the mental factors (*dharmas*) constituting it are simultaneously present in the same temporal moment, an ordinary conscious experience is not itself a single *dharma* (see also Ganeri 2012a; Chadha 2015). The Abhidharma reductionist seems to be committed to the following inconsistent triad:

S1.   Everything that is a composite is unreal.
S2.   Conscious experiences are real.
S3.   Conscious experiences are composites.

Most philosophers reject S1 but the Abhidharma nihilist, according to Siderits, must accept S1 and so must reject either S2 or S3. It is not always clear whether Siderits thinks Abhidharma Buddhists should reject S2 or S3. On the one hand, Siderits notes that mereological nihilism does not stand in the way of affirming the ultimate existence of conscious *dharma*s (2011), which suggests rejecting S3. The rejection of S3 is not straightforward though. The problem is that simple *dharmas* are not available as contents of ordinary conscious experiences. For example, although *hiri* (often translated as shame) which, as we saw in the Abhidharma typology above, is a simple *dharma*, it is not experienced as a standalone *dharma*. The experience of *hiri* is accompanied by other *dharmas*, positive feeling (*vedanā*) and intention to avoid evil acts (*cetanā*); the feeling component and the right intention are part and parcel of the emotion of *hiri*: the constituent *dharmas* are not experienced as separate *dharmas* in ordinary awareness. Ordinary conscious experiences are composites of multiple *dharmas*. Indeed, it seems that rejecting S3 also requires us to reject ordinary sensory perceptions as ultimately real. For the Abhidharma, however, sensory perception is the paradigm of conscious experiences and sensory experiences always involve the universal *dharmas* and perhaps more. We might choose to focus on other examples from the tradition, but then we need an alternative analysis of conscious experiences in terms of simple *dharmas* on behalf of the Abhidharma. Siderits does not offer any such analysis.

On the other hand, were Siderits to reject S2, the Abhidharma reductionists would need to maintain that conscious experiences are at most useful fictions. Siderits seems not concerned by this implication. He suggests that Buddhist reductionists do not have a good explanation of the phenomenal aspect of our conscious states.[4] Siderits raises the following question: How can the Buddhist

---

[4] Vasubandhu, unlike later philosophers like Dignāga and Dharmakīrti, does not want to subscribe to the self-illumination or reflexivity thesis.

reductionist explain the phenomenality of conscious experiences? He offers the following as a solution to the Abhidharma reductionist:

> By way of an abductive inference from the global availability of objects. Since global availability is just an aggregation of distinct causal pathways, it will come as no surprise that consciousness is a conceptual fiction, a single entity posited in order to simplify the task of data management. Just as it seems to us that there is a chair when the parts are assembled in a certain way, so it seems to us that there is the conscious state of seeing a chair in my path to the door when the chair is made available not only to the action-guidance system (as in blind-sight) but also to the memory system, the speech system, etc. We can thus understand why it is that, despite there being no such thing as what-it-is-like-ness, it would seem to us that there is such a thing. Subjectivity is a useful fiction.
>
> (2011, pp. 326–7)

Siderits claims that Abhidharma reductionism implies that ultimately there is no subjectivity, and no conscious experience. These are just useful fictions, like persons, pots, and chariots. Siderits writes:

> The Buddhist Reductionist stance on consciousness and the self depends crucially on mereological reductionism, the view that the composite entities of our folk ontology are conceptual fictions, conventionally but not ultimately real.
>
> (2011, p. 315)

There are key elements of the Abhidharma tradition that run strongly against the idea that conscious experiences are merely useful fictions. Conscious mental states are responsible for guiding behavior and action. For example, conscious experiences of *hiri* partly consist in forming the intention to avoid evil acts and partly in feeling good about forming that intention and perhaps more. Such an experiential state is a mereological whole of many *dharmas* (*hiri, vedanā, cetanā,* etc.). And this whole is causally efficacious. Therefore, it must be regarded as real by the criterion for reality adopted by the Ābhidharmikas (Gold 2021). This criterion of "causal efficacy," as noted in Chapter 2, is used by Vasubandhu to argue for the non-existence of selves and persons. Since conscious experiences are causally efficacious, they are good candidates for being real.

Siderits' version of Buddhist reductionism forces the Ābhidharmika account of conscious experiences to its logical conclusion to deny the ultimate reality of conscious experiences. But I doubt that the Ābhidharmika philosophers would want to go that far. Siderits might not be worried by the implication that conscious experiences are merely useful fictions, but I think that the Ābhidharmikas would want to backtrack and reconsider the commitments that led them to the conclusion that meditative states and ordinary conscious experiences are just useful fictions. They may want to re-examine the analyses which have led them to this conclusion and be cautious about endorsing a thoroughgoing mereological nihilism. The Abhidharma tradition aims to offer analytical methods for exploring and transforming human experience. On Siderits' picture, the basic unit of interest—human experience—turns out to be nothing but a useful fiction. I think the Abhidharma Buddhists would (or should) consider rejecting S1. Denying the reality of human experience is to deny the very fabric of what it is to be human; no Buddhist would want to go that far. In section 3.6, I will offer a nuanced rejection of S1 which requires minimal revision of the Abhidharma analysis of conscious experience. We will see that the proposed revision uses resources made available by later Abhidharma philosophers to solve other internal problems faced by the Ābhidharmikas.

3.4 The Phenomenological Challenge

Zahavi (2012) explicitly raises the concern that the Abhidharma view of conscious experiences is incoherent because of its commitment to momentariness. Though Zahavi is not directly addressing the ancient Abhidharma school, his challenge to Dreyfus' analysis of the Abhidharma account of subjectivity is germane to their account of conscious experiences. Dreyfus' interpretation of the *Yogācāra-Sautrāntika* doctrine allows for synchronic unity of experiences: self-specified experiences that at any given moment are reflexively transparent to the momentary conscious state itself.[5] However, he denies diachronic unity since there is no temporally extended and persisting self:

> This [Buddhist] response rests on the distinction between two senses of who we are: the subject, or, rather subjectivity, that is, the continuum of momentary mental states with their first-personal self-givenness, which are central to being a person...and the self, which is an illusory reification of subjectivity as being a bounded agent enduring through time, rather than a complex flow of fleeting self-specified experiences. Hence, the perceptions, thoughts, and memories that arise within the continuum of my mind are not impersonal. They are clearly mine in the sense of there being no possible doubt about who is the subject of

---

[5] Dreyfus' discussion is focused mainly on a Yogācāra inspired view of consciousness rather than a Sautrāntika view. Dreyfus ignores the question whether the Yogācāra view entails a form of idealism or not. His concerns are different, being limited to "cognitive and phenomenological considerations, which are not always usefully connected to metaphysical or ontological questions" (2011b, p. 116). In effect, Dreyfus is ignoring the major point that differentiates the Sautrāntika and Yogācāra views: the former's representative realism versus the latter's idealism. As far as cognitive and phenomenological doctrines are concerned, the Sautrāntika and Yogācāra views agree with each other. What is important for my purposes here is that Zahavi's criticism applies to the Abhidharma doctrine of momentariness, which is shared by the Sautrāntika and Yogācāra views.

these experiences. But this does not entail that there is an act-transcendent pole of identity, an entity that endures before and after the moment of experience, in relation to which I can establish that these experiences are mine, for all that there is is a succession of self-aware subjective states. (2011b, pp. 130–1)

Zahavi's challenge to this position, what I call a version of the Phenomenological Challenge, is motivated by Husserl's claim that "the perception of succession and change is impossible if perception only provided us with access to a momentary or now-slice of the object and if the stream of consciousness itself was a series of unconnected points of experiencing, like a line of pearls" (Zahavi 2012, p. 151). There are two distinct targets here: our consciousness of temporally extended objects and our awareness of our own conscious states. Husserl maintains that our phenomenology makes clear that we are directly experiencing succession and change, rather than remembering or imagining it. Regarding the first target, Husserl asks: How is it possible for us to be conscious of objects with temporal extension, e.g., melodies which unfold over time? He answers this by arguing for the width of presence: the basic unit of temporality is not a knife-edge present—a moment, as the Sautrāntikas would say—rather, it is a field in which the now, not-now, and not-yet-now are given in a horizontal *gestalt*. Just like time, consciousness itself, according to Husserl, has a temporal structure which is spelt out using the semi-technical triad: protention-primal impression-retention. A primal impression is narrowly directed towards the contemporaneous now-slice of the object. However, it is an abstraction never directly given in experience, but extracted from within a past (retention) and a future oriented (protention) temporal context. The primal impression is always embedded in the temporal context of a retentional aspect, which provides a consciousness of the just-elapsed slice of the object, and a protentional aspect, which in some way intends the slice of the object about to occur. This triad is given as a unified whole in our ordinary conscious experiences.

Regarding the second target, Zahavi following Husserl claims that retention, for example in hearing the past notes of a melody, is not accomplished by literal re-presentation of the notes, but by retention of my just-past experience of the melody. The so-called present consciousness retains not merely the just-past tones but also the just-past phase of consciousness. The point can similarly be extended to protention: the so-called present consciousness protends (intends in the future) not merely the just-future tones, but also the just-future phase of consciousness. These retentional and protentional processes do not merely supply a temporally extended object for our conscious experience; they constitute the very identity of an object in a manifold of temporal phases, and also provide us with non-observational, pre-reflective, temporal consciousness (Zahavi 2012). According to Husserl, consciousness is not in need of any transcendent principle of unification, a reflective metacognition, or a synthesizing ego, because consciousness is by nature temporally extended and self-unified. The principles that constitute experience have a dual function as they are also the glue for the diachronic unity of consciousness. The central point is summarized by Zahavi thus:

> For [Husserl]...even the analysis of something as synchronic as a present experience would have to include a consideration of temporality, since every experience is a temporally extended lived presence. For the very same reason, we should reject Dreyfus' attempt to make a clear-cut distinction between synchronic unity and diachronic unity. You cannot have synchronic unity without some kind of diachronic unity (if ever so short-lived). To claim otherwise is to miss the fundamental temporal character of consciousness.   (2012, pp. 153–4)

To summarize: the general upshot of the Phenomenological Challenge is that the content of a minimal experience must have some temporal width; it cannot be the knife-edge present. If Zahavi and Husserl are right, then phenomenological analysis of experience spells serious trouble for the Abhidharma (at least the Sautrāntika) account of conscious experience.[6] However, before I offer a response on behalf of the Abhidharma Buddhist to these concerns, I will discuss another challenge to their view: the Metaphysical Challenge.

3.5 The Metaphysical Challenge

Unlike the Subjectivity Challenge or Phenomenological Challenge, the Metaphysical Challenge is not directly aimed at a Buddhist or Abhidharma account of conscious experience. Instead, it aims at theories of time: McKinnon (2003) aims it at presentism, whereas Le Poidevin (2011) presents it as a challenge for the A-Theories of time, which treat presentness as not being a matter of perspective. What is

---

[6] A similar worry which draws its inspiration from James' slogan that a succession of awareness is not an awareness of succession has been raised by Dainton (2000) and Tye (2003). The thought is that instantaneous experiences cannot account for the phenomenology of the experience of succession. Dainton puts the point thus:

> We are constantly aware of phenomenal contents undergoing passage, there is constant flow and continual renewal of content. This experienced passage is both continuous and homogeneous...If experiences were packaged into discrete units this would not be the case. (2000, p. 129)

Dainton offers the phenomenologically primitive relation of *diachronic co-consciousness* as the glue for the unity of consciousness. It is hard to understand this "*sui generis*," "unanalyzable," basic experiential relation because Dainton does not do much more than characterize it in negative terms. Co-consciousness is not itself an experience, nor does it depend on further experiences (except those it relates) or any other sort of awareness. Diachronic co-consciousness, it seems, is meant to provide the phenomenological glue that confers phenomenal unity and continuity but, as far as I understand, it adds no explanatory value to the phenomenological account offered by Husserl. The pre-reflective consciousness that accompanies every experience provides the common factor that binds together all of one's experiences over a reasonable breadth of time; positing the relation of co-consciousness over and above such a consciousness is multiplying relations without necessity.

important, however, for our purpose here, is that this challenge is premised on the empirical claim that conscious states are non-instantaneous. Insofar as the Ābhidharmikas claim that conscious states, like everything else in the Abhidharma Buddhist universe, are momentary, their account must face up to the Metaphysical Challenge.

The examples which motivate the Metaphysical Challenge are ordinary experiences of temporally unextended objects like feeling the prick of a needle as you get your flu jab, hearing a door bang as someone leaves the room, sensing an itch in your right toe, having the thought that all these experiences are co-conscious right at this very moment. An appeal to the phenomenology of one's present experience offers good reasons to argue that its having non-zero duration is an essential aspect of one's experience. We can strengthen this claim by appeal to evidence from the "hard" sciences: neuroscience and neurophysiology. Le Poidevin and McKinnon argue that instantaneous experiences are impossible because of constraints on thresholds for stimulus detection (conscious sensation) and for conscious perception. In what follows, it is useful to think of conscious sensations as the raw registration of some conscious event within a particular sense-faculty and conscious perception as a more complicated process which requires recognitional capacities and other conceptual abilities and is articulable as a judgment. The term "conscious experience" is used to cover both conscious sensations and perceptions. The simple model requires that a minimum level of energy impinges on some sense organ triggering a neural process that results in conscious perception. The neural processes happen at such high speed that subjectively they seem virtually instantaneous. Experimental evidence, however, reveals otherwise. A much researched and experimentally confirmed hypothesis called the *global neuronal workspace model* for conscious access imposes a temporal granularity on neural states in a stream of consciousness. This framework postulates that, at any given time, many modular cerebral networks are active in parallel and process information in an unconscious manner. Information becomes conscious when the neural population that represents it is mobilized by top-down attentional amplification into a brain-scale state of coherent activity involving many neurons distributed throughout the brain. The long-distance connectivity of these "workspace neurons," when they are active for some minimum duration, makes the information available to a variety of processes including perceptual categorization, long-term memorization, evaluation, and intentional action. This global availability of information through the workspace is what we subjectively experience as a conscious state. Dehaene and Naccache say:

> This [implementation of the workspace model] ... suggests the existence of two thresholds in human information processing, one that corresponds to the minimal stimulus duration needed to cause any differentiated neural activity at all, and another, the "consciousness threshold," which corresponds to the

significantly longer duration needed for such a neural representation to be mobilized in the workspace through a self-sustained long-distance loop. Stimuli that fall in between those two thresholds cause transient changes in neuronal firing and can propagate through multiple circuits (subliminal processing), but cannot take part in a conscious state.   (2001, p. 19)

Empirical evidence shows that the threshold for conscious sensation is different from the threshold for conscious perception. Pockett (2002, 2003) suggests that stimuli can produce conscious sensations in as little as 50–80 milliseconds (ms), while complicated judgments concerning the stimuli may require as much as 500 ms. This is in line with earlier studies. Efron (1967) estimated that a minimum of 60–70 ms of neural processing time is required for simple auditory and visual stimuli reaching the brain to result in any kind of experience. Regarding the threshold for conscious perception, Thorpe et al. (1996) report in a study published in *Nature* that the human visual system takes about 150 ms after stimulus-onset to process a complex natural image (to decide whether a previously unseen photograph of a natural scene, flashed on for just 20 ms, contains an animal). A more recent study by Sekar et al. (2013) suggests that it takes somewhat longer. The earliest response signal peak that correlates well with stimulus perception was observed at around 240 ms after stimulus presentation. This evidence suggests that all conscious states are temporally extended. But if conscious states are temporally extended, the Abhidharma view is in trouble.

According to the Abhidharma, more specifically Vasubandhu's Sautrāntika view, everything, including all conscious experiences, is composed of complex causal interactions among numerous momentary *dharmas*. This, however, does not entail that the resulting composite conscious experience made up of those *dharmas* must also be momentary. However, Vasubandhu is also committed to the view that only the present *dharmas* have causal efficacy. This is the reason why the Sautrāntikas are motivated by the "time-lag" argument to reject direct realism in favor of representationalism. If we accept Vasubandhu's thesis that all *dharmas* that compose a conscious experience must be co-temporally present in an infinitesimally short moment (as Sautrāntikas do), and that a moment is shorter than the threshold for conscious sensation, let alone a conscious perception (as the brain scientists tell us), then we are led to conclude that Vasubandhu's view lacks the resources to adequately explain conscious states; a serious shortcoming. The Abhidharma philosopher might respond by saying that our conscious experience of blue consists in a sequence of momentary proto-conscious *dharmas* that lie just below the threshold of conscious awareness. Just as there is my experience of being in the process of typing this paragraph, there is an experience of being in the process of having an experience of blue. A certain number of these momentary proto-conscious *dharmas* must occur in a sequence for us to have a conscious experience of blue. The brain scientists can tell us just how many of these are likely to constitute our conscious experience of blue. But there is a problem with this response. The Abhidharma philosopher should not agree that our conscious experience of blue is a series of momentary proto-conscious *dharmas*. For according to the Abhidharma view, only the present moment constituents are real. Being spread out over time, a series of such constituents is a fiction and thus unreal. While the elimination of such things as persons and pots is quite acceptable to the Buddhist, the elimination of conscious experiences should not be. If conscious experiences are eliminated, then the principal Abhidharma project to give an account of conscious experience collapses: phenomenological data are explained away, rather than explained.

In view of all this, the Metaphysical Challenge yet again forces the Abhidharma philosophers to face another inconsistent triad:

M1. Everything that is temporally extended is unreal.
M2. Conscious experiences are real.
M3. Conscious experiences are temporally extended.

While most philosophers reject M1, the Abhidharma philosopher accepts M1. The task then is to see whether she can defend M2, which means that she must reject M3. The challenge is then to offer a nuanced rejection of M3 on behalf of the Abhidharma in a way that does not compromise the reality of conscious experiences while accommodating the scientific evidence that conscious experiences are temporally extended.

3.6 The Mature Abhidharma Solution

In this section, I will explore a solution to all the three challenges raised above by combining resources made available by later Yogācāra-Sautrāntika philosophers and the general notions of supervenience and representationalism. In particular, I will refer to Asaṅga, a noted Yogācāra philosopher, the author of *Abhidharmasamuccaya* and at least the compiler of *Yogācārabhūmi*. I will also be relying on the work of Saṃghabhadra, a later representative of the Sarvāstivāda tradition, well known for his trenchant criticism of Vasubandhu's doctrine. The aim is to argue on behalf of Abhidharma philosophers that conscious experiences, contra Siderits, are ultimately real. It will be clear that the account is not incoherent as Zahavi suggests, nor empirically unviable as McKinnon and Le Poidevin may lead us to believe.

The canonical Abhidharma account of the mind reduces it to fundamental atoms constituted by six kinds of conscious experiences (*vijñānas*). Five of these correspond to the five sense organs (sight, touch, hearing, smell, and taste) and the sixth is mental cognition (*mano-vijñāna*). Asaṅga, the Yogācārin, introduced

two kinds of consciousnesses to add to this list: the basic or storehouse consciousness (*ālaya-vijñāna*) and afflictive mind or ego-consciousness (*kliṣṭa-manas*).
In another work, the *Karmasiddhiprakaraṇa* (treatise on action) Vasubandhu
endorses the storehouse consciousness (*ālaya-vijñāna*) to suggest a solution to
the problem of the relation between action and its *karmic* consequences (more on
this in Chapter 6). The storehouse consciousness is a neutral baseline consciousness that serves as a repository of all basic habits, tendencies, and *karmic* latencies
accumulated by the individual. The doctrine of basic consciousness is, in large
part, an attempt to show that there is mental continuity within a lifetime and across
lifetimes despite the *dharma* ontology in which there is no enduring substance.[7]
The afflictive mind can be thought of as an innate sense of self arising from the
apprehension of basic consciousness as being a self (Dreyfus & Thompson 2007).
This self, however, is not an ontological reality for Buddhists. It is merely a conceptual fabrication resulting from the (mis)apprehension of basic consciousness.
Basic consciousness is essential to explain the full bodied Abhidharma Yogācāra
notion of conscious experience. For my purpose here, it is sufficient to present a
philosophical reconstruction of this notion, rather than a historically accurate
rendering or an exhaustive account of the literature.

Basic consciousness is introduced as the "mind with all the seeds." Ordinary
perceptions (e.g., seeing, hearing, etc.) depend on basic consciousness in that it
provides the substratum for the sense-faculties and also fuels them (Waldron
2003). In turn, basic consciousness is fueled and seeded by the objects of ordinary
perceptions and reflection. There is, therefore, a two-way dynamic between basic
consciousness and ordinary perceptions. Basic consciousness, insofar as it contains
seeds or predispositions, produces conscious states (sometimes in association
with sense-faculties and their objects), say of seeing a mango, which, in turn,
accumulates further seeds, say the desire for a mango, into it. Thus, the Yogācāra-
Sautrāntika presents a dynamic model of the mind, wherein conscious perceptions
and other mental dispositions are tied together in a continuous feedback cycle
(Waldron 2003). Furthermore, basic consciousness is postulated as encompassing
the entire life of an individual as it is connected to our sense of embodiment and
described as pervading the entire body. It is the background awareness of more
than just the material body. It also includes the awareness, mostly subliminal, of
the predispositions (cognitive and affective conditionings persisting from the
past) and one's immediate environment (i.e., the surrounding world).

---

[7] The posit of "*ālaya-vijñāna*" is introduced primarily in what Schmithausen (1987) calls the "initial
passage" in the Basic Section of the *Yogācārabhūmi*. In this initial passage, basic consciousness is
described as a kind of unmanifest consciousness that persists within the material sense-faculties
during the highest meditative state ("*nirodha samāpatti*," literally translated as the "attainment of
extinction," signifying the extinction of perception and feeling). The later sections of the *Yogācārabhūmi*
also offer other proofs for the existence of *ālaya-vijñāna* some of which aim to provide a fix for the
problem of *karmic* continuity. However, it is important to note that *ālaya-vijñāna* is one of a number
of fixes proposed to deal with this problem.

As Dreyfus puts it, "basic consciousness is the baseline of consciousness, the passive level out of which the more active and manifest forms of awareness arise in accordance with the implicit preferential patterns that structure emotionally and cognitively this most basic level of awareness" (2011b, p. 144). Basic consciousness is, like everything else in the Abhidharma universe, a series of moments; it arises from moment to moment in dependence on conditions similar to those that give rise to ordinary manifest conscious perceptions. This background awareness is both subtle and continuous. To fix ideas, it is useful to think of proprioception which makes us continuously, though nebulously, aware of our bodies in relation to the surrounding world. Like proprioception, basic consciousness goes unnoticed as it is always present in the background. Although basic consciousness arises continuously in a stream of moments, it would be a mistake to regard it as a single unity (*ekatva*). The introduction of basic consciousness also marks a major departure from the traditional Abhidharma model of conscious awareness, according to which ordinary perceptions occur sequentially depending on nothing more than the contact between the sense-faculty and its object. Since the awareness of the embodied mind and the surrounding world is always present, it must occur simultaneously with other ordinary perceptions which, as we have noted above, in turn, depend on and are supported by basic consciousness. Once this "single awareness at each moment" requirement is abandoned, the Yogācārins accept multiple awarenesses, and indeed that all six kinds of manifest awarenesses, and countless many subtle ones in the background, could be simultaneously present. Basic consciousness is best thought of as background awareness—subtle but indistinct and continuous perception—of cognitive and emotional factors and bodily states that provides a rich inventory of proto-cognitive and proto-affective *dharmas* as support for any conscious state.

My interest here is to see whether the inclusion of basic consciousness in the Abhidharma model of the mind can help us respond to the above challenges. Basic consciousness makes available many more mental *dharmas,* co-temporal with current sensory inputs and conscious sensations, to constitute conscious experiences. The *dharmas* are not identical to conscious perceptions, although the perceptions, like everything else, are "made up" of momentary *dharmas*. The notion of being "made up of" can be captured by a supervenience relation between the tropes and the conscious experiences constituted of them. Saṁghabhadra notes that each *dharma* is potentially able to have two causal operations: one for bringing about the next momentary *dharma* in its series and another which transcends the series to bring about effects by combining with other co-temporal *dharmas* of other parallel series. P. M. Williams (1981, p. 246) helpfully labels these as "horizontal" within-the-series causality and "vertical" transcending-the-series causality, respectively. For example, a momentary *dharma* of a musical sound horizontally produces the next moment of musical sound and might, depending on the presence of other universal mental factors (e.g., attention, pleasant feeling, recognition of the note, etc.) vertically produce an auditory perception of a melody. Ganeri suggests that it is best to think of *dharmas* themselves as proto-intentional (proto-cognitive and proto-affective) processes that combine to constitute conscious experiences (2012a). The relationship between mental *dharmas* and conscious experience is described as one of joint-occurring (*sahabhu*) and enveloping (*anu-pari-vartante*) which is best cashed out in terms of supervenience.

However, it is important to note that *dharmas* or tropes are only logically, and not temporally, prior to the conscious experience: only present *dharmas* are real, they alone can be constituents of a conscious experience. Consider a present conscious experience of a mango. The *dharmas* that constitute color, shape, firmness, etc., are simultaneously provided by visual consciousness. But there are countless many other co-temporal mango-relevant *dharmas* available in the storehouse or basic consciousness (*ālaya-vijñāna*) that have evolved from the seeds deposited by previous encounters with mangoes. The conscious experience of a mango does not arise in the first moment of sensory contact with the mango, but the sensory contact sets off a chain of horizontal and vertical processes which might, depending on the availability of other universal mental factors, result in the production of the conscious experience of the mango. Specifically, the visual presentation of a mango gives rise to sensible qualities that constitute color, texture, smell, etc. These sensible *dharmas* horizontally cause contiguous color, texture, smell, etc., *dharmas* in the next moment. At the same time these momentary *dharmas* vertically cause processes in the basic consciousness, which activate stored mango-relevant *dharmas*. These activations produce new *dharmas* that come together with the requisite five universal mental factors resulting in the production of the conscious perception of a mango in that unique moment when all the relevant proto-conscious *dharmas* are co-present. The conscious experience thus supervenes on the arrangement of locally present *dharmas*. To summarize: a conscious experience is triggered by parallel horizontal series of *dharmas*. It arises precisely when sufficient *dharmas* are vertically present in a knife-edge moment, courtesy of the storehouse consciousness. The storehouse consciousness provides a rich repository of *dharmas* that have time-broadening content, for example the memory impression of the mango.

It is important to note that the notions of supervenience (together with horizontal and vertical causation) and representationalism were available to, and were made use of by, the Abhidharma philosophers before the Yogācāra. The appeal to supervenience and two distinct causal relations can help resolve Siderits' Subjectivity Challenge. Taking a cue from non-reductive physicalists who say that mental properties are distinct from but nonetheless "nothing over and above" physical properties, I want to suggest that the Abhidharma might want to say that conscious experiences are distinct from but nonetheless "nothing over and above" the *dharmas*. This does not go against the basic tenet of Abhidharma metaphysics that all there is, is the *dharmas* and the causal relations between them. Conscious experiences and thoughts are "nothing over and above" the *dharmas* because their properties and valence (whether they are good, bad, or neutral) are derived from the underlying *dharmas*. But conscious experiences and thoughts are distinct in that they play a causal role in the explanation of action and behavior. That role cannot be played by stand-alone *dharmas*. So, by Abhidharma standards, conscious experiences and thoughts have causal efficacy and thus are real.

The Ābhidharmika philosophers can help themselves to a distinction between compositionally basic and explanatorily basic properties (Audi 2012). Paul Audi draws this distinction to resolve the problems faced by naturalist views of ethical properties. According to non-reductive naturalism in ethics, obligatoriness is a fundamental property; it is not composed of other properties. But it is not explanatorily fundamental; the fact that an act is obligatory can obtain in virtue of some other fact, such as the fact that it is one's duty or that it maximizes happiness. Thus, the property of obligatoriness is compositionally basic, but it is not explanatorily basic. Ābhidhārmika philosophers can appeal to Audi's distinction to argue that although conscious experiences are not mereologically or compositionally basic, they are explanatorily basic. Indeed, the later Yogācāra-Sautrāntika philosopher Dharmakīrti endorses the reality of some composites. According to Dharmakīrti, an isolated *dharma* is incapable of generating a cognition, but once it is associated with others in a complex, it gets endowed (as are the others) with a new property or capacity of generating a cognition; just as a single palanquin bearer is incapable of performing the action of lifting the palanquin which requires four palanquin bearers (Eltschinger 2010). The aggregated *dharmas* then both are causally efficacious in that they lead to perception of the real and correspond to its image in the cognition (Eltschinger 2010). The aggregate of *dharmas* that leads to perception is not compositionally basic, but it is explanatorily basic for without it, we cannot explain how cognition arises. And, insofar as the aggregate of *dharmas* is implicated in the generation of the corresponding cognition, it meets the causal efficacy criterion and must be regarded as real.

My view is that because of their other commitments, the Abhidharmikās should reject the thoroughgoing mereological nihilism proposed by Siderits. The Ābhidharmika philosophers could reject mereological nihilism or S1 above (everything that is composite is unreal) but offer a more nuanced version which allows for some composites—those that are causally efficacious and explanatorily basic—to be real. By Vasubandhu's standards this would mean that selves and persons are not ultimately real, but conscious experiences and aggregates of *dharmas* that produce those experiences are.

To avoid the Phenomenological and Metaphysical Challenges the Ābhidharmikas can appeal to the innovative notions of basic and ego consciousnesses. This is not just because basic consciousness makes available countlessly many more *dharmas* than are manifestly available in ordinary awareness, but also, and more importantly, because it is a storehouse for many additional proto-conscious impressions. To be accurate, basic consciousness can be conceived of as many constantly evolving horizontal series of causal consequents of the proto-conscious impressions, which are seeded by the ordinary manifest awarenesses from the mediate and immediate past. Conscious experience can thus be understood as vertical composites supervening on temporally coincident proto-conscious impressions mined from multiple constantly evolving horizontal series.

This analysis of conscious experiences as supervening on *dharma*-clusters, which consist of co-present momentary proto-conscious *dharmas*, with the assistance of basic consciousness and ego-consciousness can deal with the Phenomenological Challenge. On the phenomenological account favored by Husserl and Zahavi, the conscious experience of a temporally extended object is explained by the so-called primal impression, carrying the burden of the just-past impression and pregnant with the just-future impression yet to appear. On the phenomenological account favored by Yogācāra-Sautrāntika philosophers the content of the just-past and the just-future impressions is made co-temporally available in the present by virtue of the momentary present *dharma* (the vehicle) insofar as it arises on account of the just-past and is pregnant with the just-future *dharma*. The momentary present *dharmas* in the various streams of basic consciousness are representational *vehicles* that, at any given time, carry representational *content* which has genuine non-illusory width, courtesy of the just-past, and the just-future impressions. But since the just-past and just-future impressions do not really exist, only present *dharmas* are responsible for the arising of the conscious experience. The distinction between the vehicles and the content of conscious experiences salvages the mature Abhidharma thesis that the only the present momentary *dharmas* (vehicles) are causally efficacious and thus real.

But can this account be extended to explain the unity of temporally extended objects and the unity of the subject: the stream of consciousness itself? Here the Yogācāra-Sautrāntika view departs sharply from Husserl. The Yogācāra-Sautrāntika claim that the attribution of diachronic unity to objects and subjects (persisting selves) that go beyond the content borne by the momentary *dharmas* is an illusion. This illusion is a product of the ego-consciousness on account of its misapprehension of basic consciousness as a continuing stable entity rather than an ever-renewing stream of discrete momentary impressions. The misapprehension arises because of the nature of basic consciousness as a subtle but continuous awareness of one's body, cognitive predispositions, and the immediate environment. As I said earlier, the text warns us that this continuing, though ever changing, basic consciousness should not be treated as a single unified thing. The point is that we mistake what is strictly speaking a stream of awarenesses as a *single awareness* because of the continuous, indistinct, and subtle awareness of the stream. The principles that constitute conscious sensations and perceptions do not need to glue together the temporally contiguous impressions into a diachronically unified stream of experience that accounts for unity of objects and subjects. Rather, according to the Yogācāra-Sautrāntika, conscious sensations and perceptions are constituted by supervening on the local distribution of temporally co-incident *dharmas* made available by the sense-faculties, basic consciousness, and other mental factors. The reflexivity of conscious states accounts for the synchronic unity of self-aware subjective states at a time. However, it is important to note that there is no veridical awareness of succession; there is only a succession of awarenesses. Diachronic unity of successive awareness is only an illusion, a conceptual fabrication of the ego-consciousness. This addresses the Phenomenological Challenge.

To address the Metaphysical Challenge, the Yogācāra-Sautrāntika philosopher must resist the thesis (M3) that conscious experiences are temporally extended while accepting the scientific evidence that seems to support it. The Yogācāra-Sautrāntika philosopher describes (or rather redescribes) every conscious state as a momentary event carved out of a network of temporally extended processes. This network can be appropriately described as multiple series of successive combinations of momentary *dharmas*. The content of some of the momentary *dharmas* in the vertical series has temporal width, courtesy of the ever-evolving proto-conscious memory *dharmas* and proto-conscious intentions in the basic consciousness. However, it must be emphasized that the vehicles—the present *dharmas*—that carry content are momentary. Consider again our conscious perception of a mango. Suppose that the visual perception of mango happens at a certain time t_5 in a sequence of moments t_1 to t_n. In the moments prior to t_5 (i.e., t_1 to t_4), there is no visual experience of mango. Suppose further that this time-lag is about 150–200 ms. However, through t_1 to t_4 there was a mass of proto-conscious *dharmas* that comprised the causal network of parallel horizontal series that gave rise to the right sort of arrangement of *dharmas* "vertically" for the "mango-perception" at t_5. At a prior moment, say t_2 (50–80 ms), there was a sensory registration of a mango shaped stimulus. The initial sensory registration and the later visual perception are the result of vertical causal relations between interacting *dharmas* from distinct horizontal series. This is in line with the empirical evidence: it allows for a time-lag between the presentation of the stimulus, the sensory registration, and later the conscious perception of the object. Hence, the Abhidharma can potentially explain the empirical data without accepting M3 above.

The Yogācāra-Sautrāntika picture that emerges is this: we need to think of the mind as a two-dimensional matrix of parallel but interacting series of momentary proto-conscious *dharmas*. At some moments in this complex network of parallel sequences, conscious experiences or thoughts (visualize these as vertical spikes in the complex network) suddenly appear when the necessary and sufficient *dharmas* that constitute a given conscious experience or thought are simultaneously available at a single *moment*. Thus, conscious experiences are carved out of complex network of proto-conscious mental *dharmas* that are part of countless mutually interacting series of such proto-conscious moments. The conscious experience of the mango is triggered by sense-object contact, but the conscious sensation of mango-shape and mango-color, let alone the well-formed, and perhaps articulable, conscious perception of a mango, arises much after the sensory contact. The representationalism endorsed by the Yogācāra-Sautrāntika philosophers is motivated by the claim that there is a time-lag between the sense-object contact and the conscious experience. Like all the other sense-impressions, these mental representations, strictly speaking, causal consequents of the representations, are present in the ever-evolving basic consciousness. We can explain that the conscious sensations, perceptions, and thoughts are directly causally related to the initial contact, provided there is a causal network and adequate time-lag between the initial contact and the resultant conscious sensations and perceptions. The necessary and sufficient proto-conscious *dharmas* might be produced in different horizontal series but they must come together co-temporally at a given moment to produce a conscious experience or thought. In line with the empirical science, the Buddhist can claim that conscious sensations take about 50–80 ms to be registered, whereas conscious perception may require as long as a quarter of a second. This explains how a seemingly rich conscious experience is fully available at a moment. It is very likely that conscious experiences are few and far between compared to the mass of proto-conscious information available in the multitude of sequences unfolding in time. All of this fits nicely with the *global neuronal workspace model*, which supports the view that the neural basis of conscious access is a sudden self-amplifying process (vertical spike in the Abhidharma story) leading to a global brain-scale pattern of activity. There is no continuum of perception, associated with a gradual change in the intensity of brain activation, the model predicts a sharp non-linear transition from non-conscious to conscious processing (Dehaene et al. 2003). Sekar et al. (2013) also report that the threshold of around 240 ms is consistent with the hypothesis that conscious visual access is relatively sharply demarcated.

According to this picture, our ordinary manifest conscious experiences and thoughts may be triggered by sense-object contact, but conscious experiences, in the moment that they arise and cease, supervene on proto-conscious mental *dharmas*—firmly grounded in the basic consciousness—presently available in the vertical series. The reader will note that this view is but a short step from idealism, and indeed some later Yogācāra philosophers embraced idealism, but it is a step that I do not wish to endorse. This, I think, is a reasonable response to the Metaphysical Challenge on behalf of the Abhidharma Yogācāra philosophers.[8]

---

[8] That said, I do not wish to claim that all issues in the phenomenology of time can be resolved by adopting the Abhidharma ontology. For other problems that still plague such an account, see Phillips (2010).

3.7 Conclusion

This chapter has dealt with contemporary problems that may be thought to arise for the Abhidharma view of conscious experience given their commitment to mereological nihilism and momentariness. These commitments question the reality, coherence, and empirical viability of the Abhidharma account of conscious experiences. The view that conscious experiences are not real, or are just useful fictions, is no doubt available to the Abhidharma. But it is not a move, I have argued, that they endorse. In addition, the account given in this chapter shows that the Abhidharma account cannot be ruled out as conceptually incoherent or as empirically unviable. It has the resources to deal with some serious objections. In the following chapters (Chapters 4–7), I work through other objections which are serious enough to render their account of conscious experience and thought implausible due to their commitment to the no-self doctrine.

4
Episodic Memories Without a Self

4.1 Introduction

The Abhidharma Buddhist doctrine of no-self has many surprising consequences, which the Abhidharma philosophers embrace and often celebrate. But there are some alleged consequences of the no-self view that are so flatly at odds with our experience that they render the no-self view extremely implausible. In this chapter and the next, I consider the most pressing challenge for the no-self view: the challenge from unity of experiences. Conscious experiences are typically unified at a time and across time. We do not typically see colors, textures, and shapes floating about in our visual fields, we see red tomatoes and green apples. We do not typically hear punctuated sounds as an ambulance passes by, we hear a siren. Furthermore, we typically remember important events in our personal past, for example the experience of remembering one's first kiss. Somehow, the earlier experience is still available to be integrated with the current experience in a single, temporally extended, and unified episodic memory experience. The Abhidharma Buddhist alleges that there is no continuing self to unify representations across time. But she does not want to deny the phenomenological data, rather she is concerned to explain the phenomenology of our experiences.

Abhidharma Buddhists do not deny episodic memories. Indeed, in the *Abhidharmakośa-Bhāṣya*, Vasubandhu describes the problem and his purported solution in a single passage:

In the past, I was handsome (literally: I possessed physical matter). This declaration is for the purpose of indicating that the saint capable of recollecting his past lives remembers the variety of characteristics of his series of these existences. But the Buddha does not mean that he sees a real *pudgala* possessing, in a past life, such physical matter, etc.: for to think such is to fall into *satkāyadṛṣṭi* [the wrong view of a real person]. Or rather, if such is the meaning of this sentence, then its sole purpose is to reject it as non-authentic. We conclude that the *Sūtra*, insofar as it attributes the possession of physical matter, etc., to a self, has in view "a self of designation," as one speaks of a pile which, being only an accumulation, has no unity; or of a current of water which being only an accumulation,

Selfless Minds: A Contemporary Perspective on Vasubandhu's Metaphysics. Monima Chadha, Oxford University Press.
© Monima Chadha 2023. DOI: 10.1093/oso/9780192844095.003.0005

has no unity; or of a current of water which, being only a succession (of waters), has no permanence.[1] (trans. Pruden 1988, p. 1327)

This first-person report of a saint remembering his physical appearance in a past life raises many questions. Is there rebirth? Can a saint really remember his experiences in a previous life? These are legitimate questions, but they would distract us from the main point of this passage. Vasubandhu is not concerned to defend the Buddhist account of rebirth here. Rather, the passage is meant to draw attention to the problem posed by episodic memories. The point here is similar to what many of us would report reminiscing about our younger selves. The report draws attention to the fact that we have the capacity to mentally relive some episodes in our past and in doing so, we identify with our past self. This passage first presents a puzzle for our Abhidharma Buddhist philosophers: How might we explain the phenomenology of episodic memories? In the rest of the passage, Vasubandhu offers a cryptic solution to the problem. The idea put forward by Vasubandhu is to deny that alleged reference of "I," that the self or person refers to a real entity. The "I" is only a conventional expression used for the collection of *dharmas*. There is no need to posit a continuing self or person who now remembers that he was handsome in the past. That is the result of ignorance, a *satkāyadṛṣṭi*. There was and there is just a pile of physical *dharmas*, without any unity. There is no continuing self that had the experience and now remembers that earlier experience, there is just the succession of experiences; just as a current of water is a succession of waters. The solution requires unpacking. There is a huge gap in the phenomenology of the rememberer and Vasubandhu's dismissal of any continuing self that remembers the earlier experience. The task of this chapter is to develop Vasubandhu's insight to explain the phenomenology of episodic memories.

As we have seen in Chapter 2, ancient and contemporary Buddhist philosophers often disagree about the interpretation of the no-self doctrine. Nevertheless, all of them agree that, at the very least, the no-self doctrine implies the denial of identity with a past self. Endel Tulving, the psychologist who introduced the notion of episodic memory in the 1970s, regards dependence on a remembering self as the distinguishing and central feature of episodic memory. More recently, he warns philosophers and scientists attracted by the popular no-self views against the exorcism of self. He writes:

Some thinkers prefer a philosophical framework for the scientific approach to mental life in which the phenomena to be explained are expressions of processes, but in which the entities that do the processing (agents) are not permitted. Thus, thinking occurs without thinkers, knowing without knowers, and

---

[1] *Abhidharmakośa-Bhāṣya*, Chapter 9.

consciousness without anyone being conscious. The idea is to avoid using structural terminology...Besides, "self" sounds like the dreaded homunculus that
needs to be exorcised by all means possible. But until such time that we have
better ways of explaining the phenomenal existences of things such as pain,
smell, and recollection of the past, we need an agent such as self for the sake of
the completeness of the story. Eventually, self may turn out to be like phlogiston
or aether—a convenient temporary prop. But the problem today is that the story
of the mind is incomplete and awkward to tell if a concept like "self" is omitted
from it. This is why it should not be exorcised yet.   (2005, pp. 14–15)

Tulving thus presents a very clear challenge to the Abhidharma Buddhist philosopher: she must present a better way to explain the phenomenal existence of things
such as pain, smell, and recollection of the past. As a matter of fact, in the
millennium-long debate between Buddhist and Hindu philosophers in ancient
India, similar challenges were continuously thrown at the Buddhists. This chapter
takes up the challenge to explain the recollection of the past, or episodic memory,
without a self on behalf of Abhidharma Buddhist philosophers.

The phenomenology of episodic memory requires an account of two distinctive features: the rememberer's capacity to mentally relive the episodes she
remembers and the use of the term "I" in the description to intimate that the
rememberer identifies with the subject of the original experience. In section 4.2,
I give an overview of the philosophical debate between Buddhist and Hindu philosophers on the self implicated in episodic memory. Then, in section 4.3, I present Vasubandhu's no-self view to make clear that episodic memory presents a
difficult challenge to it. In section 4.4, I show, using resources from contemporary
psychology and the Buddhist Madhyamaka tradition, that the sense of self in
episodic memory is a product of narrative and social construction. Although
there are significant doctrinal differences between the Abhidharma and the
Madhyamaka traditions, the resources I will be using here do not depend on their
doctrinal differences. The central claim of this chapter is that the sense of self as
being the same one as a past self is an illusion. Furthermore, there is no positive
phenomenology associated with the experience of an identity with a past self in
episodic memory experiences. Thus, the Abhidharma Buddhist philosopher can
offer an explanation of the phenomenology of episodic memories without appeal
to self-representations.

4.2 The Challenge to the Abhidharma View

The debate between the Buddhists and the Hindu philosophers on the nature of
self hinged on the memory argument from roughly the second century CE.
Gautama, the founder of the earliest Brahminical school, the Nyāya, composed

the famous *Nyāyasūtra*: "Desire, aversion, volition (*prayatna*), pleasure, pain, and cognition are characteristics of the self"[2] (Jha 1984, p. 110). This *sūtra* is interpreted by ancient and modern commentators to contain an implicit inferential proof of the self on the basis of memory. One of the earliest commentaries on the *Nyāyasūtras*, *Nyāya-bhāṣya*, by Vātsyāyana, suggests the following interpretation: Desire is indicative of the self in the sense that desire for an object perceived now is possible on account of the same agent having perceived the object on an earlier occasion and having experienced pleasure by coming into contact with it. Desire would not be possible without a single agent that cognizes and recognizes the object; and, this single agent is the self (Chadha 2013). Taber (2012) calls this the argument from memory, according to which the volitional, affective, and cognitive states imply a "connector," a single self that ties past and present mental states together. For the Nyāya, the single self is the substratum of qualities like desire, aversion, and volition, etc. Contrarily, the Abhidharma Buddhist no-self theorists argue that there is no need of a single unifying "connector" self to explain memory; causal connections between discrete momentary conscious states do the work. The Abhidharma Buddhist denies the existence of a perceiver separate from perceptions and of a substratum separate from qualities. In Chapter 9 of the *Abhidharmakośa-Bhāṣya*, Vasubandhu responds to the hypothetical Nyāya opponent:

Objector: If a self does not exist, whose is the memory? "Whose" designates the owner.

Response: Explain by example how you understand that someone is the owner of the memory?

Objector: As Caitra is the owner of the cow.

Response: In what sense is Caitra the owner of the cow?

Objector: In that he directs and employs the cow as he pleases...

Response: One says that the "Caitra" series owns the "cow" series because the Caitra series is the cause of the geographic displacement and the various changes of the cow-series. There is not there any one, real entity "Caitra," nor another entity "cow" and there is not, for the Caitra series, any quality of owner or master outside the quality of being the cause of the movement, etc. of the cow-series.

Conclusion: There is no being-an-owner (of memory or cognition) above and beyond being-a-cause. (trans. adapted from Kapstein 2001, pp. 368–9)

Vasubandhu claims that there is no need to posit an ontologically distinct persisting single self as the owner of memories and experiences; memories can be explained by manifold causal relations between discrete conscious events.

---

[2] *Nyāyasūtra*, 1.1.10.

This Buddhist position was contested by other Hindu schools, notably Mīmāṃsā, on the grounds that a causal account cannot explain the phenomenology of episodic memory. The Mīmāṃsāka philosopher Śabara, in the fourth century CE, introduced the concept of "recognition of the past" (*pratyabhijñā*), or episodic memory, which includes one's ability to recognize oneself as an ineliminable component in the recollection of events in one's personal past. The Mīmāṃsā version of the memory argument, "establishes the existence of a continuous self not insofar as it presupposes a single subject of experience that both had the remembered experience and now remembers it, but insofar as it directly reveals one" (Taber 1990, p. 37). The thought is that the phenomenological content of episodic memory is not just captured by the proposition "I remember singing at a school concert in 1975" but the more complicated content that "I(now) remember that I(then) was singing at a school concert in 1975." Furthermore, the content of the memory directly reveals that I(now) = I(then).

The notion of direct revelation of self in introspection is epistemologically suspect because there is no independent hold on the phenomenology. It is well known that we are prone to gross error, even in favorable circumstances of extended reflection, about the phenomenology of current conscious experiences (Schwitzgebel 2008). Phenomenology cannot offer infallible, perhaps not even reliable, evidence; but it is uncontroversial that it provides data: the challenge in philosophy and sciences of the mind is to explain this data. In section 4.4, I return to explaining the phenomenology of episodic memory on behalf of the Abhidharma philosophers. For now, we see how the ancient debate between the Hindu and Buddhist philosophers unfolded.

The later Hindu philosophers of the Kashmir-Śaiva tradition, notably Utpaladeva in the tenth century CE, reignited the memory debate. The Kashmir-Śaiva philosophers agree with the Buddhists that there is no ontologically distinct subject over and above consciousness. However, they disagree with the Buddhists in that they do not identify consciousness with discrete conscious events. For Utpaladeva, consciousness itself is a dynamic but unified subject of experiences and memory. The focus of the debate now shifts from the content of memory to the nature and role of memory.

The Abhidharma Buddhist view, as we saw above, is that memory is not a literal re-presentation of the past; rather, it is a present cognition that is related to the past cognition through the causal continuity of dispositions or formations (*saṃskāras*). The Buddhist is very clear that there is no re-manifestation of the past cognition in the present memory; all cognitions are momentary. Episodic memory does not require that the earlier cognition reappears at a later moment, only that the content of the cognition is passed to successive cognitions in the stream of consciousness. Against this, Utpaladeva asks if consciousness consists in no more than distinct and discrete awarenesses, which are present and entirely self-confined, how can we make sense of comparing, contrasting, and synthesizing cognitions? In his seminal text, *Īśvarapratyabhijñākārikā* and *vṛtti* (commentary), Utpaladeva writes:

> How could we explain memory, which conforms to direct perception when the latter is no longer present, if there were not a permanent self, who is the subject of the perception?
>
> Since the former direct perception has disappeared at the moment of the memory, the memory, whose essential quality is precisely its dependence on that former perception of the object, could not arise, unless one admits the persistence of the awareness of this perception also at the moment of the memory. And this lasting awareness at different times is precisely the self, the experiencing subject.[3]   (trans. Torella 2002, p. 91)

Utpaldeva continues:

> It would not be possible to speak of the manifestation of the object being remembered if it appeared as separate from the memory; therefore the unity of cognitions that occur at different times is necessary, and this unity is precisely the knowing subject.
>
> In fact, in memory the former perception is not manifested separately—like the object—since it appears as resting on the self, as the expression "I perceived in the past" indicates.[4]   (trans. Torella 2002, pp. 106–7)

Utpaladeva makes the point that episodic memory is not simply awareness of the object but remembering the object "embedded" in our past perception. This embedded structure, Utpaladeva insists, cannot be explained without reference to unity of cognitions and this unity requires a persisting consciousness as the subject of experience (self). The point is that without such a synthesis or unity we cannot explain the subjective phenomenology of our episodic memory experience: the feeling that I have experienced this in the past.

Furthermore, Utpaladeva argues that memory cannot be dismissed as an error since it plays a very important role in the structure of our experience and our functioning in the world. We learn through memory: memory enables organizing and interpreting experience, conceptualization, driving purposeful action, language, and culture. Utpaladeva says:

> And it cannot even be claimed that memory has these as its object only erroneously, in the sense that it makes the object of its own determinative activity the

---

[3] *Īśvarapratyabhijñākārikā* and *vṛtti*, I.2.3.
[4] *Īśvarapratyabhijñākārikā* and *vṛtti*, I.4.3 and I.4.4.

former direct perception and its object, which in reality are not experienced, as happens when one states that one sees silver when faced with mother-of-pearl.

How is it possible to reduce the true nature of memory to this? And how is it possible that the establishment of objects should come about thanks to error? ...

And moreover, [if it is a question of "error"] why insist so much on the fact that memory—conceived of as error—arises from the latent impressions, when, on the contrary, it is different from the former direct perception from every point of view, not coming into contact with it in any way?

Thus, the functioning of the human world—which stems precisely from the unification of cognitions, in themselves separate from one another and incapable of knowing one another—would be destroyed.[5]   (trans. Torella 2002, pp. 100-1)

Utpaladeva argues that the problem with the Buddhist account of memory is that it is incapable of explaining the phenomenology of memory. Irina Kuznetsova explains the point clearly:

The Buddhist cannot properly account for the subjective synthesis experienced in memory, namely the certainty that "I have experienced this in the past" without which a cognitive event by definition cannot be one of remembering, or the oneness of the objective world, which memory reveals insofar as, provided that my remembered cognition was valid, I can rely on it for successful practice in the present.   (2012, p. 352)

The Buddhist no-self theorist might insist that the subjective certainty experienced in episodic memory in the "feeling of pastness" issues from an error: past cognition cannot enter our current memory experience in any form whatsoever. The Kashmir-Śaiva philosophers generalize this concern in claiming that the no-self view makes it impossible to explain *janasthitih* (the human condition). Utpaladeva centers his critique of the no-self theory on episodic memory because it requires the synthesis of cognitions at the subjective and the objective levels. At the subjective level, memory requires immediate recognition of the self as the subject of temporally distinct experiences: I remember that I have seen this in the past. At the objective level, memory explains the success of our intentional actions, predictions, plans, and practices on the basis of what we have learnt in the past.

The upshot of the debate between Hindus and Buddhists in ancient India is that the Buddhist no-self theorist is forced into a corner. An adequate explanation of the distinctive phenomenology of episodic memory requires a unity of cognitions at the subjective level. This is not possible for the Buddhist as the memory cognition bears no relationship to the remembered cognition apart from causal

---

[5] *Īśvarapratyabhijñākārikā* and *vṛtti*, I.3.4 and I.3.5.

continuity. Causal relations are not transparent to our minds and thus are unable to explain the subjective unity and phenomenology of memory. This leads the Buddhist to claim that memories are erroneous.

The Kashmir-Śaiva philosophers put forward a further challenge: We cannot question the veridicality of memory for without it we would be left without an explanation of learning from the past, which has an important role to play in our adaptive success in the world. But is this right? Must we accept the veridicality of memory to explain its role in learning? I will take up this challenge on behalf of Buddhist philosophers in section 4.4 of the chapter. But first, I turn to the explanation of the Abhidharma no-self view and why it is susceptible to the challenges posed by the Hindu opponents.

4.3 Is the Abhidharma Buddhist Susceptible to This Challenge?

In this section I shall reiterate certain key aspects of Vasubandhu's no-self doctrine, touched upon in section 2.3, that will bring it into direct contact with recent work in philosophical psychology and phenomenology of memory.

Recall, Vasubandhu's central argument in section 2.3 is a direct attack on the inferential proof for the self in the *Nyāyasūtra* (1.1.10) quoted above. The concern raised by the Hindu opponents is: How can we make sense of agents of physical actions and that of cognition without there being a self? Vasubandhu responds to these concerns by offering an alternative explanation of the phenomena that does not require us to postulate a self. In the *Treatise* Vasubandhu addresses the specific questions: Is there a subject of conscious cognition? Who cognizes? etc. His response is simply to say that there is no subject of experiences; perception arises on account of its appropriate causes: sense-faculty, object, and attention. The discussion in the *Abhidharmakośa-Bhāṣya* goes thus:

Objector: But it may be said, because states of being have reference to beings, all states of being depend on beings. e.g., "Devadatta walks"—here the state of walking refers to the one who walks, Devadatta. In the same way consciousness is a state of being. Therefore, he who cognizes must be.

Vasubandhu: What is this "Devadatta?" It remains to be proven that it is a self or unified subject. "Devadatta" does not refer to a single thing, it is just the conventional name for the collection of conditions that are the cause of resulting states. Devadatta walks just as he cognizes.

Objector: And how does Devadatta walk?

Vasubandhu: The instantaneous conditions in an unbroken continuum— grasped as the single, unified thing, the so-called Devadatta—are the cause of coming-into-being-elsewhere, which is spoken of as "Devadatta walks." For "walking" is the "very coming-into-being-elsewhere." Similarly, too there are causes of consciousness, they are spoken of as "Devadatta cognizes."[6] (trans. adapted from Kapstein 2001, pp. 368–9)

Clearly, Vasubandhu conceives of "subjects" as mere constructions which are nothing over and above disparate causes, in this case the collections of conscious events. Persons or subjects exist in "name only," i.e., they are denominations for the sake of convenience. The claim is that we need not postulate a self as the subject of experience since we cannot infer it as a cause. A single unified self contributes nothing to the arising of an experience. The causes of experience—sense-faculties, objects, and causal relations between them—are sufficient explanations. In our ordinary talk we use names such as "Devadatta" for convenience to signify the agent of action and the cognizer of an experience, but there is no single thing that Devadatta refers to. Devadatta is a shorthand for the series of mental and physical *dharmas* that cause the movement of the physical *dharmas* to a different position, so we say "Devadatta walks." Similarly, the movement of the mental *dharmas* in response to internal or external causes in the series that constitute the continuum we refer to as "Devadatta" results in a conscious cognition. For convenience we say "Devadatta cognizes," but really, there is no single unified being that is the cause of the cognition; conscious cognition arises because of the coming together of various causes in a continuum of *dharmas*.

There is no need to invoke the self as an experiencer at any point in this explanation. For the Abhidharma Buddhist, the self is an ontological dangler without a causal or explanatory role. Vasubandhu says that by the very fact that we cannot apprehend the capacity of the self "any more than a capacity of the various chants uttered by a quack to cure when it is established that the effect has been brought about by the use of certain herbs" (Pruden 1988, p. 1347). We must conclude that the hypothesis of the self is problematic. Vasubandhu offers an alternative explanation for ownership of experiences and agent of action which shows that it is redundant to postulate a self.

Hence, Vasubandhu concludes, there is no inferential basis for a belief in a self. The Buddhist can explain apparent facts about experiencers completely in terms of ultimately real momentary events and the relations of cause and effect; nothing more is needed. The rest of the work is done by conventional practices, including the way we talk about the phenomena themselves. In effect, Vasubandhu's strategy here is alluding to the Abhidharma Buddhist criterion for reality. The criterion for something being real is that it must have "causal powers" (*arthakriyāsamartha*) and "perform causal roles" (*arthakriyākāritva*). The self is not real because it is causally impotent. According to this view, there are only innumerably many distinct streams of awareness, each of which is devoid of a

---

[6] *Abhidharmakośa-Bhāṣya*, Chapter 9.

self; that is, devoid of anything that would be the "subject" of awarenesses and be the "thinker" of thoughts and the "doer" of deeds.

The Ābhidharmikas argue that the illusion of a continuing self arises from the sense that there is a subject present at each moment of experience and that it is the *same* subject from one moment to the next. In reality, however, no "I" or subject is present at any moment. The sense of self is a conventional construction to support our interests and needs. Most of us would be tempted to think that our sense of self, even if a construction, is a useful construction, for practical and prudential reasons. The Buddhist Ābhidharmikas disagree. They warn us that constructing the sense of self as the unified subject of experiences and agent of actions at a time is likely to bring with it the sense of self as a continuing subject. A continuing self is the source of moral defilements: greed, conceit, pride, jealousy, and so on. It should be quite obvious that the Abhidharma view faces a tough challenge: the radical no-experiencer and no-agent view makes it difficult to even begin to offer an explanation of the phenomenology of episodic memory. On behalf of the Buddhist Abhidharma philosophers, I argue that the sense of self is a narrative construction.

4.4 Abhidharma Explanation of Episodic Memory

Here, I turn to a more specific explanation on the nature and phenomenology of episodic memory in the light of the no-self view. I begin by addressing the concern raised by the Kashmir-Śaiva philosophers that memory must be assumed to present a veridical account of the past, otherwise we cannot explain its role in learning and our adaptive success in the world. The Buddhists claim that memory is not a re-presentation of the past, because there is no past to be re-represented in our memory experiences. Kashmir-Śaiva philosophers claim that the Buddhist account is mistaken because it fails to explain the adaptive success of memory in facilitating learning and knowledge. I then turn to the more difficult challenge of explaining the phenomenology of episodic memory. This challenge was first raised by the Mīmāṃsāka philosopher Śabara, in the fourth century CE and then reiterated by the Kashmir-Śaiva philosopher Utpaladeva. The latter challenge shows the inadequacy of Vasubandhu's attempt to explain episodic memories because it fails to account for one's ability to recognize oneself in the recollection of events in one's personal past.

4.4.1 Constructive Memory: Questioning the Veridicality Assumption

The very influential "constructive memory" account of contemporary psychology questions the veridicality assumption:

The first notion to get rid of is that memory is primarily or literally reduplica-
tive, or reproductive. In a world of constantly changing environment, literal
recall is extraordinarily unimportant...memory appears to be an affair of construction rather than reproduction.   (Bartlett 1932, pp. 204–5)

The central idea is that the "retrieved memory content is not a fixed and faithful
transcription of the past, but rather a fluid, imaginative reconstruction that knits
past experience with current beliefs, knowledge, motives, goals and even external
suggestion to fill gaps in a less-than-permanent record" (Klein 2014b, p. 429). For
example, eyewitness accounts of recent events, despite their high confidence rat-
ings, are often found to be prone to error and distortion.

Schacter (2012), in a review of the constructive memory research, notes that
the recent research in cognitive psychology and neuroscience has led to acceler-
ated progress in this field. There is evidence now to support the idea that certain
kinds of memory distortions reflect the operation of adaptive cognitive processes.
In other words, the processes that contribute to efficient functioning of memory
systems also produce distortions. Gist-based and associative memory errors,
though classified as errors, facilitate the ability to abstract and generalize. These
are linked to creativity and, most importantly, are involved in the processing of
"context frames," which facilitate recognition of other objects in the environment
by allowing predictions about what is likely to occur in a given context (Schacter
2012). In addition, there is evidence that post-event misinformation effects
(Schacter et al. 2011), and imagination inflation (Loftus 2003), although again
classified as errors, are adaptive. Post-event misinformation contributes to
"updating" our knowledge and beliefs in response to new information, while
imagination inflation proves adaptive because of its role in simulating future events.

Furthermore, episodic memory, which is traditionally associated with recollection of personal experiences, also plays a key role in imagining possible future
scenarios or episodic simulation. Patient K.C., perhaps the most documented
case of almost complete amnesia, cannot recall anything from his personal past
and cannot imagine his personal future. When asked questions like "What did
you do yesterday?" or "What will you do tomorrow?," K.C. reports that his mind
is blank. This hypothesis is also supported by neurocognitive evidence. Recent
neuroimaging studies reveal that the same brain areas are active when remembering the past and imagining the future. Studies in aging and psychopathology
show that reduction in the retrieval of episodic details for past events because of
aging, depression, or post-traumatic stress disorder is also observed for imagining the future. Losing memories of one's past is mirrored in losing hope for one's
future. Episodic simulation requires flexible retrieval and recombination of elements from stored episodes to imagine possible future episodes, but the possibility of errors in memory increases when elements from various past experiences
are reorganized (Schacter & Addis 2007).

However, episodic simulation is so beneficial that it is worth the cost of resulting in memory errors. Several lines of evidence point to adaptive functions and benefits of episodic simulation: planning and problem solving; psychological well-being and empathy; and farsighted decision making (Schacter 2012). For example, when episodes overlap extensively with one another, individuals may recall the general similarities or gist common to many episodes but fail to remember distinctive item-specific information that distinguishes one episode from another. Gist-based processes support retention of themes and meanings that facilitate generalization and abstraction of features that are relevant to farsighted decision making. But these are the very factors responsible for distortions (Bartlett 1932).

These processes are not only adaptive but also beneficial to the individual and society. There is evidence to believe that when presented with a situation depicting another person's plight, participants who imagined an event in which they help the person (episodic simulation) or remembered a related past event of helping others (episodic memory) showed increased prosocial intentions (Gaesser & Schacter 2014). This evidence is also supported by neuroscience research (van Kesteren et al. 2010; Winecoff et al. 2013; Benoit et al. 2014). Both cognitive and neuroimaging evidence support the conclusion that episodic simulation, and the brain network on which it depends, serve adaptive goal-directed functions without any commitment to veridicality of memories. Indeed, it seems that the very opposite is the case and veridical memory is the exception rather than the norm (Kirberg 2022). Neuroscientific evidence suggests that neuronal firing sequences are not simply replicated when we recall an event from the past but are always combined with new firing patterns: to remember something involves changes to the very same memory (Duvarci & Nader 2004; Gupta et al. 2010). This indicates that error is an inherent characteristic of memory processes. Furthermore, original replays of episodic memories as in immersive flashbacks commonly experienced in PTSD, indicate maladaptive processes of remembering (Berntsen 2021; Hoel 2021).

This research shows that the Kashmir-Śaiva philosophers' dismissal of the Buddhist Abhidharma position on memory on the grounds that memories are not veridical reports of the past is not tenable. The Abhidharma philosophers' claim that episodic memory, insofar as it gives the subjective sense that the remembered object is embedded in the past awareness of that object, is erroneous, since the past cognition no longer exists and thus cannot be synthesized in memory. The Kashmir-Śaivas argue that it leaves us without explanation of learning and our adaptive success in the world (objective aspect) and the phenomenology (subjective aspect) of episodic memory.

The constructive memory research shows that memory being in error is not necessarily in conflict with its adaptive efficacy (objective aspect): error and adaptation go together in memory. This should not be interpreted to mean that there are no accuracy constraints on memory. Neuroimaging studies show that there is greater sensory/perceptual detail associated with accurate memories than inaccurate memories. Using fMRI, Slotnick and Schacter (2004) demonstrate that early visual processing activity is already differentiated for accurate and inaccurate memories. Similarly, accurate recognition of abstract shapes elicits greater visual cortical activation than would false recognition. But as this sensory signature, spanning early and late visual processing, might rely on implicit memory it is very likely that it may not be accessible to conscious awareness and thus there are no differences between accurate and inaccurate memories at the subjective level.

4.4.2 Explaining the Phenomenology: It Was Me! and Mentally Reliving the Past

This still leaves open the harder problem of explaining the phenomenology (that is, the subjective aspect) of episodic memory. This section will focus on explaining how episodic memory, which includes the identification of the self that was experiencing and the self that is remembering, results in the sense of a persisting self. I approach this issue by questioning whether this subjective sense is grounded in experiential phenomenology. My strategy is to show that there is no experiential phenomenology associated with the sense of self in episodic memory; rather, the sense of self is a product of narrative construction. So, the first question to ask is what kind of self is implicated in episodic memory experiences?

Most psychologists and philosophers agree with Tulving that recollection or episodic memory implicates a notion of self. However, they do differ on the kind of self that is implicated. Shaun Nichols (2014) argues that episodic memory implicates a thin conception of self. He affirms Kant's claim that the "I"-representation in episodic memory is "the poorest of all representations" (Kant 1998 [1787], B408). Though characterized as "poor," this representation does much work in the cognitive and affective landscapes: it is responsible for our sense of identity accompanying typical episodic memory and it is responsible for triggering self-conscious emotions like guilt, pride, and shame. The question to ask, then, is whether the thin conception of self can perform these weighty functions?

Nichols introduces the episodic sense of self by distinguishing it from the trait conception of self in psychology. He argues that the sense of self delivered in episodic memory is much more impoverished than the trait sense which is "chock full of aspirations, convictions, affections and affiliations" (Nichols 2014, p. 137). The argument rests on showing that there is a double dissociation between the episodic sense of self and the trait sense of self. Radical changes in one's traits do not uproot the sense of identification delivered by episodic memory. Patient H.M., who underwent brain surgery to remove his hippocampus to alleviate epileptic seizures, was a very different personality from the earlier self he recollected in his memories. But he continued to identify as the same person who had radically changed.

Furthermore, knowledge of trait continuity does not ensure a sense of episodic identity. Patient R.B., after a bicycle accident which resulted in significant head trauma, was able to recollect experiences from his past but did not feel that he "owned" his memories. He reported no trait change. But recalling a scene from his past of being on a beach holiday with his family in New London, he reported that it felt like he was looking at a photo of someone else's vacation. Nichols concludes that trait continuity is neither necessary nor sufficient for tokening the episodic sense of self (Nichols 2014). He also suggests that the episodic sense of self is importantly different from the biological sense of identity. The R.B. case illustrates this too. R.B. had no doubt that he is the same biological organism that had the earlier experience and now remembers it, but still the memories do not bring with them the sense of the same self. Nichols concedes that the episodic sense of self is "a very imperfect guide to metaphysics" (Nichols 2014, p. 149).

Nichols does, however, say that the episodic sense of self plays an important role in our psychology in that it is activated in episodic memories together with some self-conscious emotions like pride and guilt (Nichols 2014). These functions require one to reflect and to evaluate one's experiences and doings in the past. Nichols takes this to mean that the episodic sense of self is, at the very least, a sense of a being identical with a past self.[7] This seems to present a problem for the Abhidharma Buddhist for the onus is on her to explain our purported experience of identity with a past self. However, we must be more cautious here. All that has been established so far is that my episodic memories *seemingly* come with the sense that I am the one who underwent the experience in the past. But is there really an experience of identity with one's past self, an experience that underlies our episodic sense of self? The question to ask, then, on behalf of the Abhidharma Buddhist, is whether the episodic sense of self results from an experience of identity or whether it is merely an illusion of identity?[8]

Philosophers and psychologists do not have much to say about the specific experiential phenomenology associated with the episodic sense of self. But it can

---

[7] One might think that this argument is a non sequitur; one can feel moral responsibility on account of actions of our ancestors. Nichols, however, thinks that the trait sense of self seems to be central to issues like responsibility. But the episodic sense of self generates guilt even when the trait-self has changed radically. Nichols argues that some primitive notion of identity is presupposed by self-conscious moral emotions; trait-continuity or causal continuity is too weak to generate emotions like guilt (2014).

[8] Jay Garfield (2015) has addressed this question recently. He argues that the self is not phenomenologically given, it is a narrative construction. The view developed here agrees with Garfield's position: the important difference is that Garfield dismisses the self as an illusion and therefore does not make a serious attempt to explain the phenomenology. The account developed here takes the phenomenology seriously and explains how the narrative conception sustains our sense of self.

be shown that there is a rich and vivid phenomenology associated with a tempo-rary loss of the episodic sense of self. It may be instructive to look at the recovery process in such cases to see if we can get a hold on the specific experiential phe-nomenology of the episodic sense of self. There are reports of patients (other than R.B.) in which loss of sense of self targets "memory." Klein (2016) notes that mal-function of the mechanism(s) responsible for feeling that one owns one's mental states is a well-documented clinical phenomenon: there is a loss of sense of self, for example, in anosognosia, somatoparaphrenia, depersonalization, and schizo-phrenic thought insertion, etc. During the acute phase of depersonalization, indi-viduals report that what normally would be taken as memory feels like an alien intrusion (Sierra et al. 2005). Klein (2015b) also mentions post-traumatic stress disorder (PTSD) as symptomatic of the loss of sense of self.

4.4.3 A Case Study for Episodic Sense of Self: Brison's Trauma and Recovery

To focus on the temporary loss and recovery of episodic sense of self, it is useful to consider Susan Brison's case as someone who suffered from PTSD. In her 2003 book *Aftermath*, Brison presents an illuminating example for exploring the phe-nomenology of the loss of episodic sense of self and its recovery, especially because her personal reflections are intermingled with philosophical concerns about identity over time. In July 1990, Brison was attacked from behind, severely beaten, sexually assaulted, strangled to unconsciousness, and left for dead. After the incident, she experienced profound alienation from the world, feeling she had outlived herself, and even uncertain as to whether she had died. Her account of losing one's sense of self is not isolated. Other PTSD patients report similar sto-ries. Trauma survivors often say they have lost themselves, or even that they have died.[9]

Brison's testimony makes clear that the loss of sense of self is that of the epi-sodic sense of self: "The undoing of the self in trauma involves a radical disrup-tion of memory, a severing of past from present and, typically, an inability to envision a future" (Brison 1999b, p. 214). Brison also quotes Primo Levi, a Holocaust survivor who suffered from PTSD and took his own life decades after he was liberated from Auschwitz. He says that at Auschwitz: "We had not only forgotten our country and our culture, but also our family, our past, the future we had imagined for ourselves, because, like animals, we were confined to the pres-ent moment" (Levi 1996, p. 43). Trauma experience, quite literally, involves the

---

[9] See "Understanding the Impact of Trauma," available at: https://perma.cc/BL9E-L4FA.

feeling of not being able to identify with one's former self and an imagined future self.

In writing about the process of recovery, Brison stresses the importance of empathetic listeners and explores the performative aspect of speech: how *saying* something about the memory *does* something to it. She explains that under the right conditions, *saying* something about traumatic memory *does* something to it: defuses it, renders it less intrusive, less disruptive, and transforms it into narrative memory that can be integrated into a self in the process of being rebuilt (Brison 1999a, p. 47). Again, this description of the process of recovery is not isolated. The ability to recreate a narrative in PTSD and depersonalization disorder recovery is widely acknowledged in psychiatric treatments (Pickard 2014).

The process of recreating the narrative is linked to recovery, but it should not be mistaken for a return to the past self. Brison notes:

> Am I back to where I was before the attack? I have to say *no*, and *I never will be.* I am not the same person who set off, singing, on that sunny Fourth of July in the French countryside. I left her in a rocky creek bed at the bottom of a ravine. I had to in order to survive. The trauma has changed me forever, and if I insist too often that my friends and family acknowledge it, that's because I'm afraid they don't know who I am.   (2003, p. 21; emphases added)

People, even close friends and relatives, fail to listen to or empathize with the victims of rape and trauma because listening to the victims makes people realize how little control one may have over what happens to them. But others must understand, Brison emphasizes, that they have a role to play in the reconstruction of the narrative that creates the *new* self and thus the recovery; the narrative is not created by oneself in isolation but is entangled with the narrative of others, the stories that others tell about us. Recovery does not consist in picking up the shattered pieces of the self and putting them back together. Rather recreating the narrative, for Brison, is the making of a *new* self that reconstructs the past, including the traumatic event, and is able to imagine a future. Brison explains this by saying that:

> Narrative, as I now think, facilitates the ability to go on opening up possibilities for the future through retelling the stories of the past. It does this not by reestablishing the illusions of coherence of the past, control over the present, and predictability of the future, but by making it possible to carry on without these illusions.   (2003, pp. 103–4)

There are many lessons to learn from this insightful account: two are most important for our purposes here. First, it tells us that the episodic sense of self is not the result of a mysterious persisting subject of experience that underlies our episodic memories. Instead, the episodic sense of self depends on the ability to (re)construct our narrative self-conception. The inability to construct a narrative, as in Brison's case, signals a loss of sense of identity with a past self and inability to imagine a future self. Recreating the narrative marks the return of the sense of identity with a past and an imagined future self. Second, it tells us that narrative self-conception sustains one's sense of self in episodic memory—the sense one has that tells us: *it was me*. Brison's case study also shows that the narrative self-conception is not something that we create in isolation; others too have a role to play. Who we and others think we are—the co-authored narrative—sustains the episodic sense of self; there is no otherwise mysterious underlying subjective self that grounds the phenomenology of a persisting sense of self. The lesson to be learnt, then, in Dennett's words is:

> [W]e are virtuoso novelists, who find ourselves engaged in all sorts of behavior, more or less unified, but sometimes disunified, and we always put the best "faces" on it we can. We try to make all our material cohere into a single good story. And that story is our autobiography. The chief fictional character at the center of that [co-authored] autobiography is one's self. And if you still want to know what the self really is, you are making a category mistake.   (1992, p. 114)

Some may be concerned that one case study is not enough to establish the claim that episodic sense of self depends on narrative conception. The claim, however, finds extensive support in psychology research. Martin Conway proposes that memory is strongly influenced by demands of coherence between memories and the self (2001, 2005; Conway et al. 2004). The self, according to Conway, has a bi-directional relationship with episodic memories: it employs transient goals to govern autobiographical retrieval but is at the same time constrained and grounded in memories. The self and memories have to form a coherent system, in which each component informs and constrains the other; what is encoded, maintained, and retrieved in priority is information that is consistent with an individual's goals, self-images, and self-beliefs. Reciprocally, beliefs and knowledge about oneself are grounded in memories of specific experiences. Similarly, McAdams (2001) argues that the evolving story of self is based on autobiographical memories as well as future expectations; he is emphatic that life stories are constructions. People's memories are not completely disconnected from reality, but they tend to be altered, distorted, and even fabricated to support the story of the self (Conway 2005; Greenwald 1980; Wilson & Ross 2003). As McAdams says: "To a certain degree, then, identity is a product of choice. We choose the events that we consider most important for defining who we are" (2001, p. 110). The bi-directional relationship of episodic memories with the self signals that if memories are constructed, so too, as I will argue, must be the self.

4.4.4   A Narrative Conception of the Episodic Sense of Self

So far, I have established that the episodic sense of identity is not a result of some mysterious persisting subject of experience; rather it is sustained by our narrative self-conception. However, I need to clarify what exactly is meant by saying that the narrative "sustains" the episodic sense of self. Episodic memories and our narrative self-conception have a bi-directional dependence. On the one hand, it is obvious that episodic memories have a special place in the narrative even though the events we episodically remember are few and far between. Some cognitive scientists, for example Pribram (1999), suggest that a properly functioning episodic memory is essential for cashing out the non-fictional aspect of the narrative. This issue, however, is moot in light of the reconstructive nature of memory. Episodic memory and episodic simulation play a special role in the narrative, I contend, because they function as supports to hook the narrative to events in the reconstructed past and the imagined future.

To fix ideas, it might be useful to think of episodic memory and episodic simulation and their role in the narrative conception of the self as analogous to occasion sentences (especially those with a pure indexical "I") that play central role in constructing Quine's translation manual (1960). Just as occasion sentences constitute the most direct link between language and the recurrent macroscopic objects of human attention and interest, episodic memories and episodic simulation constitute the most direct link between the narrative and reconstructed events from the past and the imagined events in the future. The reconstruction and imagination are derived from human interest and attention; not much more. In a sense, therefore, the reconstruction contributes to the narrative.

Episodic memory, on the other hand, is the result of reflecting on past experiences, and such reflection, I propose, introduces a self in the original experience by appropriating the experience as part of one's narrative. This appropriation requires linguistic and conceptual resources which, in turn, are provided by the narrative. Such an appropriation view has been defended by Madhyamaka Buddhist philosophers—for example, Nāgārjuna and Candrakīrti. Jonardon Ganeri labels this the "Appropriativist Theory of Self" and explains it as follows:

> [T]he language of self – use of words like "I", "mine", "you", and so forth – is not properly understood as having a representational function.... What, then, is the use of the language of self? The word "I" is used, it seems, to perform an appropriative function, to claim possession of, to take something as one's own (compare *upādāna*: "the act of taking for one's self, appropriating to one's self"). The appropriation in question is to be thought of as an *activity of laying claim to*, not the making of an assertion of ownership. When I say, "I am happy", I do not assert ownership of a particular happy experience; rather, I appropriate the experience within a stream [of experiences], and in doing so lay claim to it.
>
> (2004, p. 70; emphasis added)

Appropriativist theory of self neatly explains that the function of the term "I" is not to refer, but rather to *lay claim to, appropriate* experiences and actions *as if* they are owned by oneself. Thus, the sense of self as the subject of experiences (including memory experiences) and agent of actions is the result of the metacognitive operation of appropriation. This clarifies the sense in which the narrative sustains the episodic sense of self. The narrative imposes/inserts a self on/in reconstructed experiences in one's past and imagined future. Thus, the narrative functions as the fabric that ties together various episodic memories and episodic simulations as belonging to *me*.

This account explains that self-conscious emotions like pride and guilt follow naturally from the activity of laying claim to actions in the past as one's own. However, the account also shows that Nichols' proposed disassociation between the episodic and the trait conceptions of self must be questioned. The narrative conception includes the knowledge of one's traits and much more. Furthermore, the notion of narrative at issue here does not suffer from the usual problems faced by narrative accounts of self. A pressing concern about narrative theories is that presumably some narratives get it wrong. What do we say about cases where that happens, where the narratives are false? We need to have some truth makers—why is it the case that one narrative truly characterizes what I did while another does not? The account of narrative presented above shows that the question itself is confused.

A further concern is that the concept of narrative appears to imply coherence, but such a coherence is only an imposition on otherwise fragmented life histories (Strawson 2015). Again, the reliance on reconstructive memory shows that coherence is not an imposition; it is built into the fabric of our episodic memories. It is important to emphasize that my account does not aim to provide a narrative theory of self; rather the account is aimed at debunking the very idea of identity with a past self. My account might suggest a mutual dependence between episodic and narrative senses of self, but it is important to clarify that this is not the case. The episodic sense of self comes with the sense of identity with a temporally distant self. The narrative account proposed here shows that this sense of identity is a mere construction. This is good news for the Abhidharma no-self theorist because according to her the sense of self is a product of social and narrative construction. But the Abhidharma Buddhist needs to go further to show that it is an illusion. She is not there yet.

4.4.5 The Illusory Sense of Self

The narrative is not meant to function as evidence for our sense of identity with a past self; there is no delineable evidence for the episodic sense of self. Klein makes the stronger claim that one's sense of (subjective) self is not directly based on memory or any other form of evidence. I agree, there is no direct evidence for the episodic sense of self. However, Klein also warns us that because "the self of sub-jectivity is not experienced as a changing self [it does not follow] that the self of subjectivity is not experienced at all" (Klein 2014a, p. 12). He offers two reasons: First, our sense of self is the most salient feature of everyday experience. This first-personal pre-reflective awareness of the self is part of the datum of every experience and cannot be denied. And secondly, patients with various levels of cognitive impairment can maintain a coherent sense of diachronicity (Klein 2014a). This shows that what underlies the episodic sense of self is the constancy of subjectivity. However, I believe that it is a mistake to think that the self of sub-jectivity is experienced. There is no phenomenological marker of the self in expe-rience. Zahavi and Kriegel (2015) argue that there is no separate self-quale that one can consult in one's phenomenology in isolation from the content of con-sciousness. The pre-reflective self-awareness does not deliver a datum or a quality like the smell of fermented garlic. They claim that:

> [I]t is not supposed to be any specific feeling or determinate quale at all....Our view is not that in addition to the objects in one's experiential field—the books, computer screen, half empty cup of coffee, and so on—there is also *a self-object*. Rather the point is that each of these objects, when experienced, is given to one in a distinctly first-personal way. On our view, one does not grasp for-me-ness by introspecting a self-standing quale, in the same way one grasps the taste of lemon or smell of mint....In other words, the "me" of for-me-ness is not a sepa-rate and distinct item but rather a "formal" feature of experiential life as such.
>
> (2015, p. 38)

In this sense, the sense of self is a structural and formal feature of experience, rather than a datum of experience. The view that the self, though not given as a "datum" in experience, is a formal feature of experience is also defended by some Hindu philosophers, specifically the Nyāya-Vaiśeṣika philosophers. Their argu-ment for the self takes the form of an inference as discussed in section 4.2. However, as we have seen, that argument is not successful in establishing the self as identical across time. The relevant point for our discussion here is, contra Klein, that the self of subjectivity is not a datum of experience.

Klein's second argument can be questioned by pointing to many cases in which patients cannot maintain a coherent sense of diachronicity. Brison's PTSD case and many other similar cases point to loss of constancy of subjectivity, the so-called "living in the moment." The illusion of constancy arises, I believe, from the fact that the sense of self seems to be embedded in every experience, albeit implicitly. And, because it seems to be always present in every experience, we mistakenly experience it as being the sense of the *same* self. Since there is no experiential phenomenology associated with the sense of self, experience cannot be the evidence for the sense of self. And since there is no experiential phenomenology associated with the episodic sense of self, episodic memory experiences cannot be the evidence for an identity with a past self. Rather than providing the evidence, the function of the narrative account is to ground the illusion of the episodic sense of self. This might be what Kant has in mind in thinking that the poor "I" representation engenders the illusions of rational psychology; illusions that there is a self that is simple, substantial, and identical across time. The episodic sense of self as identical across time is, as the Abhidharma Buddhists say, an illusion.

4.4.6 It Was Me!

There is one last issue to which we must attend before I conclude this chapter: What about the sense of "mentally reliving" the experience in episodic memory? Klein, following Tulving, explains that in episodic remembering the retrieved content is accompanied by autonoetic consciousness (Klein 2013). Autonoesis is the "unique awareness of re-experiencing here and now something that has happened before at another time and place" (Tulving 1993, p. 16). Episodic memory is crucially identified in terms of the manner in which content is given in awareness rather than the content per se (Klein 2015a).

Autonoetic consciousness endows the memory with the "feeling of pastness" on account of a direct acquaintance relation with the reconstructed content. This explains the "mentally reliving the past," an important phenomenological feature of episodic memory. This feature too has an adaptive benefit. Klein contends that autonoesis may be evolution's answer to how we decide whether our memories track the past. There are evolutionary advantages in believing that one's memories make contact with a past "reality." Assuming the veracity of episodic memory will save valuable time in acting on environmental contingencies, without having to verify whether the memories are "true" and "correct." Autonoetic awareness may be the source of our confidence that our recollections track the past. This, in turn, enables us to deal promptly and effectively with the circumstances for which recollection was naturally selected (e.g., future-oriented responses). Autonoesis informs consciousness that the content of a recollection is tied to its source in one's past (Klein 2014b).

4.5 Conclusion

The view proposed here is a narrative deconstruction of the sense of self, combined with a degree of skepticism about introspection and the veridicality of memory. This disturbing combination seems to suggest that, according to the

Abhidharma Buddhists, we are completely cut off from the reality of our lives. But disturbing as it might seem, there is reason to think that the "reality" of our lives is an active construction or controlled hallucination rather than passive perception. Anil Seth proposes that experiences of the world around us and ourselves within it are "controlled hallucinations" that have been shaped over millions of years of evolution to keep us alive in worlds full of danger and opportunity.[10] The Abhidharma no-self view goes further than this. It tells us we can not only survive but do "better" all things considered if we give up on the conceit of self. In what sense is this better? This is a question I will postpone; we must press ahead with other challenges for the Abhidharma no-self view. But it is a question to which we will return in the last two chapters in this book.

In this chapter, I have offered an explanation of episodic memory on behalf of the Abhidharma Buddhist philosophers. The response here takes account of the concerns raised by ancient Hindu philosophers (section 4.2) and contemporary philosophers (e.g., Tulvig). My episodic memory experiences seemingly come with the sense that I was the one who underwent the original experience. But is there really an experience of an identity with a past self—namely, an experience of being a subject that underlies our episodic sense of self? I have argued that there is nothing that it is like to be identical with oneself in the past: there is no experiential phenomenology associated with the episodic sense of self. There is thus no onus on the Abhidharma philosopher to explain the episodic sense of self.

---

[10] Anil Seth, *Your Brain Hallucinates Your Conscious Reality*, available at: https://perma. cc/6UGQ-B4BU.

5

Synchronic Unity Without a Self

5.1 Introduction

The early Nyāya unity arguments, as we saw in the previous chapter, depend on diachronic unification of distinct representations, but later Nyāya philosophers explicitly widened the scope to incorporate new unity arguments that invoke synchronic unification. In this chapter, I tackle the question of synchronic unity of experiences.

But first we must be clear about what we mean by synchronic unity. There is considerable disagreement in the recent philosophical literature about the scope and extent of the synchronic unity thesis. The argument of the Nyāya opponents is based on a fairly uncontroversial synchronic unity thesis which demands an explanation. The examples used by the Nyāya philosophers include everyday examples like seeing and smelling the same flower, Devadatta's cognition of form, flavor, odor, and texture (say of a mango), etc. These momentary experiences often seem to be composed of multiple multimodal features and multiple objects. This unity was lodged as a key argument for the causal indispensability of the self by the ancient Nyāya philosophers. Some of these arguments have been resuscitated in contemporary literature (Chakrabarti 1992; Ganeri 2000) but they have been discussed from the Nyāya point of view. Here, I want to discuss how the Abhidharma Buddhist might address the objection raised by the synchronic unity of experiences. The question I want to address in this chapter is: If there is no self then how do we explain the manifest fact that individuals typically have unified conscious experiences involving multiple features, multiple modalities, and multiple objects? I will argue that there are different kinds of synchronic unity and that once we distinguish between the various kinds of these unities, the Nyāya argument for the causal indispensability of the self becomes difficult to sustain.

I begin in section 5.2 by describing various notions of synchronic unity in the literature to delineate the one of interest. This groundwork allows me to introduce the Nyāya arguments from synchronic unity of experiences against the Buddhist no-self views in section 5.3. Sections 5.4 and 5.5 consider some responses that have been offered by Buddhist philosophers in the ancient Indian tradition. These responses do not offer an adequate solution to the problems raised by the Nyāya. In section 5.6, using some resources from contemporary cognitive science, I offer a new solution to the problem of synchronic unity on behalf of our Abhidharma

Selfless Minds: A Contemporary Perspective on Vasubandhu's Metaphysics. Monima Chadha, Oxford University Press.
© Monima Chadha 2023. DOI: 10.1093/oso/9780192844095.003.0006

Buddhists. Section 5.7 addresses some concerns about the solution to the problem of synchronic unity put forward in this chapter.

5.2 What Do We Mean by Synchronic Unity?

Contemporary discussions of synchronic unity of experiences have been influenced by Tim Bayne's *Unity of Consciousness* (2010). Bayne distinguishes between three kinds of synchronic unity: representational unity, subject unity, and phenomenal unity. Representational unity concerns not the subjects but the objects of consciousness. Unimodal and multimodal perceptual features are not experienced as isolated states of consciousness but bound together as integrated perceptual objects. We do not see the color and shape of a tomato, we see a tomato. We do not see the rocky terrain and feel the rocks under our feet while walking cautiously in rugged terrain, we simply experience the rugged terrain. This kind of unity is not only restricted to objects but also encompasses perceptual fields. We do not just see a cup of coffee on the table, we see it in front of the computer and within easy reach. Representational unity is commonplace and intuitively plausible, and it seems that this is what the Nyāya philosophers have in mind.

Bayne's discussion of unity of consciousness goes much further and deeper. Bayne is principally interested in phenomenal unity. Bayne explains the notion of phenomenal unity by drawing our attention to a description of a conscious experience:

> I'm sitting in the Café Cubana (47 Rue Vavin, Paris). I have auditory experiences of various kinds, I can hear the bartender making a mojito; I can hear the dog behind me chasing his tail; and there's a rumba song playing somewhere on a stereo. I am enjoying visual experiences of various kinds, I can see these words as they appear in my notebook; I can see the notebook itself; and I have a blurry visual impression of those parts of the room that lie behind the notebook. Co-mingled with these auditory and visual experiences are olfactory experiences of various kinds (I can smell something roasting in the kitchen); bodily sensations of various kinds (I am aware of my legs under my chair; I can feel my fingers on the table); and a range of cognitive and affective experiences. The bartender is talking to an old woman at the bar, and I have a vague sense of understanding what he's saying. I am soon to embark on a lengthy trip, and a sense of anticipation colours my current synchronic state. Finally, I am enjoying conscious thoughts. I realize that the bar is about to close, and that I will be asked to leave if I stay for much longer.   (2010, p. 5)

The stream of consciousness described by Bayne is rich and varied, it encompasses some manifest experiences and conscious thoughts but also a vague sense of embodiment and a background experience of anticipation of a forthcoming trip. Each of these synchronic elements, Bayne suggests, is phenomenally unified with the others within his overall phenomenal field. This unity is not itself an object of experience, nor is it something that a subject reflects on while enjoying the experience. Nonetheless, Bayne claims, it is a necessary feature of ordinary human experience that each of the experiences enjoyed at a particular time are phenomenally unified with other experiences at that time. In terms of evidence, he simply points to introspection. He says:

> The plausibility of the unity thesis derives largely from introspection. Consider the structure of your overall conscious state. I suspect that you will be inclined to the view that all your current experiences are phenomenally unified with each other—that they occur as components of a single phenomenal field; to put the same point in different terminology, that you enjoy a single phenomenal state that subsumes them all. (2010, p. 75)

Bayne's unity thesis is quite strong, suggesting that at any given point of time there is a single total conscious state experienced by a subject. This thesis implicates the notion of subject unity. All phenomenally unified experiences form a single synchronic state, and that state belongs to one subject. The notions of subject unity and phenomenal unity, insofar as the latter implicates the subject, might seem to be a worry for the Abhidharma Buddhist philosophers. Bayne's presentation of the unity thesis suggests intuitive plausibility. Reflection, however, shows otherwise. First, a close look at Bayne's description of his conscious state while sitting at a café in Paris shows that the unified conscious state he is in includes manifest experiences that are at the forefront of his awareness, and a host of other peripheral conscious experiences, which can perhaps be thought of as background states. Compare another total conscious state that most academics are familiar with while giving a lecture: there is awareness of words coming out of one's mouth, reading and perhaps pointing to material on the slides, facial expressions and body language of the students, and what to say next. All of these have to be in sync for a lecture to be delivered smoothly and it seems fair to say that they are part of the total conscious state of the academic even though she does not reflect on this while delivering the lecture. But now ask the further question: Is she also aware of the feel of the pointer on her fingers, or the feeling of her feet in her shoes? Not really, or at least not aware of them at the same level as the other conscious states. Following the Abhidharma analysis offered in Chapter 3, we may think of this difference in the level of awareness as a difference in degree—being more conscious or less conscious. The academic is manifestly conscious of the words coming out of her mouth and the words on the screen because they are at the center of her attention. The bodily feelings, such as the feel of the feet inside the shoes and the pressure on the fingers from the pointer, are felt in a vague, almost subliminal sense as they are at the periphery of her consciousness. She can be reminded that these background feelings persist in the periphery even though she is not consciously aware of them. For example, if she were to trip on a bump in the carpet, she would suddenly become consciously aware of the position of her feet. Given that there are many parts of any given conscious state, and we are not fully aware of all the parts or not aware of all the parts to the same degree, it is hard to make sense of these states as part of the total conscious state at any given moment of time. It is better to say that there is no total state but there are different composite states at different levels of awareness. We cannot even begin to think what it means to say that there is a total state that encompasses the feeling of pressure on my feet while walking in the lecture theatre and seeing the expressions on the faces of my students as I talk to them about the paradoxes of time travel.

Second, as Bayne himself appreciates, there are a number of clinical and experimental phenomena that seemingly pose problems for his strong unity thesis. He argues for the "switch model" of split-brain consciousness, according to which a split-brain subject possesses only a single stream of consciousness, unified at and across time, that shifts from one hemisphere to another from moment to moment. According to Bayne, the split-brain subject has a single stream of consciousness whose physical basis shifts from one hemisphere to the other as a function of which hemisphere has momentarily won the battle for attentional resource (2008a). So, just like ordinary subjects a split-brain subject has only a single stream of consciousness unified at a time and across time. Schechter (2012) and more recently Hill (2018) have given various reasons to question whether the switch model provides the general explanation of split-brain consciousness. In a recent review article co-authored by Bayne, the authors recognize the current consensus that there is insufficient evidence to give a definite answer to the question whether split-brain patients have one or two consciousnesses (de Haan et al. 2020).

In the light of this I think we can safely put aside the strong unity thesis as a potential objection to the Abhidharma no-self view. But there still is the concern over the manifest fact that conscious experiences often seem to be composed of multiple features, multiple modalities, and multiple objects. I will call this the manifest fact of synchronic unity. This fact demands further explanation.

5.3 A Nyāya Challenge: Synchronic Unity

In Chapter 4, we looked at the most prominent articulation of the argument for the existence of the self as presented in *Nyāyasūtra* 1.1.10. The Naiyāyikas argue that the self is indispensable for the explanation of desire, memory, etc. We may call this argument the Causal Indispensability (CI) argument for the existence of the self. A schematic version of this Nyāya argument is as follows:

CI1. The self is presupposed to be a single persisting conscious agent.[1]

CI2. The Naiyāyika notion of self must be posited in order to causally explain phenomena like desire, etc.

CI3. If an entity must be posited for causal explanation, that shows that the entity exists.

CIC. Thus the self (as presupposed by the Naiyāyikas) exists.

In Chapter 4 we were concerned with answering the challenge from episodic memory. Vasubandhu, as we have seen, agrees with CI3. His argument against the indispensability of the self is focused on premise CI2. If Vasubandhu is right, we can explain memory, desire, etc. without adverting to an enduring self over and above the states of consciousness. Thus, we can undermine the Causal Indispensability argument for the self presented in the original *Nyāyasūtra*.

Following Vasubandhu's response to the Causal Indispensability argument, the sixth-century Nyāya philosopher Uddyotakara develops a new argument designed to show that the self is indeed causally indispensable. In his commentary on *Nyāyasūtra* 1.1.10, Uddyotakara argues that we must appeal to the self to explain *pratisandhāna*. The term "*pratisandhāna*" has often been translated as "recognition" or "putting together." Though the term is initially introduced in the commentaries on the *Nyāyasūtra* in the context of discussion of memory, in the commentaries it is used in a broader sense than recognition. In the more inclusive sense, "*pratisandhāna*" is translated as "mental integration" (Ganeri 2007, p. 179), "synthetic cohesion" or "synthesis" (Kapstein 2001, p. 148), and "connecting up" (Taber 1990, p. 52). The inclusive reading allows for putting together or synthesizing diachronic and synchronic sensory impressions. In what follows, I use *pratisandhāna* in the broader sense and translate it simply as "synthesis."

Uddyotakara explicitly raises the challenge from synchronic unity against Vasubandhu's claim that the self is explanatorily redundant. That is, synchronic unity is presented as a new basis to support CI2 in the Causal Indispensability argument, suggesting that the causal explanation of synchronic unity requires appealing to a self. Vasubandhu never takes up this challenge directly, but as we shall see later, Buddhists do respond to the challenge.

A bit of background is necessary. Uddyotakara develops the challenge by reference to Vātsyāyana's commentary on *Nyāyasūtra* 3.1.1. That *sūtra* invokes cross-modal cognition to offer another argument for the existence of the self:

3.1.1.   Because one grasps the same object through sight and touch, there is a self that is distinct from the body and the sense organs. (trans. Dasti & Phillips 2017, p. 80)

---

[1] *Nyāyasūtra*, 1.1.10.

Vātsyāyana comments:

> Some particular object is grasped by sight and the same object is also grasped by touch, "That very thing which I saw with my eyes, I am now feeling through my sense of touch" and "that very thing that I felt through my sense of touch, I am now seeing with my eyes." The two instances of mental content that are each directed towards one and the same object have—in being comprehended—a single subject.... Thus, the grasper of one and the same object by the visual organ and the organ of touch comprehends the two instances of mental content about one and the same thing, two instances of mental content that have distinct causal complexes and distinct instrumental causes, but have no other subject other than the grasper. That one, in a special category, is the self.
>
> (trans. Dasti & Phillips 2017, pp. 80–1)

As is reflected in the above comment, Nyāya philosophers argue that mind and sense organs form the causal complex for perception, but they are just instrumental causes. The self, in contrast, is the agent unifying the percepts delivered by the sense organs. Vātsyāyana continues:

Question: How, again, is it that the mere functioning of the sense organs cannot bring about the single subjectivity for both instances of content?

Response: It is true that a sense is capable (in a sense) of comprehension in terms of grasping and repeatedly transmitting its peculiar content itself to a subject who endures the passage of time. But it does not grasp the other content which belongs to another sense faculty. (trans. Dasti & Phillips 2017, p. 81)

Thus, sense organs transmit content to the self, but they cannot transmit that content to any other sense organ. For instance, sight transmits the color and shape of a cup, but it cannot transmit the feel of the cup; nor can touch transmit the color of the cup. The eye cannot feel, and the skin cannot see.

The subsequent *sūtra* is put in the voice of a hypothetical (Buddhist) opponent who draws on this very restriction of the sense organs to argue that there is no need to posit a self over and above the sense organs:

3.1.2 Objection: This is wrong. (There is no self that is distinct from body and sense organs) because sense organs are restricted to their own proper content. (trans. Dasti & Phillips 2017, p. 81)

Let us dub the criterion that sense organs are restricted to their proper content as the "Restriction Assumption." Vātsyāyana elucidates the Buddhist objection raised in the *sūtra* and offers a response:

Objection: Other than the aggregates of the body and the rest (the sense organs) there is no consciousness....the sense organs have objects or content that is strictly demarcated. When there is no organ of sight, no colour is grasped....Just these several sense organs are conscious, because what is grasped is the content restricted to the specific sensory modalities....what's the point of positing something else as the experiencer.

Response: ...your contention remains doubtful, since there is an alternative, there is a conscious self *because* the sense organs are instrumental for conscious awareness but not themselves sufficient for conscious grasping that occurs. (trans. Dasti & Phillips 2017, pp. 81–2)

The hypothetical (Buddhist) opponent is suggesting that since we only grasp modality-specific content and sense organs themselves are conscious, what is the need of positing a self? Vātsyāyana's response does not challenge the Restriction Assumption but objects to the Buddhist claim that sense organs are conscious. Rather, he proposes that sense organs are only instruments of conscious awareness, they are not themselves sufficient for conscious awareness. Thus, the need for a conscious self. The next *sūtra* then turns the opponent's argument on its head:

3.1.3.   The very restriction of sense organs to their own proper content is a reason to suppose the existence of a self. (trans. Dasti & Phillips 2017, p. 82)

In his commentary on 3.1.3 Vātsyāyana ties this all together, "it is *because* the sense organs are restricted in content that there has to be something else, a conscious being capable of cognizing anything, a grasper of content of whatever sort" (Dasti & Phillips 2017, p. 82). Indeed, he maintains that if sense organs did not have content restricted to a single modality but could grasp all sorts of contents, then "we wouldn't have to infer a conscious being over and above that" (Dasti & Phillips 2017, p. 82). Thus, we can put Vātsyāyana's argument as follows:

V1. I feel through my sense of touch the same thing I saw with my sense of sight.

V2. These different sense organs, while not themselves conscious, grasp their content and transmit it to consciousness.

V3. Moreover, each of the sense organs is restricted to its specific objects.

VC. Thus, the conscious awareness that I touch what I saw can only be explained by appeal to a conscious being (a self) that provides the synthesis of the contents of the different sense organs.

The conclusion of this argument is a causal indispensability result. The first premise emphasizes the multimodal nature of the experiences. The second premise affirms the basic function of sense organs. The third premise asserts the restricted nature of the different sense organs to their own domain. This Restriction Assumption is shared by both the Buddhists and the Naiyāyikas.

As we will see shortly, Uddyotakara articulates a version of this argument that invokes synchronic unity as the explanandum (premise 1). Uddyotakara is aware of Vasubandhu's objections to the memory argument presented in *Nyāyasūtra* 1.1.10. So, first, Uddyotakara attempts to buttress the memory argument by drawing on Vātsyāyana's discussion of cross-modal cognition; Uddyotakara adverts to the Restriction Assumption in arguing that the self is the *agent* that unifies the cognitions across sensory modalities,

> For recognition could not occur if there were a plurality of subjects, a plurality of cognitively fixed contents, and a plurality of causes for ideas put together. The ideative flows of sights, tastes, smells, and touches are not made to come together (*pratisandhāna*) to form a recognition on their own. Nor is it true that my visual experience in the past is something I am able to touch later. And it is also false that my tactile experience from the past is the sight now.
>
> Furthermore, it is wrong that when something has been seen by Devadatta that very thing is recognized (*pratisandhāna*) by Yajñadatta....What's the reason for all this. It's because distinct cognitions have fixed content of their own. Having fixed content of their own, cognitions mutually exclude one another by nature. This is accepted by those who deny the self's existence. On their view, we should not expect any acts of recognition. Therefore, that which brings together (*pratisandhāna*) contents into a recognition is precisely a self.
>
> (trans. Dasti & Phillips 2017, p. 77)

Uddyotakara then rejects Vasubandhu's account of memory and strengthens the Nyāya argument further by explicitly drawing attention to examples of synchronic unity as additional phenomena that causally implicate a self:

> On your side, memory is not at all possible, and without memory there is no unification. But (in fact) there is unification (*pratisandhāna*)...Devadatta's cognitions of visible form, flavour, odour and texture bear the mark of one and many for they are synthesized by the cognition "I." Similarly, the cognitions of many persons, who having previously entered into an agreement (are linked together) during the single instant when the dancing-girl raises her brow.
>
> (trans. Kapstein 2001, p. 383)

Uddyotakara's argument moves from the unification of many simultaneous cognitions by a single agent that is the referent of "I" to the unification of many simultaneous cognitions belonging to different agents. There are many different nuances in this passage and thus many different interpretations in the literature, but one point is clear: Uddyotakara argues that we need to posit a self to causally explain examples of synchronic unity of cognitions.[2] And that is what matters for my purposes here. Uddyotakara appeals to "synchronic synthesis" as a further argument for the existence of a self. Thus, we arrive at what we can call *Uddyotakara's argument*, the causal explanation of synchronic unity requires invoking the self. Taking the lead from Vātsyāyana, Uddyotakara's argument can be presented thus:

U1. Devadatta sees the shape and color and feels the texture of a mango through the sense organs of sight and touch.

U2. These different sense organs, while not themselves conscious, grasp their content and transmit to consciousness.

U3. Moreover, each of the sense organs is restricted to its specific objects.

UC. Thus, Devadatta's conscious awareness that "I am seeing and touching a mango" can only be explained by appeal to a conscious being (a self) that provides the synthesis of the contents of the different sense organs.

Uddyotakara's argument clearly articulates the challenge from synchronic unity. How might the Buddhist answer this challenge? Vasubandhu does not directly respond. However, the Nyāya-Buddhist debate about the existence of the self continued in ancient India. In what follows, I discuss two responses that the Buddhists might offer. The first is developed by Siderits on behalf of the Abhidharma Buddhist, the second by the later Buddhist Śāntarakṣita. Though Śāntarakṣita is better known as a Madhyamaka philosopher, he is credited with bringing together the important insights of Abhidharma and Madhyamaka schools. So, it is worth considering his response to Uddyotakara's challenge.

5.4 A Conventionalist Reply on Behalf of Vasubandhu

One kind of response to Uddyotakara's argument is simply to deny the ultimate reality of synchronic unity and to maintain that any talk of synchronic unity is merely conventional. This response is developed by Siderits (2006, 2014) and is backed by resources available in the Abhidharma Buddhist tradition. Abhidharma philosophers, including Vasubandhu, posit a two-tier ontology: (i) the ultimately

---

[2] Uddyotakara's very dense and difficult example of the dancing-girl's raising of the eyebrow can be interpreted in ways that go beyond cases of synchronic unity that I am concerned with here. For instance, the example of the raised eyebrow seems to be a case where many persons undergoing different experiences nonetheless end up experiencing the same aesthetic emotion (e.g., of sexual desire) with respect to the same object, that is the raising of the dancing-girl's brow since that object causes their distinct experiences. That may well be right, but it is beyond the scope of this discussion, which is more narrowly focused on the basic phenomenon of synchronic unity.

real entities (the *dharmas*) that are genuinely non-composite and (ii) the conventionally real composite objects (for example, chariots) to which we express ontological commitment in our everyday speech and thought. Two features of composites are important in this context. First, composites are merely conceptual constructions, which group together real *dharmas*. Some of these groupings of real *dharmas* are useful fictions insofar as they serve human interests and purposes. For example, the chariot as a whole is not ultimately real. But insofar as it can be used by humans to get from one place to another, it makes sense to treat co-occurring *dharmas* as a whole and refer to it by the term "chariot." The second important feature is that properties of composites supervene on properties of the ultimately real *dharmas*, and the ultimately real parts do all the causal work (Siderits 2006).

If multimodal experiences are simply groupings of percepts with no ultimate reality,[3] then a Buddhist can just dismiss the grouping as a convention. That is, a Buddhist can perfectly well say, "if all you mean by 'synchronic unity' is a conventional grouping of percepts that serves human interests and purposes, then fine. Group all you want. Synchronic unity would only challenge a Buddhist if the group of states turned out to be *really* causally explanatory."

Although the conventionalist move would provide a direct response to the challenge from synchronic unity, the move is implausible. Take the example of watching a movie. We simultaneously hear a character talking and see their lips moving. That there is a single integrated audio-visual experience is suggested by the fact that when the dubbing is off, it is phenomenologically evident that the sound and the lips are out of sync. In this case, the synchronic unity of complex audio-visual experience is clearly causally explanatory. Audio-visual perception provides other commonplace examples. We have audio-visual experiences of hands' clapping, vehicles' colliding, and so on. The composite percepts in these multimodal experiences have causal potency. For instance, if we perceive that the video and audio are out of sync in a movie, we might turn it off in a fit of irritation. The irritation cannot be explained by the individual causal contributions of the auditory percept and the visual percept.[4]

The shortcomings of the conventionalist reply are also revealed by having a simultaneous experience of diverse objects. I currently have the experience of a laptop and a book on the table in front of me. If you would ask me how many objects I see on the table, I will say "two." If you take the book away and ask again,

---

[3] The Naiyāyikas also hold that each sense-faculty produces its own distinctive kind of cognition, so that no perceptual cognition can involve more than one modality. Both parties agree that multimodal percepts are groupings; they disagree whether these groupings are ultimately real or not.

[4] Furthermore, it may be argued that these multisensory percepts enhance perception by improving accuracy and reliability and allowing for perception of novel features (O'Callaghan 2017b). It seems there is a good explanation for why perception delivers these integrated multimodal percepts— it's an adaptive way of representing the world. Thus, it seems plausible to suppose that the synthesizing work done by sensory systems is a result of natural selection rather than mere convention.

I will give a different answer. It is worth adding that unconscious percepts, if there are such things, will not be included in the determination of these verbal responses. The significance of this synchronic unity is strikingly revealed by pathologies. People with simultagnosia can only see one object at a time. In one demonstration, a patient was shown a comb and a spoon. The patient was asked what he saw, he says "comb." When asked whether he sees a spoon, he says "no." The experimenter then sets both items down and picks them up again. Now the patient says that he sees the spoon but does not see the comb (Rafal 1997). In a different demonstration, when presented with an array of several red and green discs, a patient with simultagnosia claimed that he saw only one color; but when the differently colored discs were connected with a bar, thereby constituting red-green dumbbells, he reported seeing two colors (Humphreys & Riddoch 1993).

Simultagnosia is visually debilitating. Imagine being unable to see both the sofa and the coffee table at the same time. As you might expect from imagining this, people with this condition are functionally blind. It is because you simultaneously see the table and the sofa that you are able to effectively navigate between them. This reinforces the point that our ability to see multiple objects simultaneously is functionally important. So, the conventionalists' attempt to deny the reality and causal potency of unified experiences seems inadequate as a response to Uddyotakara's argument.

5.5 An Intellectualist Reply

Another prominent Buddhist response to Uddyotakara's argument was developed by the later Buddhist philosopher Śāntarakṣita and his pupil Kamalaśīla. Śāntarakṣita accepts that there is unity of consciousness at a time, perhaps even that "there is indeed a single centre of consciousness, one that is conscious, all at once, of the various objects of the senses and of the intellect"[5] (Kapstein 2001, p. 150). As a Buddhist, he denies that the single center of consciousness is a persisting conscious self. Rather, he posits a single mental cognition that immediately succeeds the distinct sensory cognitions, and it is this subsequent mental cognition that is responsible for synthesizing the preceding sensory cognitions into a single whole. So, in effect, synchronic unity is explained by appeal to a causal link between the preceding sensory cognitions and a single succeeding act of "intellectual consciousness" that takes the sensory cognitions as its object. Kamalaśīla explains Śāntarakṣita's response:

> Thus, from a single succeeding act of consciousness, which is the condition of immediate continuity, the (preceding) occurrence of the six consciousnesses of

---

[5] *Tattvasaṁgraha*, v. 198.

eye, etc., are clearly known. So it is that what sees the dancing girl's figure, also hears the sounds of the drum and other instruments, smells aromas like that of the blue lotus, tastes camphor, and so forth, feels the breeze of the fan, etc., and thinks of presenting a gift of cloth. It is not correct to assert that this is due to the extreme rapidity of movement, as one sees a circle formed by a whirling torch.[6]

(trans. Kapstein 2001, pp. 150–1)

The whirling torch example, originally Vasubandhu's, is often used in the Buddhist tradition as a strategy for handling cases of seeming synthesis. A rapidly whirling torch is seen as a ring of fire, though there is fire only at the tip of the torch. This strategy might be deployed to explain multimodal synthesis by suggesting that there is rapid alternation of percepts from different modalities which is blurred into a unified percept. Śāntarakṣita rejects this because this strategy suggests that there is an enduring observer, over and above the cognitions, that blurs rapid succession into unity. Rather, he wants to distinguish his response by claiming that synchronic unity is brought about by a single mental cognition which takes the preceding sensory cognitions as its object. As we saw in section 5.3, the Buddhist holds that the sense organs are capable of cognizing (or grasping) their own specific contents. Nonetheless, these diverse causes can produce an intellectual recognition of a unity of disparate contents. Kapstein interprets the view as follows: "Śāntarakṣita holds that there will be a phenomenal unity of consciousness whenever an act of intellectual consciousness occurs, but there will never be a real unity of consciousness" (2001, p. 151). Instead of a real unity of consciousness, Śāntarakṣita maintains the unity is "conceptually imputed" (Edelglass & Garfield 2009, p. 329). In contemporary parlance, we might characterize Śāntarakṣita's notion of intellectual consciousness as a form of "higher-order cognition" (see for example, Garfield 2015, p. 103).

Although Śāntarakṣita's intellectualist proposal gives the Buddhist a way of acknowledging that synchronic unity is real without allowing a causal role for the self, the proposed solution carries controversial implications. Many philosophers and cognitive scientists would likely reject the claim that synchronic unity only occurs as the content of a higher-order state. Rather, synchronic unity is plausibly a basic feature of experience that does not depend on higher-order capacities or conceptual imputation. Monkeys, cats, and rats seem to navigate through multiple obstacles in the way that patients with simultagnosia cannot. On the assumption that the basic structure of visual consciousness is continuous in other mammals, there is reason to think synchronic unity is present and functionally critical in all mammals. To sustain the higher-order account of synchronic unity, one would have to maintain either that cats and rats lack synchronic unity or that

---

[6] *Tattvasaṁgrahapañjikā*, 110–11.

they possess capacities for higher-order cognition. Both options are highly controversial. I think there is a less precarious way for the Buddhist to respond to Uddyotakara's argument, to which we turn in the next section.

5.6 The Generation and the Effects of Synchronic Unity

To review, Uddyotakara's argument holds that diachronic unity (as in the case of memory) and synchronic unity can only be explained by invoking a self. The Naiyāyikas claim that some sort of synthesis is required for memory and synchronic unity. My concern in this chapter is with the synthesis required for synchronic unity.[7] According to Uddyotakara, if there were no single self, "there would be no synthesis (*pratisandhāna*) of diverse agents, diverse objects, and diverse stimuli. For the cognitions of form, taste, odour, and texture would in that case not be synthesized" (Kapstein 2001, p. 148). Kapstein glosses the argument as follows:

> That is to say, assuming no identity of agency, there can be no synthesis of the diverse cognitions of form, odour, etc., into an organic whole—in what sense, then, could we understand ourselves to be both seeing and smelling the same rose? We would not be able to say that the very object I see is the very same object I feel, unless we can affirm that it is one "I" that does both the seeing and the feeling.   (2001, p. 149)

There are two prominent Buddhist responses to this argument—conventionalism and intellectualism. I have argued that neither of these replies works. The task now is to offer a new response to the Naiyāyikas synchronic unity argument for the self. So, what is the notion of self defended by Nyāya? In his explication and defense of *Nyāyasūtra* 1.1.10, Uddyotakara makes clear that the Nyāya notion of self is that of an enduring conscious substance.[8] With this Nyāya conception of self in the background, I will respond to Uddyotakara's synchronic unity argument on behalf of the Abhidharma Buddhists.

Before proceeding, I want to distinguish between the *generation* of synchronic unity and the *state* of synchronic unity itself. Notice that this distinction is not just technical jargon, it is already implicit in the usage of the English word "synthesis," which can mean either a process or a state. The OED defines synthesis as: "The putting together of parts or elements so as to make up a complex whole... [a]lso, the state of being put so together." I argue that the *generation* of synchronic unity does not show that there is an enduring conscious self, over and

---

[7] Elsewhere, I have argued there is no real unity in the case of memory (Chadha & Nichols 2019).
[8] For details of Uddyotakara's argument see Chakrabarti (1982) and Taber (1990).

above the perceptual apparatus ("sense organs" in the Nyāya terminology) because the generation of that unity can be explained by the perceptual apparatus without appeal to the self. And I argue that the *state* of synchronic unity itself does not show that there is a self because that unity is momentary and ever changing.

5.6.1 The Generation of Synchronic Unity

Synchronic unity is a phenomenon of experience that calls for an explanation. When looking at a tennis ball, we have a unified experience of a yellow sphere, not merely separate experiences of yellow and sphere. The synthesis of color and shape seems to be an intrinsic feature of our experience of objects like tennis balls. Visual object perception provides the paradigm example of intra-modal feature binding, but we also find examples in audition and touch, as when a sound is audibly high-pitched but wavering (O'Callaghan 2017a) or when a surface feels smooth and warm to the touch (Fulkerson 2011).

Thus, in everyday life we experience features as bound together. Indeed, intra-modal feature binding seems to be a pervasive characteristic of our experience. As Anne Treisman, one of the pioneers in research on feature binding, puts it:

> Experienced objects have colours, locations, orientations. They may not always be correctly bound; in fact, when we first look at a complex multi-object scene they probably are not. But it seems impossible to even imagine free-floating shapes, colours, or sizes. Using language or other symbols, we can abstract particular properties (a kind of unbinding), but this is not part of our perceptual experience.   (2003, p. 97)

Of course, we also experience *inter*-modal binding. The fact that we experience inter-modal binding is nicely exposed by cross-modal illusions, ventriloquism[9] being the most familiar (Bertelson 1999). A subtler demonstration of inter-modal binding is found in the auditory-flash illusion, in which subjects misperceive a single flash of light as two flashes when it is paired with two beeps (Shams et al. 2000). A similar interaction has been found between touch and audition, where participants who are presented with multiple tones will experience a single tap as two taps (Hötting & Röder 2004). Inter-modal integration also occurs for high-level, categorical information. The best known is the McGurk effect, in which dubbing the phoneme /ba/ onto the lip movements for /ga/, produces, in normal

---

[9] Ventriloquism is a performance act which involves the art of "throwing" the voice, i.e., speaking in such a manner that the sound seems to come from a source other than the speaker. A ventriloquist creates the illusion that the sound is coming from another source, say a puppet.

adults, an auditory percept of the phoneme /da/ (McGurk & MacDonald 1976). Of course, illusions are not the only examples of inter-modal binding; there are plenty of cases of veridical inter-modal binding, as when we look at and listen to each other.

The Abhidharma Buddhist aims to account for the phenomenology of experiences, so they should be concerned. The point at issue in the Nyāya-Buddhist debate is whether such an explanation necessarily invokes the self, conceived of as an enduring conscious substance. Can we explain the intra-modal and inter-modal binding without the self? Yes, we can.

There is abundant evidence that undercuts the Restriction Assumption, according to which each sense organ is restricted to its own proper content. Perceptual processing in one modality is often modulated by perceptual processing in other modalities (Bertelson 1988; Calvert et al. 2004; de Gelder & Bertelson 2003). For instance, in the McGurk effect the alveolar /da/ is a compromise between the visible velar /ga/ and the audible bilabial /ba/. So, conflicting information from different sensory systems is reconciled in order to reduce or resolve conflict. Crucially, this conflict is resolved before the percept is transmitted to consciousness (see e.g., O'Callaghan 2017a; Cinel et al. 2002).

Furthermore, there is reason to believe that the perceptual system integrates information across modalities in such a manner that the representations in question are neither confined to auditory nor to visual cortices but are instead located in areas that are inherently audio-visual. Consider the sound-induced flash illusion again: the visual and the auditory systems are not generating representations of a visual object and an auditory object respectively; rather, the interaction generates a representation of an audio-visual object. O'Callaghan (2008) suggests that the perceptual experience of the sound-induced flash illusion shows that the flash and the beep are manifestations of a single event, not distinct visual and auditory stimuli. More generally, it is plausible that integrated multisensory representations are characteristic of conscious experience. In the words of one review article, multisensory integration "is the rule and not the exception in perception" (Shimojo & Shams 2001, p. 505).

A common factor in both intra-modal and inter-modal binding is that the binding process is unconscious. Patients with blindsight are capable of binding together primitive features in their blind field (Kentridge et al. 1999; Kentridge 2004). We also find evidence for unconscious binding from work on priming in patients exhibiting unilateral neglect. Processing of a word presented in the right visual field can be facilitated by the brief presentation of an associated word in the neglected left visual field, even though the neglected word appears not to enter consciousness. In order for the neglected word to facilitate right visual field processing, it needs to be represented as such, and this of course requires the binding of its constituent features (Ladavas et al. 1993; Farah 1994). This shows that there is some unity in representations before they become conscious. One natural explanation of at least some instances of synchronic unity is that features (e.g., yellow; triangle) are bound unconsciously into a representation and then this representation becomes conscious. Indeed, Bayne argues that the "binding constraint" requires that perceptual features *cannot enter consciousness* without first being bound together unconsciously in the form of objects (Bayne 2010).

Similarly, in the case of inter-modal binding, the integration happens at an unconscious level. We do not consciously hear the sound and see the flash and subsequently consciously perceive two beeps and flashes. We consciously perceive the audio-visual object consisting of two beeps and flashes (for further discussion see, O'Callaghan 2008; Bayne 2014).[10] Bayne cites examples of the McGurk effect and ventriloquism as evidence for the claim that multisensory integration can occur "outside" of consciousness in the sense that a subject need not be conscious of the sensory cues responsible for modulation of perceptual content (2014). Visually presented lip movements that are presented in the ipsilesional hemifield of a person suffering from hemineglect can give rise to the McGurk effect when combined with the auditory speech stimuli presented in the patient's neglected contralesional hemifield (Soroker et al. 1995a, 1995b; Bayne 2014). More generally, the prevailing view is that multisensory integration happens unconsciously—features are bound into a multisensory representation before the representation becomes conscious.

The revealed nature of perceptual integration raises a problem for the Restriction Assumption. The Nyāya seem to assume that our sensory apparatus entrusts the job of integrating sensory data and adjudicating inter-sensory conflict (as suggested by the McGurk effect) to the conscious executive self. Cognitive science tells us that this is not the case. Instead, sensory systems resolve inter-sensory disputes prior to consciousness with the result that the conscious subject is unaware of the very existence of the disputes (Alais & Burr 2004). This arrangement has its advantages: eliminating inconsistencies prior to consciousness frees up post-conscious mechanisms for other tasks (Bayne 2010).

The Nyāya view cannot be squared with the emerging picture of intra-modal and inter-modal integration. We cannot account for the interplay between the contents of various modalities if the senses are working independently of each other. Inter-modal integration suggests that the sensory apparatus is not composed of sense-specific tributaries that generate experience in isolation from each other. Bayne claims that:

---

[10] There are different views about inter-modal integration and the nature of inter-modal objects. O'Callaghan (2008) distinguishes two versions. According to the first, there's nothing internal to the content of the visual and tactile experiences which demands that it is one and the same object that is both seen and felt. On this view, the logical structure is something like, x is red and y is smooth, and then it is an open question whether $x = y$. On the other model, the content of perception requires that it is a single object that is both seen and felt, that is, x is red and smooth. O'Callaghan defends the second version.

The senses are not hermetically sealed off from each other, but function as highly interdependent channels. A subject's perceptual experience in any one "modality" is the result of complex interactions between any number of sensory channels, and the hope that one might be able to identify stable, modality-specific mechanisms underlying it is, I suggest, a vain one. (2010, p. 235)

As we saw in section 5.3, Uddyotakara argues that the self must be posited in order to explain the synthesis of experiences from different sensory organs. One way to interpret this argument is that the *generation* of multimodal experiences requires the self, since, according to the Restriction Assumption, the senses are restricted to grasping their own objects and thus cannot transmit multimodal content to the conscious self. However, as we have seen, the Restriction Assumption is false. The perceptual apparatus is capable of generating multi-modal content. Thus, the generation of synchronic unity cannot be used as reason to bolster the original argument for the existence of the self in *Nyāyasūtra* 1.1.10.

The extant work on intra- and inter-modal binding provides overwhelming corroboration for our ordinary multimodal experience of objects. However, not all aspects of our experiences are bound into single objects. We also have simulta-neous experiences of *multiple* objects. And we can have experiences in different modalities that are not unified in the way we have been discussing above, for example we sometimes smell garlic while we are looking at a tomato. This is pre-sumably not a unified experience of a garlic-smelling tomato. However, the pro-duction of each of these experiences (of the garlic smell and the tomato) presumably has its own history in unconscious sensory processes. One subset of unconscious processes generates the tomato percept, another subset of uncon-scious processes generates the garlic-smell percept. In these cases, the sensory organs are not synthesizing different sensory contents into a unity. Rather, sen-sory organs are independently transmitting different contents to consciousness. Nonetheless, in such cases, there seems to be co-consciousness of sight and smell. And the kind of synchronic unity that we find in these cases might have down-stream consequences that show the causal indispensability of a self. To explore this issue, we turn to the *state* of synchronic unity.

5.6.2 The State of Synchronic Unity

A typical perceptual state enjoys unity that is created by the processes of intra- and inter-modal feature binding. For example, we have conscious inter-modal percepts of speech. More simply we have conscious unified visual percepts, e.g., of a tennis ball. These synthesized percepts have an obvious effect on behavior. I will play with the tennis ball rather than a similarly shaped tomato or a similarly colored banana. My unified experience of the tennis ball is thus plausibly causally relevant. Thus, Vasubandhu cannot simply dismiss synchronic unity as explanatorily redundant.[11] A conventionalist might respond on behalf of Vasubandhu that the tennis ball is not perceived. What is perceived is a bundle of property-instances—ballness, greenness, etc.—which we conventionally call a tennis ball. However, such a response runs afoul of the "binding-constraint." Perception does not deliver unbound property-instances or features that we bundle together under concepts or conventions; perception delivers single perceptual objects like tennis balls.

Additionally, as noted above, a unified conscious state at a time often contains multiple percepts. I experience the smell of garlic and the visual percept of a tomato. To return to the example from section 5.4, if you present a spoon and a comb to me, I will have distinct visual percepts for each. But both percepts will be part of a single experience of mine. I will have an experience of both the comb and the spoon. The percepts are part of a unified synchronic state. Moreover, the fact that they are both part of the same unified experience makes a causal difference. If you ask me how many things I see, I will say "two." If you take away the spoon and ask again, I will say "one."

Thus, the overall conscious state will often include multiple percepts, each of which is itself a synthesis of features. And the state of the unified experience will have distinctive causal effects. Furthermore, unlike its generation, the state of synchronic unity is conscious. Might the Nyāya then maintain that this kind of synthesis proves the explanatory power of the self?

The obvious problem with identifying the self with the state of synchronic unity, from the Nyāya perspective, is that the unified synchronic state is constantly changing. The state of synchronic unity is in constant flux as we move around the world, or it moves around us. The state of synchronic unity seems to have a causal role in explanation, but it is not a plausible candidate for an enduring self. Without further argument, the state of synchronic unity does not show a causal role for the kind of self that the Nyāya seek to defend.

5.7 Synchronic Sense of Self and Soteriology

I want to close this chapter by briefly drawing attention to what might seem to some as problems that arise from the proposed explanation of synchronic unity. First, it might be argued that any such account faces the harder problem

---

[11] Vasubandhu would happily acknowledge that experience is multi-featured (as in seeing a tall woman) and can potentially involve multiple percepts. So, the problem is not the state of synthesis per se.

of explaining the synchronic sense of self. In the case of diachronic unity of experiences, I argued that the content of the episodic memory and the accompanying sense of self is a product of (narrative) construction. In the case of synchronic unity, I have argued that, at least in the cases of representational unity, there is a genuine phenomenon that calls for an explanation. Does that implicate a sense of self as the subject of experience? The second problem is how the experience of synchronic unity might bear on Buddhist soteriology (philosophy of salvation). Insofar as many Buddhist philosophers deny synchronic unity, it is important to see whether it conflicts with Buddhist soteriology.

First, is there a sense of self as the subject of synchronically unified experiences? Do synchronically unified experiences of the sort discussed here, for example seeing a mango or multiple percepts, say a mango and knife, presuppose the self as the subject? I think not. The kind of unity explained here is representational unity which involves what we might call object unity and spatial unity (Bayne 2009). Experiences are object-unified insofar as they represent objects as unified entities. For example, my visual experience of the mango color and mango shape and my olfactory experience of the mango odor are object-unified insofar as they are directed at one and the same object. Similarly, my visual percepts of the mango and the knife as I see them next to each other on the table are spatially unified. Such cases of representational unity are accounted for by unconscious sensory processing including some multimodal sensory processes. None of these cases seem to implicate a sense of a self as subject of experience. There is of course the more general concern that the very having of an experience implicates a subject. Experiences, insofar as they are conscious states, must always be the states of a particular subject of experience. This general concern will be dealt with in Chapter 7.

Second, how might the experience of synchronic unity bear on Buddhist soteriology? The primary aim of Buddhist teachings is the elimination of suffering. The *Four Noble Truths* summarize Buddha's teaching: there is suffering, suffering has a cause, suffering can be removed by removing the causes, and there is a Path to freedom from suffering. The First Noble Truth describes suffering as a universal fact: all existence is bound up with suffering. The Second Noble Truth describes craving and clinging as the root causes of suffering. All possible objects of clinging, including one's own being, are impermanent. However, we cling to objects, including our own being, as if they are permanent. This results in sorrow and disappointment. The Abhidharma philosophers developed this theme in their writings in that elimination of suffering is brought about by abandoning the distorted projections created by imagination including, most importantly, the distorted idea that there is a self.

The centrality of the no-self doctrine for Buddhist soteriology is evident when Vasubandhu begins his discussion of soteriology with:

Question: Now, then, is no liberation (from the round of *saṃsāra*) to be found outside of this (teaching of the Buddha)?

Response: No, it is not.

Question: Why so?

Response: Owing to preoccupation with false views of self. For (our opponents) have not determined that the conceptual construction "self" refers to the bundle-continuum alone.

Question: What then?

Response: They imagine that the self is a discrete substance. Moreover, the negative affections are born from grasping-as-self. (trans. Kapstein 2001, p. 350)

Vasubandhu claims that the most important hurdle for liberation is preoccupation with false views about the self. The tendency to regard the self as a real substance results in (mistakenly) identifying it as an enduring conscious entity which persists through change in properties and experiences. This, in turn, leads to negative attachments in the form of craving and clinging to objects and labeling them as "me" and "mine." The soteriology recommends that we give up the belief in an enduring self, which entails the denial of diachronic unity over time.

As an antidote to attachment, the Abhidharma Buddhists are concerned to show that the belief in the enduring self is false. I worry about whether *I* will be miserable, whether *I* will obtain wealth, whether *I* will die next year. However, it is less clear that the belief in synchronic unity would facilitate attachment in the sense important for Buddhist soteriology. Of course, it might be that the belief in synchronic unity inevitably facilitates the belief in an enduring self. However, if we bracket that possibility, it is worth reflecting on whether the basic phenomenon of synchronic unity conflicts with the soteriological aims of Buddhism. To affirm synchronic unity is to say, for example, that color and shape are bound in some experiences, that vision and audition are bound in some experiences, or that multiple objects appear simultaneously in some experiences. It hardly seems like a problem for Buddhist soteriology aimed at elimination of suffering to acknowledge these commonplace aspects of experience. The Second Noble Truth locates the source of suffering in craving and clinging. But craving and clinging are characteristically directed towards future states of affairs involving the self. Insofar as we have thoughts about a persisting self, craving and clinging will lead to suffering. But if we can blunt this presupposition of a self, it is hard to see why acknowledging momentary unified experiences would contribute to suffering.[12]

---

[12] It is perhaps useful to compare Vasubandhu's Buddhist view with Metzinger's (2003) *Self-Model Theory*. According to Metzinger, no such things as selves exist in the world, selves and subjects are not part of the irreducible constituents of reality. He agrees with the Buddhists that the body and the mind are constantly changing. Nothing in us is ever really the same from one moment to the next. Yet there

5.8 Conclusion

The Nyāya argument from synchronic unity is one of the most powerful and influential arguments for the causal indispensability of the self. Nonetheless, I have argued here that this argument does not establish the causal indispensability of the kind of self presupposed by the Naiyāyikas. Additionally, I have suggested that the existence of synchronic unity does not invoke the sense of self as a subject of experiences and that seems to be consistent with Buddhist soteriology. As is well known, the debate between the Naiyāyikas and the Buddhists does not end here. Nyāya philosophers offered further arguments against the no-self view, including the argument from agency and ownership of experiences. I will take up these arguments in the following chapters. My aim is more modest here; we only want to claim that the synchronic unity argument offered by the Naiyāyikas can be rebutted by the Abhidharma Buddhists. The existence of synchronic unity is consistent with the Buddhist denial of the self as the enduring subject of experiences.

---

is the experience of self which represents a very strong phenomenal experience of sameness. This feeling of being the same enduring self is illusory. Nevertheless, Metzinger argues, it is a useful fiction because it has adaptive value for beings like us. As beings that work towards securing a better future, we would not do that if we did not have the very strong feeling that it is going to be "me" in the future. Metzinger agrees with the Buddhists that the feeling of being the same self is based on non-veridical experience of sameness. But here is an important difference: Metzinger thinks that the belief in the same self persisting over time has an important adaptive function. Unlike Metzinger, the Buddhists hold that the belief is pernicious as it is the source of existential suffering.

6

No-Self and the Phenomenology of Agency

6.1 Introduction

The aim of this chapter is to defend the Abhidharma no-self view as a no-agent view. The no-agent view appears to be counterintuitive. That the view is counterintuitive might not concern our Abhidharma Buddhist philosopher, but she ought to be concerned by the fact that the no-self doctrine denies that actions originate from an agent. Most contemporary philosophers writing on Buddhist philosophy take a middle way: although there are no selves, conventionally real persons seem to have the right kind of temporal extension to serve as surrogates for agents and therefore as bearers of moral responsibility (Siderits 2007). But, as I have argued in Chapter 2, this kind of solution fails to recognize the full force of the revisionary no-self metaphysics. Vasubandhu rejects persons on the same grounds as selves, persons are not ultimately real because they are causally inefficacious. The whole point of the no-self doctrine is to deny a real distinction between "oneself" and "others," to deny any privilege to one's own interests over those of others. Yet it appears that without such a distinction, we are left without any ground for the attribution of agency and moral responsibility. In what follows, I will explore Vasubandhu's solution to this quandary.

In section 6.2, I present Vasubandhu's no-agent view. While the no-agent view is widely endorsed by contemporary Buddhist philosophers, there is a schism whether we regard our ordinary talk of agency and responsibility as mere talk pertaining to conventionally real persons or we resuscitate real agency and moral responsibility without appealing to persons or selves. On the former view, persons exercise agency and free will and thus stand in as surrogates for agency and bearers of moral responsibility (notably Goodman 2016; Siderits 2013). I disagree with this view for reasons already discussed in Chapter 2. The latter view takes the no-agent view seriously. It attempts to recover notions of agency and responsibility by building intentionality and moral significance into the *dharmas* (notably, Gold 2015; Meyers 2017). My defense of Vasubandhu falls into this camp but is distinctive in that it brings in Vasubandhu's *Karmasiddhiprakaraṇa* (The Treatise on Action), a later text which deals specifically with this issue. In section 6.3, I present Thompson's (2014) reconstruction of the no-self view with elements of Abhidharma and Madhyamaka views that endorses a minimal self as the

Selfless Minds: A Contemporary Perspective on Vasubandhu's Metaphysics. Monima Chadha, Oxford University Press.
© Monima Chadha 2023. DOI: 10.1093/oso/9780192844095.003.0007

subject of experiences and agent of actions. The minimal self is conceived of as pre-reflective feeling that a given movement/action is performed by me (sense of agency), or that a given perceptual experience/thought is owned or had by me (sense of ownership). Insofar as the minimal self is understood phenomenologically, that is, in terms of how one experiences it, Thompson argues that the Abhidharma Buddhist will have no problem accommodating it. I disagree. I argue that although introducing the minimal self makes the Buddhist doctrine sound intuitively (and perhaps empirically) plausible, it undermines the spirit of the Buddhist no-self views in general and of the mature Abhidharma Buddhist views in particular. The denial of the minimal self certainly leaves the Abhidharma Buddhist philosopher with the additional burden of explaining the phenomenological sense of agency and sense of ownership. But is there really an experience of agency? Section 6.4 argues that there is nothing it is like to be an agent in the sense that there is no experiential phenomenology associated with our sense of agency; our sense of agency is a conceptual construct. The upshot is that the Abhidharma Buddhist philosopher need not burden herself anymore with explaining the sense of agency as it will be explained away by the end of this chapter. A similar treatment of the sense of ownership follows in the next chapter.

6.2 Vasubandhu on Responsibility Without Agency

I begin by revisiting Vasubandhu's argument for the no-agent view in the *Abhidharmakośa-Bhāṣya* before turning to his defense of agency and responsibility without persons or selves in his *Karmasiddhiprakaraṇa* (The Treatise on Action). In Chapter 9, *Refutation of the Theory of Self*, of the *Abhidharmakośa-Bhāṣya*, Vasubandhu addresses the concerns raised by Hindu philosophers: How can we make sense of agents of physical actions and of knowledge without there being a self? The questions go on: cognition, happiness, and pain are qualities had by a substratum, what is the substratum of these qualities? Who is the referent of the notion of "I"? Who is the one who is happy or unhappy? And finally, who is the agent of *karma* and the enjoyer of the results of *karma*?

Vasubandhu's strategy is to respond to each of these questions by giving an alternative explanation of the phenomena at issue by appeal to nothing but (the only ultimately real) momentary events and causal relations between them. In the context of discussing how *karma* arises without a self serving as its agent (*kartṛ*), he says:

Objector: There being no-self, who is the doer of these deeds? And who is the enjoyer of their fruit?

Response: What is the meaning of "doer"?

Objector: The doer is the one who does, the enjoyer is the one who enjoys.

Response: Synonyms have been offered, not meaning.

Objector: The grammarians say this is the mark of the "doer": "the doer is autonomous."

Response: Now whose autonomy is there with respect to what effects?

Objector: In the world, Devadatta is seen with the respect to bathing, sitting, locomotion, etc.

Response: But what is it that you term "Devadatta"? If the self, then that remains to be proven. Then the five bundles? In that case, those are the doer. Moreover, this action is threefold: action of body, speech, mind. There, with respect to the actions of body [speech], they are undertaken depending upon the mind. And those of mind are undertaken depending upon a proper cause with respect to body [and speech]. That being so in that case, nothing at all has autonomy. For all things coming about depending on conditions.... Therefore, no doer characterized [as autonomous] is apprehended. That which is the dominant cause of something is called its doer. But the self is not found to be a cause, with respect to anything. Therefore, there cannot thus be a self. For from recollection there is interest; from interest consideration; from consideration willful effort; from willful effort vital energy; and from that, action. So, what does the self do here?[1] (trans. Kapstein 2001, p. 373)

Vasubandhu's response is that there is no need to postulate an agent for bodily actions. So, for example, actions like eating, bathing, walking, etc., are explained in the following manner. A self contributes nothing to the arising of an action, such as eating a mango. The desire arises from a memory of enjoying a mango in the past. If one has not tasted a mango or for some reason one has no memory of it, one might not be moved to eating a mango. From this desire arises a consideration as to how to satisfy this desire, what follows is an intention to move the body for the sake of satisfying the desire. This movement, of the hand to acquire and cut a mango, finally leads to the action of eating a mango. There is no need to invoke the self as an agent at any point in this explanation. We do not need a self or person as the agent of an action of the body since we cannot infer it as a cause. For the Abhidharma Buddhist, person or self is an ontological dangler without a causal role in an explanation. Vasubandhu says that by the very fact that we cannot apprehend the capacity of the self, any more than the capacity of the various chants uttered by a quack doctor when it is established that the effect has been brought about by the use of certain herbs, we must conclude that the hypothesis of the self is untenable (Pruden 1988). We may add that for the same reason the hypothesis of person is untenable. The point of these explanations is not just that there is a better alternative explanation of the phenomena, but that these

---

[1] *Abhidharmakośabhāṣya*, Chapter 9.

alternative explanations show that there is no need to postulate or infer a self or person to explain these phenomena. Thus, Vasubandhu concludes, there is no inferential basis for a doer, an agent. What then about moral responsibility?

The terms "consideration" and "willful effort" in the quote above refer to "mental actions" in the series of *dharmas* leading up to the physical action. In contemporary philosophy, we speak of such states as forming intentions or volitions. According to the Abhidharma philosophers, however, intention is itself a simple *dharma*, whereas consideration and willful effort are complexes of *dharmas*, that partake in the series leading up to action. To understand these concepts fully, I turn to the *Karmasiddhiprakaraṇa* where Vasubandhu takes up the question of how to account for responsibility in the absence of selves and persons. Vasubandhu begins with a simple exposition of the Buddhist account by reference to the canonical Buddhist *sūtras* in the *Aṅguttara Nikāya*:

1. The nature of action: Action is essentially thought, voluntary and conscious, and as a consequence morally qualifiable as good or bad.
2. The mechanism of retribution: Action produces a fruit or result of retribution (*vipākaphala*) either in this life, or in a future life.... This means that the retribution of action is certain: there is a necessary relationship (*karmaphalasaṃbandha*) between an action and its result. But this relationship is not always immediate: action does not necessarily ripen in this life; more frequently, it gives forth its result in the course of a future existence. If we thus suppose that action is accomplished, then there will be a transmigration (*saṃsāra*) during which the result of retribution (*vipākaphala*), agreeable or disagreeable, will appear.
3. The retributed entity: Actions ripen for their author, or more exactly, in the series where it has been accomplished. In other words, there is a retributed entity. (trans. adapted from Pruden 1987, pp. 15–16)

Before moving on to Vasubandhu's explanation of these three points, it is worth noting that in the third point he talks about the "author" of the action as the attributed entity. This reference to an "author" should be a cause for alarm. Vasubandhu introduces his discussion by referring to the *Aṅguttara Nikāya* and it is well known that in these dialogues the Buddha talks about persons as real centers of living experience, engaged in a quest for happiness and freedom from suffering rather than as aggregates. In the following commentary, he gives a careful paraphrase of the "author" in terms of a series of mental *dharmas*. This introduction and reference to the *Aṅguttara Nikāya* does well to serve his purpose here because in this text his main opponents are fellow Buddhists, Mādhyamikas, Pudgalavādins, and other schools in the Abhidharma tradition.

Vasubandhu elaborates on his definition of *karma*: "action (*karma*) as volition or intention and action-after-having-being-willed." According to him, there are three kinds of volition: deliberation, decision, and movement-volition. Deliberation and decision constitute mental actions. Movement-volition is of two kinds: volition which moves the body and volition which emits a voice. They are called bodily action and vocal action respectively, but this, Vasubandhu claims, is misleading since one might think they are not volitional actions. But they are insofar as some bodily and vocal actions are moral actions in that they might harm another being, for example hunting animals or hate speech. Since such actions are produced with the volition or intention of hurting another being they are essentially volitional actions. Volition is the basis of morality. Actions lacking the essential factor of intentions are not morally charged and cannot be evaluated as good or bad. Vasubandhu explains with an example, "[i]f the deed of killing were not essentially a volition, it would not be a morally qualifiable action, since intention is at the basis of morality"[2] (Pruden 1987, p. 27).

It is standard in philosophy to define moral action as associated with an intention. But the difference here is that for Vasubandhu intention is a momentary *dharma*. How, then, are we to understand the process of its role in the production of moral action and retribution? Vasubandhu defines intention (*cetanā*) as "that which conditions, informs and that shapes the mind"[3] (Pruden 1988, p. 189). Furthermore, he explains "mental volitional action which is active, projects a new existence; this new existence, thus projected, is produced from the seed which is the consciousness 'informed' through action."[4] (Pruden 1988, p. 444). In other words, he claims that intention is the primary factor in activating a mental state to create the potential for rebirth and from which a new existence is projected. By activating a mental state, Vasubandhu has in mind the formation of an active manifest conscious state which, as we saw in Chapter 3, consists of other *dharmas*. So, the moral valence of the intention is determined by the *dharmas* that constitute the mental state. Good intentions derive their moral valence from wholesome *dharmas*, for example compassion, and lead to good actions like that of charity. The *dharma* of intention in this sense has the role of bringing together *dharmas* like attention, contact, discrimination, compassion, etc. which are necessary for the production of a conscious volition which in turn leads to the moral action of giving charity. What about moral retribution? In *Karmasiddhiprakaraṇa* Vasubandhu explains:

> The mechanism of the ripening of action is to be sought in the internal evolution of the mental series. The action, which is a thought associated with a special volition is momentary (*Kṣaṇika*): it perishes immediately upon arising. But it "perfumes" (*vāsanā*) the mental series (*cittasamtāna*) which is its point of departure; it creates in it a special potentiality (*śaktiviśeṣa*). The mental series

---

[2] *Karmasiddhiprakaraṇa*, I.   [3] *Abhidharmakośabhāṣya*, 2.24.
[4] *Abhidharmakośabhāṣya*, 3.41.

thus perfumed undergoes an evolution (*pariṇāma*) occasionally long, the end point (*viśeṣa*) of which is a state of retribution, a result. The process is thus the following: an action (thought), a mental series in evolution, a state of retribution of the action, and ultimate transformation of the mental series. In this same way, the seed is the cause of the fruit, but there is a series with all of its transformations placed between the seed and its fruit: shoot, trunk, branch, leaf, flower.

(trans. Pruden 1987, p. 28)

The point here is that retribution for morally valenced actions is not always produced instantaneously, there is a time-lag and sometimes the result or the moral retribution might be experienced much later in this life or even in the next life. But here a problem arises for our Abhidharma Buddhist philosopher which was raised by her Hindu counterparts. The objection was originally raised by the Nyāya philosopher Uddyotakara in his *Nyāyavārttika*, followed up by Naiyāyika philosophers Jayanta and Udayana and the Mīmāṃsā philosopher Kumārila.[5] For the Hindus, the main problem with the Buddhist "perfuming" theory is that it requires causation between momentary entities that occur at different times. How can the effect arise after the cause has completely disappeared? Uddyotakara notes that the consciousness that arises in the next moment cannot be "perfumed" by the preceding consciousness, since the preceding consciousness has vanished and has no relation to it. In short, there is no relation of perfumer and perfumed for momentary consciousnesses (Taber 2012).

Vasubandhu has an ingenious response to this objection. He introduces a new kind of consciousness over and above the six kinds of consciousness listed in the early Abhidharma texts. The latter are called active or manifest consciousnesses, five of which correspond to the sense organs and the sixth corresponds to the mental cognition (*manovijñāna*). The new kind of consciousness is called the subtle mind or basic consciousness (*ālaya-vijñāna*). The reasons for its introduction and the details of its interaction with active or manifest consciousness are explained in section 3.6. My interest here is to see whether the inclusion of basic consciousness in the Buddhist model of the mind can help us respond to the above challenge raised by Uddyotakara. In paragraphs 30–2 of the *Karmasiddhiprakaraṇa*, Vasubandhu explains:

> The active-consciousnesses and the *dharmas* which are simultaneous to them, good and bad, perfume (*bhāvayanti*) the subtle mind: they deposit therein the seeds of the different consciousnesses and of the different *dharmas*. Thus perfumed, the subtle mind forms a store-mind filled with all of the seeds (*sarvabijaka*).

---

[5] For details and development of these objections see Watson (2006), Oteke (1988), and Taber (2012) respectively.

The subtle mind "subdues" the seeds deposited in it (it hinders them from ripening); but its "series" evolves: its power of domination diminishes whereas the force of the seeds grows larger. The result of the evolution is a state of retribution of the series, i.e., wherein finally ripened, the seeds of the consciousnesses and of the good or bad *dharmas* give forth a result, that is, produce consciousnesses and agreeable or disagreeable *dharmas*. The subtle mind is thus a result-of-retribution-consciousness (*vipākaphalavijñāna*). From birth until death, it forms a continuous series free from any interruption. From the fact of retribution, it passes (*saṃskrāmate*) from existence to existence, grasping different aspects. Arriving at Nirvana, it is definitively cut off.   (trans. Pruden 1987, p. 31)

These passages are an attempt to explain the so-called process of perfuming. There is a two-way interaction between active and basic consciousness. An action, or more precisely its element of intention, does not perfume a succeeding *dharma* which is yet to come into existence. Rather, it perfumes or influences co-temporal *dharmas* in the basic consciousness. The morally valenced *dharmas* that constitute active volitions determine the quality of the seeds (*karmic* influences) deposited in the basic consciousness. The basic consciousness is a subtle mind, it stores the seeds, so to say, in a dormant state for some time. That is why we do not experience the *karmic* consequences of actions in the very next moment. The basic consciousness subdues the deposited seeds temporarily. The evolution of the basic consciousness is a complex process because of its interactions with other series of manifest or active consciousnesses and influences of the stored seeds. Basic consciousness functions as a ground for the production of future active consciousnesses in the mental series. The quality of the active consciousnesses is determined by external and internal factors including the manifestation of the *karmic* effects of previous actions. For example, the *karmic* merit of giving charity to the needy may be experienced later in life in experiences of joy as a result of succeeding in one's business and accumulating wealth. The results of actions determine the kind of active consciousness or experiences, in this case joy, to be suffered or enjoyed by descendant *dharmas* in the mental series. The point is that any active conscious experience is produced by the interplay of many mental and physical *dharmas* in different mental series (including the series of the basic consciousness). These jointly cooperate to produce newer active consciousnesses depending on the moral quality of the *dharmas* evolving in the basic consciousness series. The internal mental factors include prior and subsequent intentions as well as various cognitive and affective mental factors such as desire, memory, fear of wrongdoing, hatred, envy, etc. These factors may also be neutral or morally valenced: hatred and envy are bad *dharmas*, whereas compassion and fear of wrongdoing are good *dharmas*. Additionally, external factors may determine the moral quality of the action. So, for example, in the case of giving charity to a monk who subsequently attains equanimity, a "definitive transformation" (*pariṇāmaviśeṣa*) arises in the mental series of the donor that results in totally unexpected positive *karmic* residues. The intention to give is still the necessary condition that makes such transformation possible, but the exceptionally good *karma* is acquired on account of factors that had nothing to do with the donor series.

Vasubandhu emphasizes the role of intention without underplaying the importance of other factors. Intention is emphasized because forethought is a necessary condition for actions that have determinate ethical qualities and *karmic* effects. Completion of the action is another curious factor that Vasubandhu mentions in Chapter 4 of the *Abhidharmakośa-Bhāṣya*. Completion includes not only the material performance of the action but also the performance of preparatory (*prayoga*) actions and related subsequent (*pṛṣṭha*) actions. It is a curious factor insofar as it includes preparatory and subsequent action. Here, Vasubandhu is drawing attention to the open-endedness of actions. For example, if an action of killing is followed by repentance (*kaukṛtya*), this additional action extenuates the severity of the offence resulting in wiping out some of the negative *karma* acquired by the murderer series. However, if the action of murder is followed by pride and gloating, it leads to acquiring more negative *karma* than that acquired by the action of killing. In this context, Vasubandhu mentions that actions that are subsequent parts of an original action may well merge into the preparatory parts of another action. For example, since adultery is forbidden, someone who has illicit sex with the wife of an enemy commits a bad action. If having sex with her results from the intention of subsequently using her as an accomplice in the murder of her husband, the action becomes preparatory for another forbidden action—that of killing. This open-endedness of actions within a mental series creates plenty of room for the exercise of freedom within the bounds of *karma* and the course of evolution of the mental series dictated by it. Vasubandhu does not hesitate to talk about good actions as evolving in the same way as morally wrong actions. For example, someone who takes the Buddhist vows for setting out on the Path forms the intention of exercising restraint for the cultivation of good *dharmas*, which in turn lead to good actions in the mental series, and over a period of time bring about a moral transformation in that series. But this open-endedness does not mean that actions are never completed and thus do not produce retribution.

The important point to note here is that in defining action as intention Vasubandhu wants to emphasize the role of reflection in the moral quality of the action. Since intention is taken as an ethically charged mental activity, defining action as intention bestows actions with the power of bringing about a transformation in the mental series to account for the psychological process of moral formation and soteriological cultivation as well as for the transmission of *karmic* results (Meyers 2017). That said, it needs to be emphasized that moral, and thus intentional action in Vasubandhu's sense of the term action is not always conscious and deliberate. Habitual moral actions, such as those of skilled Buddhist practitioners who have made considerable progress on the Path, also count as moral even though they may not involve any forethought. Vasubandhu does think that a mental series accrues *karmic* residues on account of habituated moral actions, although they are negligible compared to actions done with conscious intention.

This view of action, the role of intention, and the gradual evolution of the series in response to the moral quality of the action shows that there is plenty of room for freedom and responsibility in the Buddhist account. And all of this can be explained, following Vasubandhu, without any recourse to selves or persons as agents. Though Vasubandhu does mention authorship of an action in the introductory section, it is quite clear from the detailed exposition of the Yogācāra-Sautrāntika view that he does not think of the author as a centralized agent. The "author" is only a term used by the Buddha to explain the doctrine of *karma*, a mere convenient designation. Authors have only nominal existence, ultimately it is the mental *dharmas*, primarily intentions, that do the real causal work.

6.3 Abhidharma Deconstruction of the Minimal Self

According to the distinctive Abhidharma view there are no selves or persons, there are only aggregates or the sequential psycho-physical processes that supervene on collections of ultimately real momentary atoms (*dharmas*). This deeply counterintuitive view drives contemporary philosophers to qualify the Buddhist rejection of self as the denial of a substantial self that is independent of the mental and physical aggregates constituting us. This tendency is further exacerbated by the later Yogācāra epistemologists' introduction of the notion of self-awareness or reflexive awareness (*svasaṃvedana*).[6] In the absence of a self this raises the question: *What* are we aware of in self-awareness? The Abhidharma Buddhist answer is to say that self-awareness is not to be understood as awareness of a subject having or possessing different experiences, rather it is simply a conscious state being aware of itself or being given to itself in a first-person way. Some suggest that this Yogācāra view entails that there is at least a "thin subject of experience," comparable to Galen Strawson's argument that subjectivity entails a thin subject of experience (2007). To keep matters straight, I recommend that we do not muddy the waters by talking about a thin subject of experience because we cannot make sense of the thin subject without positing a subject that is distinct from the experience. In Lewisian-speak, I concede that the search for perfection deservers of our folk-psychological, semi-theoretical notion of "self" is futile, because there

---

[6] The terms "reflexive awareness" and "self-awareness" are used interchangeably in the literature.

are not any perfect occupants of the role and hence no perfect deservers of the name (Lewis 1995). The Strawsonian thin subject is equally not a good deserver of the name; if anything the subject collapses into the awareness.

The Yogācāra thesis is that awareness itself is reflexively self-aware. This notion of self-awareness in Abhidharma Buddhist philosophy is in some ways similar to the phenomenologists' notion of pre-reflective awareness. Perhaps then, we might think that the Abhidharma philosophers can endorse minimal selves as they do not have a temporal extension beyond the experience. But we need to be more careful. It is important to distinguish the Abhidharma Buddhist's notion of self-awareness from the various notions of minimal self in the literature. Zahavi equates a minimal self with the "very subjectivity of experience" (2005, 2012), but this is a notion thicker than the one that an Abhidharma Buddhist philosopher can willingly endorse. For Zahavi, conscious experiences and consciousness itself have temporal structure and an extension in time, unlike the Abhidharma Buddhist universe in which conscious experiences, like everything else, are only momentary events. The same applies to Gallagher's (2000) notion of minimal self and Damasio's (2012) notion of core self as they both include the sense of ownership and agency, which is not part of the Abhidharma Buddhist notion of self-awareness. Similarly, the notion of minimal phenomenal self, proposed by Blanke and Metzinger (2009), is too rich to be endorsed by the Abhidharma Buddhist philosophers as it involves self-location and self-identification. Our Abhidharma Buddhists are likely to resist the appeal to identification, for the notion of identification seems to illicitly smuggle in the problematic notion of self. The Buddha warns us against any identification with the *skandhas* (mental and physical states).[7] In a famous passage in the *Samyutta Nikāya* (22.59), the Buddha says:

> What is impermanent, suffering, of a nature to change, is it suitable to regard as, "This is mine," "I am this," "This is myself"? "No, Sir." Therefore, monks, I say, whatsoever form...feeling...perception...mental fabrications...consciousness, past, future or present, internal or external, gross or subtle, inferior or superior, far or near, should be looked upon as, "This is not mine," "I am not this," "This is not myself." (trans. Mendis 2007)

Here, the Buddha warns us against the natural tendency to identify with the aggregates, because we inadvertently smuggle in an independent entity self, which is anathema to all Buddhists. When we say "I identify with states x, y, and z" this suggests that I am something apart from states x, y, and z. As a result, we

---

[7] To be more precise, in the early stages of the Path it may be better to identify in certain ways rather than others: as a monk, say, rather than as a thief or a conman. Practitioners starting on the Path may be encouraged to relinquish unhealthy forms of ego-identification in favor of other identifications (as a monk, or later as an *arhat*) eventually leading up to the relinquishment of all kinds of identification.

should be cautious about embracing the phenomenal self. The only exception is Krueger's view, according to which the Yogācāra view is best interpreted as saying that there are "numerically distinct minimal selves: dependently conditioned, temporary subjects that arise, exist, and pass away within the span of an occurrent episode of consciousness" (2011, p. 51). This suggestion appears to be consistent with the Abhidharma view, but then again, the question arises whether this minimal self is distinct from the experience. I think it is better to treat all talk about the "self" as only a convenient designator which refers to the collection of ephemeral *dharmas*. The Abhidharma Buddhist notion of self-awareness is too minimal to allow for a good enough deserver for a minimal self; it is best thought of as the awareness being self-luminous or aware of itself.

Contemporary philosophers, for example, Ganeri (2007) and Thompson (2014, 2020) are inclined to argue that the Buddhist claim that the self is not ultimately real is not to say it is an illusion. Ganeri says that persons are conventionally real or "real with reference to conception" (2007, p. 173) and, therefore, are not illusions. Person-involving conceptual schemes are subject-specific or interest-specific; they are positional observations, not subjective illusions. They are ways of thinking about the real; not false but certainly imperfect. I agree with this view insofar as the self or person is a construction (like a pot). We should not think of selves and persons as real or as natural kinds but as artefacts (see also, Chapter 8). The person-involving conceptual schemes are artificially constructed; persons are real in the sense in which the Menzies building is real. The construction of the Menzies building is, however, imperfect; we could do better.[8] So too, it is with persons and selves. According to the Buddhists, the conceptual schemes containing persons and selves are morally and intellectually inadequate. These schemes are ways of thinking about the world as organized into persons, divided into me, you, ours, and others. There are no such strict divisions and boundaries at the level of reality. Furthermore, there are no good reasons to endorse such divisions. The Abhidharma view, and the Buddhist view more generally, must be interpreted as saying that the self or person is a delusion that needs to be deconstructed as we are better off without it. If we are able to get rid of this delusion, we will reduce suffering, which is the overarching aim of Buddhism.

Thompson, however, argues that a minimal notion of self, which involves thinking or experiencing of the stream of consciousness as "mine," is not a delusion (2014). According to him, the Abhidharma no-self doctrine is the denial of a substantial and independently existing thing, but not of the minimal sense of self that is the subject of experiences and agent of actions (2014). Thompson agrees with the Abhidharma-Yogācāra view that our sense of self is mentally constructed

---

[8] The Philosophy Department at Monash University in Melbourne is housed in the Menzies building. If you have visited the Menzies building you will know that the statement is true; if not, trust my word.

but does not believe that this renders the self as nothing but an illusion. Even though all illusions are constructions, the converse is not necessarily true. Thompson claims that the Yogācāra view offers an account of how the self is constructed. The afflictive mind (*kliṣṭa-manas*) misapprehends the basic consciousness (*ālaya-vijñāna*) as a self to generate a sense of self, which is articulated in "I-Me-Mine." This sense of mineness is not based on introspective attention, which requires picking out a given thought or experience and identifying it as one's own. Rather, my experiences are given to me as mine in a more basic, pre-attentive and non-identifying way. According to the Yogācāra, in introspection we attend to this sense of mineness, which in turn leads to the generation of mistaken I-thoughts. Thompson explains that the mistake consists in assuming that the "I" essentially refers to a substantial self that exists independently of the psycho-physical stream of consciousness. However, a minimal notion of self that can be said to arise dependently from the stream of consciousness cannot be faulted in the same manner. Rather, such a minimal notion of self as a subject of experience and an agent of action provides a legitimate and valuable notion of self. Legitimate, because it allows us to experience ourselves as neither the same as nor different from the stream of consciousness and valuable, because it allows us to individuate my experiences and actions as belonging to me as subject and agent without thinking of myself as a substantial entity (Thompson 2014). But the Abhidharma Buddhist philosophers view the process of "I-making" as afflicted and erroneous precisely because it takes the basic consciousness, itself a momentary series of conscious moments, and transforms it into a relatively permanent self.

In his defense of his process view of self, Thompson appeals to the *appropriativist theory* of self offered by the Mādhyamika philosopher Candrakīrti. According to Candrakīrti, the function of the term "I" is not to refer, but rather to *lay claim to* our *appropriate* experiences and actions *as if* they are owned by oneself. This appropriation does not amount to *asserting ownership of* experiences and thoughts within one's conscious stream:

> One individuates oneself as a subject of experience and agent of action by laying claim to thoughts, emotions, and feelings—as well as commitments and social practices—and thereby enacts a self that is no different from the self-appropriating activity itself. Again, the self isn't an object or a thing; it's a process—the process of "I-ing" or ongoing self-appropriating activity.
>
> (Thompson 2014, p. 363)

Thompson is right to appeal to the *appropriativist theory* to show that the sense of self arises through laying claim to experiences, thoughts, feelings, and perhaps more. He identifies the self with the self-appropriating activity, and thus creates the self as a process. Thompson treats the appropriating activity as an enactment that creates a self to serve as the subject of experience and the agent of actions. This self has a real basis in the biological and neural processes that underlie it. Thus, Thompson argues that the constructed self is a not an illusion. The identity of the process of enactment and the self is difficult to understand.

What kind of self would this be? Thompson claims that the self-appropriating activity is ongoing. But is it really? He says, "[t]o think or say 'I am happy' or 'I am nervous' is to lay claim to a feeling of being happy or being nervous that preattentively presents itself as mine and to which my attention has been turned" (2014, p. 362). Thus, the activity of laying claim to one's actions and experiences is a conscious activity, it involves paying attention. But often when I am immersed in doing something, for example, writing this paragraph, I am not simultaneously attending or laying claim to the activity of writing. Does the self cease to exist at times when I am not engaged in the activity of self-appropriating? The self then would be a sort of thing that comes into and goes out of existence quite often. Perhaps, Thompson has in mind that the self is a construction based on the self-appropriating activity. The construction of the self has real basis in the underlying brain processes, but that does not mean the product of this mental construction—the self—has a real basis in the underlying brain process. The product of the construction is nothing more than a fiction, the result of a mental activity. It is no more real than Sherlock Holmes, the fictional character created by Conan Doyle's mental activity. I have argued in Chapter 4 that the sense of self as the subject of experiences and agent of actions is the result of the metacognitive operation of appropriation which requires linguistic and cognitive resources provided by the narrative. In Dennett-speak, the self is nothing but the chief fictional character, the protagonist of the narrative.

Thompson may simply say that he is not defending a Buddhist view, his aim is to use Buddhist ideas and materials in the service of constructing a view inspired by the Buddhists. Strictly speaking, Thompson's view is not an Abhidharma view. Thompson's view is a reconstruction which in his words "combines elements from Buddhist philosophy (specifically from the Madhyamaka school), biology, cognitive science and the neuroscience of meditation" (2014, p. 24). That said, he is also guilty of ignoring the central Madhyamaka thesis that the sense of self is a delusion. In his seminal text *Ratnavali* (1.29), Nāgārjuna endorses the view that our sense of self is a delusion:

> The psycho-physical complex originated from the sense of self, but this sense of self is in reality false (*anatta*). How can the sprout be true when the seed is false.
>
> (trans. Ganeri 2004, p. 68)

Candrakīrti develops this line of thought in his *Prasannapadā* (18, 347), a commentary on Nāgārjuna's *Mūlamadhyamakakārikā*:

[F]or those who are far removed from viewing the nature of self and own as they really are, who are caught in the cycle of birth and death, in the grip of the mis-belief of primal ignorance, for such, a false thing—the self as hypostatized on the basis of the *skandhas*—manifests itself as real. But for those close by who see truth of these matters, no such false thing manifests itself.

(trans. Ganeri 2004, p. 68)

Thompson's reconstruction thus goes against the Madhyamaka view that the sense of self is a delusion. More generally, it goes against the spirit of the no-self doctrine.

The Abhidharma Buddhist philosophers' rejection of self as the subject of experiences and the agent of actions is underwritten by their denial of any entities existing over time. Also, as explained in section 6.2 above, Vasubandhu denies the need to postulate an agent of action; causal connections among series of mental states are adequate to explain mental and physical actions. The Buddhist concern is that the sense of self as the agent of actions is responsible for the delusion of a diachronically unified self that not only coordinates the psychophysical complex but also mobilizes emotional resources for actions necessary to maintain the integrity of the organism (Dreyfus forthcoming). Our actions are aimed at self-preservation of this psychophysical complex and are directed by the special, though unwarranted, concern one has for one's future self. The strength of my emotions contributes to the overriding and asymmetrical concern I have for myself and endows me with a sense of "specialness" that makes me, in the words of William James, "the home of interest" (1983 [1890], p. 285). But such a sense of self, the Buddhist argues, is a delusion because it depends on the diachronically unified and bounded nature of the self as separate from the rest of the world. This deluded sense of agency is not a faithful representation of how things really are. But the Abhidharma Buddhists are committed to giving an account of phenome-nology of experiences. So, our question is: Is there anything like an experience of agency which is grounded in the subconscious activity of the afflictive mind?[9] I will argue that there is not.

6.4 Is There an Experience of Agency?

Intuitively, the sense of agency is the sense of myself as the agent of my actions, the being that is the owner and controller of my mind and body, insofar as they are involved in action planning and execution. For healthy, well-functioning indi-viduals, actions are accompanied by a sense of being the author and controller of

---

[9] There is also the question of how we explain the sense of ownership. For Vasubandhu ownership is also strictly a causal relation among mental states. But that is the task for the next chapter.

one's actions. Recent discussions reveal that the sense of agency is complex and ambiguous, and the literature contains a variety of perspectives. While philosophers agree that it is hard to pin down an exact definition or meaning for the sense of agency, they insist that it should not be taken as mere *façon de parler* (Bayne 2011). Bayne and Pacherie (2014) include experiences of deliberation, experiences of intentionality, experiences of decision-making, experiences of freedom, experiences of mental causation, the awareness of movement, the awareness of intentions to act, the sense of control, the sense of effort and so on as aspects of agency. Gallagher (2012) talks about multiple contributories to the sense of agency, some of which are reflectively conscious, some pre-reflectively conscious, and some non-conscious. Earlier, he had suggested that the sense of agency is constituted by a sense of action control and monitoring (Gallagher 2000). De Vignemont and Fourneret (2004) take it to be the sense of initiation and the sense of one's own movements, while Pacherie (2007) simply talks about it as the experience of being in control. Bayne, however, identifies agentive experience as having at "its core the *experience* of a particular movement or mental event as realizing one's own agency" (2011, p. 357; emphasis added). In other words, simply the sense of authorship.

My interest is not in the whole complex included in the sense of agency but, following Bayne and Pacherie (2014), in the core of the sense of agency as the sense of authorship. Thus, I ignore reflective judgments and beliefs about agency. This is because the Abhidharma Buddhist philosopher is interested in explaining the phenomenology of our experience of agency as the sense of authorship (if there is any such thing). As agentive experience, the sense of authorship stands for a "special feeling," or "a positive phenomenal content associated with acting." Bayne (2011) insists on the analogy with perception. Just as we have sensory systems that function to inform us about how things are within and immediately outside our bodies, so too we have a sensory system whose function it is to inform us about features of our own agency. Bayne does not offer a direct argument for his perceptual model of agentive experience, but he does say that the existence of agentive experience can be highlighted by drawing attention to the pathologies of agency, for example, the anarchic hand syndrome[10] and schizophrenic delusions of thought-insertion and alien control. They are pathologies of experience in virtue of the fact that there is good reason to believe that these delusions are at least partly grounded in abnormal experiences of agency (Pacherie 2006). That these syndromes involve experiences of alienated agency does not entail (though it provides some support for) the thesis that unimpaired agency is accompanied by experiences of intact agency, Bayne (2011) argues. I will argue this claim does not

---

[10] Anarchic hand syndrome is a phenomenon in which a person loses control of one hand, and it acts as if it has a mind of its own (Della Sala et al. 1994).

provide much support at all for the view that there is something like an agentive experience.

I am not denying that there are anomalous experiences of agency in pathological cases; rather, I want to deny that in the normal case, in which there is no such loss of authorship, agentive experience is present. From the fact that the anarchic hand patient experiences a lack of authorship (over their hand), it does not follow that there is the presence of agentive experience. The point is that we should not immediately infer the presence of an agentive experience from the behavioral capacity to distinguish the presence of authorship from lack thereof. The behavioral capacity, and the resultant ability to judge reliably whether or not we are the authors of our actions, is proof that the experience of being the author is remarkably different from the experience of not being the author. There is a positive phenomenology associated with the case of the loss of authorship, which is absent in the case of authorship; for example while I am immersed in writing these words, I do not have an accompanying experience that constantly conveys to me that I am the author of these words. I am just writing. But if suddenly words appear that I did not write or had no intention of writing, there would be a strong feeling of loss of agency. In the first case, there is no agentive experience since there is no phenomenal content associated with being the author of the words I am writing. However, in the second there is a strong feeling of loss of control and an experience of the lack of authorship. There is no agentive experience since there is no phenomenal content exclusively associated with authorship. Rather, the sense of agency or authorship results from the absence of a feeling associated with loss of authorship. The claim is not that the feeling of authorship is not normally accessed because it is recessive, like the sense of one's body. It is important to note that the absence of the feeling of authorship is not meant to suggest that there are no sub-personal processes associated with agency. Surely, there are sub-personal and sub-doxastic processes underpinning agency, but everyone agrees that these processes are inaccessible to our awareness. The fact that experiences of alienated agency in cases of syndromes like the anarchic hand are likely to be cognitively impenetrable, Bayne (2011) argues, adds weight to the argument that there is agentive experience because the agent's experience of lack of agency does not go away in the face of rational explanation to believe otherwise. But again, the resilience of experiences of lack of agency is no proof for the existence of agentive experience. The cognitive impenetrability of experiences of alienated agency gives us good reason to believe that there are robust experiences of the lack of agency but does not tell us anything directly about the existence or otherwise of agentive experiences. My claim is that there is no agentive experience or positive phenomenology with the feeling of authorship.

My case against the presence of agentive experiences draws strong support from Paglieri's (2013) thesis that there is no specific feeling associated with free action or decision. Paglieri demonstrates that from the fact that we can easily and reliably judge whether our actions are free, it does not follow that there is a "freedom attribute" in our experience of acting freely. The judgments are based on the absence of coercion, not the extra ingredient of "feeling free" in our experience. Similarly, I want to argue that from the fact that I can judge easily and reliably whether I am the author of a given action, it does not follow that there is an extra ingredient of "agentive experience"; it may just be an absence of a feeling of loss of authorship. What I am aiming at is a defense of a default theory of agency. This default option is to consider ourselves as authors of our actions with no need for any other proof or evidence from our own experience. In contrast, only a phenomenologically salient experience of loss of authorship can lift the default and force me to judge that I am not the author of my actions. Following Paglieri (2013) I suggest the following as desiderata of a default theory of sense of agency:

1. Evidence that the phenomenology specifically associated with authorship is thin and recessive and tends to be reported in ways that sound suspiciously close to ex-post reconstructions, if not outright fabrications.
2. Evidence that the lack of authorship, in contrast, associates with a clear and rich phenomenology.
3. Arguments to the effect that presence of the sense of authorship is typical and nonproblematic, whereas the absence of the sense of authorship is the exception that needs to be promptly detected, for the individuals to perform adequately.
4. Evidence that the known pathologies and distortions are adequately accounted for by the default theory.

There is agreement in the literature on the sense of agency that the phenomenology associated with agency is thin and recessive. In noting the complexity of the experience of agency, Gallagher says:

This complexity may be surprising in light of what is usually considered to be the "thin" phenomenology associated with agency, which means that the sense of agency is short-lived and phenomenologically recessive (i.e., it remains in the pre-reflective background of experience and so not very noticeable in ordinary experience), and therefore difficult to specify.   (2012, p. 19)

In a similar vein, Bayne argues:

The advocate of agentive experience need not hold that agentive experiences are phenomenologically vivid or easy to discern; indeed, it is common for agentive experience to be described as recessive—as typically confined to the margins of consciousness.   (2008b, p. 184)

In the course of arguing that the sense of agency is generated in sensory-motor processes, Tsakiris et al. also claim that:

> The sense of ownership and sense of agency are part of a pre-reflective experience of embodied experience. They are generated in low-level, albeit complex, sensory-motor processes. They tend to remain phenomenologically recessive or attenuated. That is, they involve a thin or minimal although not necessarily simple phenomenology.   (2007, p. 660)

Thus, there seems to be widespread agreement, among those who advocate that there are agentive experiences, that the phenomenology is thin and recessive. Furthermore, the reports of such agentive experiences sound very close to ex-post rational reconstructions. Gallagher (2012) is concerned whether the various aspects and elements of agency involved in a unified qualitative experience of agency can be articulated in action. He uses the example of the actions of a cliff climber José who takes on a challenging climb in the Himalayas. After months of meticulous planning José is finally at it and totally immersed in the activity. Gallagher would agree that it is not clear that José's experience of being the author is well articulated when he is *in action*. I think Gallagher is right to worry about this, but what is more important for our purposes is not just whether José's experience of authorship is articulated, but also whether he has any sense of being the author when he is in action. Csikszentmihalyi (1978) has shown that when people are immersed in an activity, such as rock climbing, they retrospectively report that they were aware of the immediate situation but say that they cannot report the contents of their conscious awareness at the time. They also report having no sense of how much time passed during the activity in which they were immersed. Ex post facto reports of rock climbing and bushwalking in challenging terrains with their florid phrases sound a lot closer to fabrication than actual description of experience in action. For example:

> Our rope slides through the anchor and flirts with gravity before eloping into the wind. Again we're caught off guard by crashing and tearing noises overhead. Through lips chapped and bleeding, we debate the cause of these eerie sounds, rule out rockfall, and credit the anomaly to swirling gusts ripping through the canyon's narrowing walls.[11]

And,

> Our reverie upon the great trail of dust and rock was soon shaken to its very core when our bricky crew came across what proved to be a great torrent of

---

[11] Blake Herrington, *Climbing and Writing*, available at: https://perma.cc/8QYB-VG55.

water. Surely this cataract was the resulting outburst of effusive melting of great snowfalls high above us in the cradle of the unreachable Sierra peaks. Old Sol, his heat and light an all too powerful blast, turning ice to water, and the subsequent cataclysm now found its way to lower elevations, threatening to end our journey before it began. One false step and our weak manflesh would be hurled downstream, only to find purchase upon hard boulders and snag-filled pools; our lifeless bodies broken and desecrated.[12]

The foregoing presents a first indication to satisfy the first desideratum to defend the default theory of the sense of authorship. Evidence for the second desideratum is not difficult to come by as is shown by the vignettes from researchers or verbatim quotes by patients suffering from thought-insertion and anarchic hand syndromes:

I look at the window and I think that the garden looks nice and the grass looks cool, but the thoughts of Eamonn Andrews come into my mind. There are no other thoughts there, only his...He treats my mind like a screen and flashes thoughts onto it like you flash a picture.   (Mellor 1970, p. 17)

Thoughts come into my head like "Kill God." It's just like my mind working, but it isn't. They come from this chap, Chris. They're his thoughts.

(Frith 1992, p. 16)

I got up during the middle of class one day, and without telling anyone, I started to walk home—which was about five miles away—and I felt that the houses were starting to communicate with me and that they were sending me messages. I didn't hear any voices, and I thought they were putting thoughts inside my head, things like, "Walk, repent, you are special, you are especially bad." Accompanying this were feelings of intense loathing and fear.[13]

Parkin (1996) reported that his patient MP had problems in choosing television channels, because as soon as MP selected one station with his right hand, the left hand would press another button. Again, Della Sala et al. (1991, p. 1114) reported that:

Another patient of ours (GC) often complained that her hand did what it wanted to do, and tried to control its wayward behaviour by hitting it violently or talking to it in anger and frustration.

For the third desideratum, we need arguments to the effect that the presence of the sense of authorship is typical and nonproblematic, whereas the absence of the

---

[12] J. M. Jelak, *Trip Report*, available at: https://perma.cc/5FHD-JDR3.
[13] Elyn Saks, *This is What It's Like to Live with Schizophrenia*, available at: https://perma.cc/2DAH-43YD.

sense of authorship is the exception that needs to be promptly detected for the individuals to perform adequately. My first argument draws attention to the notion of "naked intention," or more precisely why we should reject it. The idea of naked intention suggests that there can be awareness of an action without an awareness of who the agent is (Jeannerod & Pacherie 2004)—or an "agent-neutral" action experience (Pacherie 2007). Jeannerod and Pacherie argue on the basis of neurological evidence that the same areas of the brain are activated when I engage in intentional action or when I see another engage in the same or similar intentional action. The signal produced by mirror neurons appears to be the same for an action performed by the self and by another agent. Moreover, mirror neurons do not constitute the only instance of shared representations. On the basis of brain imaging studies, Jeannerod and Pacherie contend that the cortical network that provides the basis for the conscious experience of intentions does not by itself provide us with a conscious experience of self- or other-agency. Thus, there is always the question "Is this intention mine?" In case of overt actions, the question is answered by answering the question: "Is this my body performing the corresponding action?" So, they postulate the "who" system in the brain, which specifies whether the agent is oneself or another.

Jeannerod and Pacherie's argument is based on an invalid inference from sub-personal brain processes to phenomenological conclusions. Even if we grant that the "who" system identifies the agent of the intention, there is no reason to think that there is an isomorphism between sub-personal mechanisms at the level of brain processes and phenomenal level of experience. The "who" question is possibly relevant at the level of brain processes, but it never comes up at the phenomenal level because there is never any doubt about who the agent is. Even if I am wrong about "who" the agent of an action is, something that happens in anarchic hand syndrome and other cases of delusions of control, I am perceiving or experiencing the action as already specified with respect to agency. There is no experience of actions without an agent. This should give us some reason to think that the default option is to consider our actions as being authored by us as agents. That is to say that there is a presumption of authorship built into one's actions, unless there is reason to believe otherwise.

My second argument for the presence of the sense of authorship as default option is based on an examination of Gallagher and Zahavi's claim that there is a first-order, pre-reflective, non-conceptual, primitive experience of agency (2012). Insofar as a sense of authorship of one's action is the core of the sense of agency, this may lead some to believe that there is some positive phenomenology or feeling associated with being the author of one's actions. But this would be an error. I draw attention to Hume's famous remark concerning the denial of self: "For my part, when I enter most intimately into what I call *myself*, I always stumble on some particular perception or other, of heat or cold, light or shade, love or hatred, pain or pleasure. I never can catch *myself* at any time without a perception, and

never can observe anything but the perception" (Hume 1975 [1739], 1.4.6.3).
Hume is complaining that he fails to find a phenomenological marker of the self
in experience. Zahavi and Kriegel (2015) argue that this way of looking at Hume's
complaint suggests that there is a separate self-quale that one can consult in one's
phenomenology in isolation from the content of consciousness. This is a mistake;
the pre-reflective self-awareness does not deliver a datum or a quality like the
smell of fermented garlic. They claim:

> [I]t is not supposed to be any specific feeling or determinate quale at all. Nor is it
> supposed to be a synchronic or diachronic sum of such contents of conscious-
> ness (or any other relation that might obtain among such contents). Our view is
> not that in addition to the objects in one's experiential field—the books, com-
> puter screen, half empty cup of coffee, and so on—there is also *a self-object*.
> Rather the point is that each of these objects, when experienced, is given to one
> in a distinctly first-personal way. On our view, one does not grasp for-me-ness
> by introspecting a self-standing quale, in the same way one grasps the taste of
> lemon or smell of mint....In other words, the 'me' of for-me-ness is not a sepa-
> rate and distinct item but rather a "formal" feature of experiential life as such.
>
> (Zahavi & Kriegel 2015, p. 38)

This implies that pre-reflective awareness of the self does not deliver self-standing
quale. In a similar vein, we might say that the pre-reflective awareness of authorship is not a specific feeling or a determinate quale that we can consult in our
phenomenology—an author that we can detect in performing an action. That
there is an author is just a formal feature of the structure of agency. To say that the
pre-reflective sense of authorship is a formal feature of the structure of agency is
to deny that there is any positive phenomenal content interlaced into the experience of authorship. But it is also to say that the presence of the sense of authorship
is the typical case of action.

Furthermore, there is reason to believe that the absence of the sense of authorship is the exception that needs to be promptly detected for individuals to perform adequately. Parnas and Handest (2003) argue that the phenomenological
manifestations of anomalous self-experience, where one's experience of being the
author of one's physical and mental actions is distorted, are symptomatic of prodromal phases of schizophrenia and psychosis. They argue that familiarity with
subtle, nonpsychotic anomalies of subjective experience of one's status as the
author of one's actions, among other symptoms, is not just theoretically significant but crucial for early differential diagnosis. It is useful here to quote some of
the clinical descriptions of the alterations of self-experience (specifically cases
that report lack of authorship) to make the case that such absence, if promptly
detected, might allow for timely diagnosis and early interventions before the
onset of psychosis. Some of these disturbances manifest themselves in motor

performance. Random verbal or motor acts may occur as if they are interfering with one's actions and speech without being clearly labeled as uttered or performed by oneself or some other external agency:

> Case 5: A former paramedic reported that many years prior to the onset of his illness he occasionally experienced—while driving in an ambulance and much to the driver's surprise—uttering words entirely unconnected with his train of thoughts. He immediately continued to speak in a relevant way or make some cliché remark to cover for this embarrassing episode.
>
> Case 6: A female library assistant reported that prior to the onset of her illness she was alarmed by a frequently recurring experience that replacing books from a trailer onto the shelves suddenly required attention: she had to think how she was to lift her arm, grasp a book with her hand, turn herself to the shelf etc.
>
> (Parnas & Handest 2003, p. 127)

These cases clearly demonstrate that such random bodily and linguistic actions, which are associated with the positive experience of the loss of authorship, need to be promptly detected to avoid full-blown symptoms of schizophrenia and psychosis.

The fourth and last desideratum concerns the adequacy of the default theory to account for known pathologies and distortions. The most striking illustrations are delusions of alien control in schizophrenia, where a subject is aware of the content of the action she is executing but denies being the agent of this action. According to the default theory, there is a presence of an experience—albeit not a veridical experience—of loss of authorship. The patient has a positive experience of some other external agent that causes their hands to move (anarchic hand syndrome) or inserts thoughts into their head (thought-insertion). The positive experience, although mistaken, accounts for the vividness and fine-grainedness of the delusional phenomenology. The patient has a positive experience of not being the author of her actions possibly because of neurological or other mental disorders.

This completes my case for a default theory of the core aspect of sense of agency. To conclude, there is no positive phenomenology associated with the experience of agency. There is nothing it is like to be an agent; thus, there is no experience of agency. The Abhidharma Buddhist philosopher can hold on to the no-self doctrine without the extra burden of having to explain the phenomenology of agency.

6.5 Conclusion

In this chapter, I have defended Vasubandhu's no-self view as the no-agent view. Abhidharma philosophers deny the need to postulate an agent of action. Vasubandhu argues that causal connections among series of mental and physical states are adequate to explain mental and physical actions. The self as the agent does not exist because it is causally impotent. While the denial of agency may seem at odds with the Buddhist doctrine of *karma*, which implies some degree of free will, moral responsibility, the possibility of moral progress, and finally liberation, Vasubandhu suggests a way out of this quandary by appeal to the notion of basic consciousness or store-mind. But he is still left with the burden of explaining the phenomenological sense of agency. But is there really an experience of agency? Using resources from contemporary cognitive sciences, I have argued that there is nothing it is like to be an agent in the sense that there is no experiential phenomenology associated with agency. The sense of agency is a conceptual construct. These are not, however, the only challenges for Vasubandhu's no-self view. The additional commitment to the no-ownership view poses further challenges. These will be explained, in detail, in the next chapter where I will also offer a defense on part of the Abhidharma philosophers against the challenges posed by the no-ownership view.

7

No-Self and the Phenomenology
of Ownership

7.1 Introduction

The aim of this chapter is defending a reading of the Abhidharma Buddhist
no-self view as a no-ownership view. The no-ownership view is deeply counterintuitive and highly implausible; after all any experience is experience *of* or *for* a
subject. In Chapter 2, I have argued that Vasubandhu's view can be plausibly
interpreted as a no-ownership view. Many contemporary Buddhists will argue
that this reading creates a vulnerable straw man, an easy target that cannot stand
ground against the opponents. My intention here is not to create a straw man; it is
to explore what contemporary no-self theorists, Buddhist and others, can
learn from a defense of the Abhidharma no-ownership view. I argue that the
Abhidharma Buddhist metaphysicians are committed to denying the ownership
of experiences and the sense of ownership.

In section 7.2, I clarify the no-ownership view and present an interpretation of
Vasubandhu's view. The no-ownership view is dismissed as absurd or self-refuting
(Strawson 1959). In section 7.3, I offer a defense of the no-ownership view on
behalf of Vasubandhu against these charges. But since the Abhidharma are also
concerned to explain the phenomenology of our conscious experience, they are
faced with the further question: What about our purported experience of ownership? In section 7.4, I argue that there is no experiential phenomenology associated with ownership, thus there is no onus on the Abhidharma philosopher to
explain the purported sense of ownership. I argue that there is nothing that it is
like to be an owner of experiences.

7.2 Vasubandhu's View as a No-Ownership View

In denying the existence of subjects of experience Vasubandhu is not saying that
subjects of experience are mythical creatures, like unicorns. What is the difference, then, between the Abhidharma Buddhist's denial that there are subjects of
experience and the ordinary denial that there are unicorns? The Abhidharma
Buddhist does not deny that there appear to be such things as subjects of experience. In fact, they concede that our ordinary beliefs and statements which entail

Selfless Minds: A Contemporary Perspective on Vasubandhu's Metaphysics. Monima Chadha, Oxford University Press.
© Monima Chadha 2023. DOI: 10.1093/oso/9780192844095.003.0008

the existence of subjects of experience are often in some sense correct—they are conventionally true. But they claim they are not ultimately true in the sense that they are not among the constituents of reality. Experiences too come with the sense that there is a "me" who is experiencing my current experiential state. The Abhidharma Buddhists agree that experiences come with a sense of ownership, but they argue that this sense of ownership is not veridical. We will return to this argument in the last section. But first we must get clear about what it means to say that there are no subjects of experience.

The central thesis of the no-subject view is that conscious events are fundamentally subjectless. Historically, in the West, this view has been ascribed to Lichtenberg, Hume, Schlick, and Wittgenstein. Peacocke (1999) notes that there are at least two different versions of the no-subject view.

The first version can be attributed to Wittgenstein, who famously argues that the term "I" lacks a reference. The use of "I" is the most misleading referential technique, particularly when used to represent immediate experience (Wittgenstein 1975). The thought is that there is no loss of content if we replace the proposition "I have a toothache" with "There is a toothache," since the term "I" (in its subject use) is not a genuinely referring expression. In its subject use, the term "I" is supposedly picking out an inner subject of experience, but since there is no such thing, it is a referring expression without a referent. The first version of the no-subject view thus denies that the first-person pronoun is a referring expression.

A second version of the no-subject view questions the transition from the occurrence of a conscious mental state to the corresponding self-ascription to a subject. It can be found in Lichtenberg's criticism of the Cartesian *cogito* when he says that Descartes was only entitled to say "there is thinking going on" or "it thinks," rather than "I think." The thought here is that seeing, thinking, and judging are events like thunder or rain that do not involve the existence of anything that thunders or rains. According to the second version of the no-subject view, the transition from the occurrence of a conscious mental state to the corresponding self-ascription to a subject is unsound. To enable a proper appreciation of the Abhidharma Buddhist view, I will label the first version as the no-reference view and the second the no-ownership view (Snowdon 2009).

Most philosophers do not distinguish between these two versions, because the point of the discussion usually is to mention the no-subject view only to dismiss it quickly as incoherent. However, the distinction is useful to my purposes for two reasons: first, as we shall see below, the Abhidharma Buddhist view can be plausibly described as the no-ownership view. Furthermore, we must note that the no-ownership view clearly involves two transitions. The first is a transition from merely having an experience to being aware of having that experience. The second is a transition from being aware of having an experience to the first-person present-tense psychological ascription of that experience expressed in statements of the form: "I am having that experience." The first transition can sometimes be justified, as in cases where one is attending to the experience. But even in cases where the first transition is justified, the no-ownership view claims that this by itself does not justify the second transition leading to the first-person present-tense psychological ascription. The first transition, when justified, only permits the Lichtenbergian phrasing: "There is F." The Abhidharma Buddhist version of the no-ownership view claims precisely that the second of these transitions is unjustified. Vasubandhu claims that the second transition requires a conceptual resource, a resource that is not available and thus can never be justified. And secondly, Ganeri's admirable reconstruction of Vasubandhu's view runs together the two versions, and that makes it harder to defend the Abhidharma Buddhist version of the no-ownership view. I will discuss this in detail in the next section.

But first let us briefly look at considerations as to why the Abhidharma view might rightly be interpreted as a no-ownership view. The simplest statement of the view is found in the *Visuddhi Magga*, a Theravāda Buddhist commentary written by Buddhaghosa: "Misery doth only exist, none miserable. No doer is there, naught save the deed is found"[1] (Warren 1896, p. 146). The thought here is that my experiences or perceptions do not require a subject of experiences or an agent of action over and above the experience or the action. There is a feeling of pain, but the feeling is not attributed to, or had by, a certain subject of experience. This suggestion is developed further in an argument presented in the *Abhidharmakośa-Bhāṣya*. After the discussion of memory and identity over time, Vasubandhu addresses the specific questions raised by the opponents: Is there an owner of conscious cognition? Who cognizes? His response is simply to say that there is no owner of experiences; perceptions arise on account of their appropriate causes—that is, sense-faculty, object, and attention. Vasubandhu claims that ownership is just a matter of causal relations between two streams. The discussion in the text continues thus:

Objector: But it may be said, because states of being have reference to beings, all states of being depend on beings. E.g., "Devadatta walks"—here the state of walking refers to the one who walks, Devadatta. In the same way consciousness is a state of being. Therefore, he who cognizes must be.

Response: What is this "Devadatta"? It remains to be proven that it is a self or unified subject. "Devadatta" does not refer to a single thing, it is just the conventional name for the collection of conditions that are the cause of resulting states. Devadatta walks just as he cognizes.

Objector: And how does Devadatta walk?

Response: The instantaneous condition in an unbroken continuum—grasped as the single, unified thing, the so-called Devadatta—are the cause of

[1] *Visuddhimagga*, 15f.

coming-into-being-elsewhere, which is spoken of as "Devadatta walks." For "walking" is the "very coming-into-being-elsewhere." Similarly, too there are causes of consciousness, they are spoken of as "Devadatta cognizes."[2] (trans. Kapstein 2001, pp. 368–90)

The text above indicates that Vasubandhu conceives of "subjects of experience" as mere constructions that are really nothing over and above disparate causes—in this case, the collections of conscious and physical events. Persons or subjects exist in "name only": that is, they are denominations for sake of convenience. They can only figure in conventionally true statements. This makes it at least plausible to think that Vasubandhu and the Ābhidharmikas in general subscribed to a version of the no-ownership view. It is typical of the no-ownership theorist to resort to analogies in order to make their view intuitively plausible. So, one finds the famous chariot and the lamp-light analogy in the Abhidharma and other Buddhist texts. Chariots can be reduced to parts—nuts, bolts, wheels, axles, etc.—related to one another in certain ways; lamp-lights can be reduced to a continuum of flames; and, similarly, subjects of experience can be reduced to collections of causes of conscious and physical events.

   In the next section, I will defend the no-ownership view by responding to the most challenging objection in the Western philosophical literature. But, before we close this section, it is worth pointing out that the a priori reflection on the notion of unified subject of experience has led many philosophers to conclude that the subject of experience must persist over time. Peacocke's argument is based on the claim that memory is *factive*, in the sense that genuine memories are really memories. Apparent memories that are not true are *merely* apparent, they are not memories. If a subject remembers its own earlier states, it must persist through time. This follows just from the fact of the correctness of a memory. Since the subject who is now remembering is identical with the subject who had the earlier experience, it follows that the subject must persist through time (Peacocke 1999). The same conclusion is drawn by Strawson (1959) simply by reflecting on the fact that we ordinarily ascribe conscious experiences and physical properties to the same thing. And, as some physical properties endure over time, so there must be persisting subjects. This is exactly the kind of reasoning that motivates the Buddhist Abhidharma philosopher to insist that having a conscious experience does not entail that there is a subject of experience: they want to block the very first move in this dialectic. The Buddhist Ābhidharmikas further warn that introducing the subject as the synchronically and diachronically unified subject of experiences and the agent of actions is likely to bring with it all manner of moral defilements: greed, conceit, pride, jealousy, and so on. This consideration may

---

[2] *Abhidharmakośa-Bhāṣya*, Chapter 9.

well be offered as practical reason in favor of the no-ownership view, but there are theoretical reasons against the view that merit consideration.

7.3 Incoherence Objections and a Response on Behalf of Vasubandhu

It is commonly assumed that the very idea of conscious experience involves the existence of a subject of experience. By definition, a mental state is conscious when there is something it is like to be in that state. The "something it is like" must mean "something it is like for the subject." The claim is that an experience is impossible without an experiencer. Peacocke calls this a "constitutive, metaphysical point about the nature of consciousness" (1999, p. 292). Galen Strawson credits this to Descartes' *Second Meditation*. Descartes' claim is that the existence of the thinker, subject, or experiencer cannot be doubted even if one is wrong about the substantial nature of experiencing something. The claim is that wherever there is an experience there must be a subject (Strawson 2003, p. 281). For Strawson, this claim has the status of an obvious necessary truth. What, then, is the nature of the subject? Strawson presents three views of the subject: the subject as a human animal (the thick view), the subject as some sort of a persisting inner locus of experience (the traditional view), and the subject as "an inner thing of some sort that exists if and only if experience exists of which it is the subject" (the thin subject) (2017, pp. 171–2). He rejects the first two conceptions in favor of the thin subject. But what is this thin subject? Strawson's answer is that the subject of an experience *is* the experience. He calls this the *subject of awareness/awareness identity thesis* (2017). This identity thesis explains his claim about the duration of the subject: the subjects lasts as long as the experience lasts, no more no less. The identity thesis is difficult to understand. Snowdon (2018), for example, points out that the identity thesis commits us to saying that an experience has an experience. Not only *is* it an experience, it *has* one. But equally, it seems to follow that the subject *has* a subject. Put this way, we seem to lose hold on what it means to be a subject.

What exactly is the force of saying that the experience has a subject? By way of argument, Strawson uses the old adage that an experience has "what-it-is-likeness," and that requires a likeness *for* a subject. But the claim that 'likeness is for a subject' requires an argument. No such argument is forthcoming in contemporary analytic philosophy. For now, it will suffice to say that in saying that subjects are experiences, Strawson robs subjects of any genuinely explanatory role beyond, as Snowdon puts it, speaking with the "vulgar." Our Abhidharma Buddhist philosopher will agree that, conventionally speaking, we might say that experiences have a subject. But we should be very clear that there is no ultimately real subject since it does not play a role in causal explanation.

One way of cashing out the incoherence of the no-ownership view is to say that the very idea of an experience that was not a state of anything is incoherent. Experiences are like dents: just as there could not be a dent without a dented object, there could not be an experience without a subject of experiences. Olson (2007) reminds us of the Cheshire cat in *Alice in Wonderland*, who disappears and leaves behind its grin—no head, no lips, just the grin. But you cannot have a grin without anything grinning. This much seems right, but Buddhists do not need to embrace a Wonderland metaphysic. Experiences are not like grins or dents; they are not physical things. Rather, we can think of experiences as many unthinking things combining to produce an experience. Olson offers examples of a group of people putting on a play or a collection of cables supporting a suspension bridge. Olson concludes that the no-ownership is not only defensible but survives scrutiny to stand among the three best accounts of *what we are* together with the temporal parts view and animalism (2007). The no-ownership view is not without further difficulties, but it is not prima facie untenable.

Taking a clue from Olson, the Abhidharma Buddhist philosophers can claim that the *dharmas*, that is the physical and psychological atoms which by themselves would not count as conscious experience, cooperate in a way that these lesser contributions add up to an event of experiencing, without making up any subject of experience. In that case, there is an experience without a subject of experience. A detailed account of the Abhidharma account of conscious experience without any mention of a subject of experience has been developed in section 3.2 and some challenges to the account are answered in Chapter 3.

Philosophers who reject the no-ownership view as incoherent implicitly make assumptions that are questionable, if not outright mistaken. These assumptions require argument, but no such defense is forthcoming from those who regard the no-ownership view as incoherent. P. F. Strawson (1959), for example, does not argue but simply asserts that the subjects of experience, in his case persons, are primitive basic particulars. It is assumed that the concept of a person is a primitive concept of a *single* two-sided thing that cannot be analyzed in terms of an ego and a material body (in some sort of relation). This concept seems indistinguishable from that of a simple self. One may ask, why must persons be simple, *single*, primitive basic particulars that cannot be further analyzed? Strawson does not offer a defense but as we shall see, it plays an important role in his argument against the no-ownership theorist.

P. F. Strawson (1959) famously argues that the no-ownership theorist cannot state her position coherently. The no-ownership theorist needs to be able to say it is a contingent fact that a certain experience is causally dependent upon the states of a particular body. It is contingent in the sense that the same experiences could have been dependent on states of another body as well. But the theorist cannot, according to Strawson, coherently state her position that "All *my* experiences are (contingently) had by body B." He says:

It [the no-ownership view] is not coherent, in that the one who holds it is forced to make use of that sense of possession of which he denies the existence, in presenting his case for the denial.   (1959, p. 96)

P. F. Strawson argues that the no-ownership theorist cannot refer to the set of experiences at issue without the help of some possessive expression such as "my," "yours," "theirs," etc., which uses the sense of possession that she denies. For any attempt to get rid of "my" will result in trivial and necessarily true statement that "all experiences that are causally dependent upon body B are causally dependent upon body B." Thus, Strawson concludes that "the requirement of identity rules out the logical transferability of ownership" (1959, p. 97). This is not a welcome consequence. Strawson's point is that experiences owe their identity to the identity of the person whose experiences they are. This allows for the possibility that experiences are owned by a person in the logically non-transferable sense of "ownership." Thus, it is not possible that an experience which actually belongs to me, could have belonged to somebody else.

Strawson simply claims that the no-ownership theorist cannot come up with a way of identifying experiences without using the sense of being possessed by someone. But there are some possibilities that he fails to consider. We can perhaps pick out certain experiences in some demonstrative way and then designate the rest using some relational description (Snowdon 2009). There is nothing wrong with identifying a sensation as "this orange sensation" and saying of it "that it is irritating." Indeed, our Buddhist Abhidharma philosopher will go further than Snowdon and identify experiences using pure demonstratives "this," "that," and perhaps complement them by using temporal location rather than categorize them by using descriptive terms. Descriptive expressions as class terms are to be avoided as they bring with them the tendency to reify spatio-temporal particulars as persisting entities and classes thereof as universals. So, the Buddhist Abhidharma philosopher will be tempted to use expressions like "this experience now" and saying of it "that it is painful."

Ganeri (2012b) argues that the Abhidharma no-ownership theorist can sidestep Strawson's objection by acknowledging that a sense of ownership accompanies experience. He points to Vasubandhu's work in his later Abhidharma Yogācāra phase. Vasubandhu posits the notion of afflictive mind (kliṣṭa-manas), or simply mind (manas), as an aspect of experience that presents my experiences to me as mine in a more basic, pre-attentive, and non-identifying way. This sense of mineness is not based on introspective attention that requires picking out a given thought or experience and identifying it as one's own. Instead, the afflictive mind (manas) takes the basic or storehouse consciousness (ālaya-vijñāna) as its foundation. Storehouse consciousness is a baseline consciousness that serves as a repository of all basic habits, tendencies, and karmic latencies accumulated by the individual. This basic consciousness is misapprehended by the afflictive mind as a self (Dreyfus & Thompson 2007). According to Ganeri (2011), Vasubandhu argues that the "mind" undergoes a transformation into something that we metaphorically call a self; there is, in fact, no such thing as a self. This transformation is a cognitive fabrication since it requires a new conceptual resource, one that is not in fact available in our experience. So, in Ganeri's view, Vasubandhu identifies a gap between my first-person view on my own mental life (my sense of ownership) and my ability to use this primitive way of being self-aware as a justification for making first-person present-tense psychological ascriptions—for example, "I am hungry" or "I have a headache."

One may think, as in fact Zahavi (2005) does, that the transition in question involves only paying attention to the mineness inherent in my experience; that there is no need for the exercise of any new conceptual resource. The Buddhist Abhidharma can in fact appeal to conscious attention (*manovijñāna*): for example, attention can be directed to processes in the basic consciousness, as in consciously attending to a disposition—say, anger. Buddhists, however, will stop short of saying that this is a mode of self-awareness: there is just the conscious awareness of "being angry." Ganeri does refer to conscious attention as a distinct mental activity, but he is quick to label it as a phenomenon involved in self-consciousness—that is, one of consciously attending "to one's own state of mind" (2011, p. 178). This is misleading because the mineness is not something one can *attend* to; it is simply a subtle background presence. What we *attend* to is the content of the conscious experience. When we think and talk of awareness of one's own inner mental states, as a joint activity of the pre-attentive mind and conscious attention, there is only conscious awareness of the content of experiences. There is no distinct quale associated with mineness inherent in one's inner experiences and thus no experience of a subject even when we attend to inner experience. There is just the sensation of "being angry" but no additional sense of "I am feeling angry." This is exactly Hume's point when he says that conscious reflection never reveals anything but the perception (Hume 1975 [1739]). It is precisely this lack of a subject that presents the demand for an extra conceptual resource.

I think it is best to regard Vasubandhu's view as a no-ownership view that claims that transition from the occurrence of a conscious mental state to the corresponding self-ascription to a subject is unsound. Vasubandhu claims that conscious attention to the mere having of experience gives us the license to think, for example, "this feeling is pain," "this feeling is anger," etc., since there is no distinct self-quale to be found as part of the content of the experience. According to Vasubandhu, the transition from "this feeling is anger" to "I am feeling angry" requires importing a conceptual resource that is unavailable in our experience. Ganeri fails to recognize this two-step transition here because, like many, he is convinced that it makes no sense to think "there is an inner experience occurring, but is it occurring to me?" Or *à la* P. F. Strawson: "This feeling is anger; but is it I who am feeling it?" (1966, p. 165).

Ganeri thinks that one way for the Abhidharma Buddhist philosopher to avoid the charge of incoherence raised by P. F. Strawson is to offer an account of the sense of ownership. He then goes further to stretch the Abhidharma explanation to reconstruct a Buddhist explanation of "immunity to error through misidentification" of self-ascriptions. Ganeri writes:

> If I cannot be mistaken about whose inner experience it is that I am experiencing, this is because no identification of a subject, and so no possibility of mis-identification, is involved at all. What I am suggesting, then, is that our Buddhist philosophers explain "immunity to error through misidentification" (Shoemaker, 1984) of self-ascriptions, by acknowledging that when my experience presents itself to me as my own, *no representation of myself as a subject takes place.* Asaṅga and Vasubandhu postulate, instead, the existence of a primitive mode of self-awareness, a basic awareness of the contents of my inner life (my "store-consciousness") as mine. And, this, in turn, is what makes it possible for me to have a first-person rather than a merely third-person, perspective on my mental life.   (2011, p. 180; emphasis added)

I think that it is a mistake to assume that Vasubandhu, or indeed any of the Buddhist Abhidharma philosophers, postulate a primitive mode of self-awareness. According to Vasubandhu, the primitive mode of self-awareness is an error on part of the afflictive mind (*kliṣṭa-manas*) to mistakenly regard the evolving storehouse consciousness as a continuing self. Accordingly, they would not want to explain the immunity to error through misidentification, rather they want to claim that misidentification is ubiquitous. Shoemaker introduces this notion to explain why one cannot be mistaken in saying "I feel pain" because one cannot be mistaken about who is the referent of that use of "I." This would commit the Buddhist to the claim that, in making statements like "I am feeling dizzy," we cannot be mistaken about who the "I" refers to. But Vasubandhu claims that in the case of names like "Devadatta"—and presumably the first-person pronoun will be treated similarly—we are mistaken in thinking that the name refers to a single unified thing. This is because names like "Devadatta" and "I" are only conventional expressions that refer to a collection of causes. This claim can be further substantiated by the Abhidharma distinction between ultimate reality and conventional reality. Just as terms like "chariot" and "lamp-light" are only conventional expressions that signify entities constructed from material elements assembled together to serve an interest or purpose, so, also, terms like "person," "self," etc., are only conventional expressions to signify mental and physical elements assembled together to serve certain social and legal purposes and interests. We should not be misled into thinking that there are such things in the world.

The Buddhist distinction between ultimate and conventional reality is widely used in the contemporary literature to suggest that "I" refers to the person. Armed with the *Two Truths*, Ganeri might think he can explain why "I" does not refer to any real entity, and also explain our ordinary talk of pain as belonging to a subject, in this case a person. Ganeri might say the referent of "I" has the tendency to cause serious harm if we take it as referring to an ultimately existing simple continuing self. But not so, if we take it as referring to conventionally real persons. In this sense, persons are best regarded as useful fictions. In Chapter 2, I have argued that persons are not useful fictions, and in fact are just as harmful as selves. So, the Abhidharma Buddhist would be better off not positing a self or person as a useful fiction to provide an owner for conscious experiences like pain.

I suggest that the Abhidharma no-ownership view is restricted to the claim that the transition from being aware of a conscious experience to self-ascribing that experience is unsound. That is, the transition from "being in pain" to "I am feeling pain" or "my feeling of pain" is unwarranted. Therefore, I think that Ganeri is mistaken to introduce the sense of ownership to explain the immunity of error through misidentification. Rather, it is best for the Buddhist to give up all talk of ownership of experiences, for it brings with it the danger of introducing more or less unified and enduring subjects as owners of these experiences. But one might think that the Buddhist Abhidharma philosophers are obliged to give an account of the sense of ownership since there is something in our experience that signals to us that we own our experiences—a phenomenological ingredient that is the basis of our sense of ownership. Next, I argue that there is no such thing.

7.4 Is There an Experience of Ownership?

Intuitively, the sense of ownership is the sense that it is I who am experiencing this thought or that movement. For healthy, well-functioning individuals, mental and bodily awareness is typically accompanied by a sense of ownership. For my purposes here, I shall focus on the sense of ownership of bodily awareness, since it is much more tangible and there is extensive literature available on bodily ownership in cognitive neuroscience, phenomenology, and analytic philosophy. There are two opposing conceptions of this sense of ownership—called, aptly, the deflationary and the inflationary conception (Bermúdez 2011). Both parties in the debate agree that we make mostly reliable judgments of ownership. Defenders of the deflationary conception (Martin 1992, 1995; Bermúdez 2011, 2015) argue that there is nothing that it is like to experience one's body as one's own. According to this view, "the sense of ownership is exclusively judgmental; it has no counterpart at the experiential level...no distinctive positive phenomenology of ownership as such, no felt myness that goes over and above the mere experience of bodily properties" (De Vignemont 2013, p. 643). According to the defenders of the inflationary conception, there is a distinctive quale of ownership that is incorporated into our experience of our own bodies, and it is through this quale that we experience our bodies as our own (Bermúdez 2015). The core of the debate is the question of whether there is an experience for ownership that signals to us that we own our bodies—some distinctive quale that is present when we experience our bodies as our own, and absent in disownership pathologies.

This debate should be important to the Buddhist Abhidharma philosopher, as she is required to explain the phenomenology of our experience of ownership (if there is one). De Vignemont's argument for the inflationary conception posits the experience of ownership as an explanatory tool "which allows for a single unified explanation of ownership illusions, for phenomenological differences between sensations in one's limbs and in tools, and for disownership pathologies" (2013, p. 650). The argument is, at root, an inference to the best explanation. The experience of ownership is posited as the best explanation of the available phenomena: ownership illusions, disownership pathologies, etc. The argument for the deflationary view, in contrast, rests on Anscombe's *separability thesis* (1962). The idea is that a judgment of ownership cannot be grounded in a quale of ownership unless the latter can be described independently of the judgment. Bermúdez (2011) claims that there is no explanatory gain in positing the experience of ownership since it cannot be described independently of our judgments of ownership. Either our descriptions of bodily sensations such as pressure here, a tension there, a tingle in another place (Anscombe 1962) are too vague to serve as an epistemic basis for the judgment, or they simply recapitulate the very knowledge they are supposed to be describing and so are not sufficiently independent to serve as an epistemic basis. The deflationists argue that there is no reason to posit the experience of ownership, for it cannot do the explanatory work for which it is designed. So, the question is: How might the explanatory work be done?

I argue that the work can be done by postulating an experience of disownership. Phenomenologically, the experience of disownership is accompanied by a vivid and rich phenomenology, unlike the experiences of ownership. Here, I will focus on explanation of disownership pathologies because other phenomena alluded to by the inflationist—namely, ownership illusions and phenomenological differences in sensations in one's limbs and in tools—can be explained. Recently, Alsmith (2015) has argued that the illusory experiences of body ownership, as in the Rubber-Hand illusion,[3] may be best explained as imaginative perceptual experience. Cardinali et al. (2021) have argued that phenomenological differences in sensations in one's limbs and tools can be explained using the same principles as the Rubber-Hand illusion. The deflationist is left with the burden of explaining disownership pathologies, and the phenomenological differences between sensations in one's limbs and in tools, without positing the experience of ownership. In this section, I argue that the vivid experience of loss of ownership

---

[3] The Rubber-Hand Illusion evokes the feeling of ownership of a rubber hand displaced from a participant's real occluded hand by synchronously stroking both hands with paintbrushes.

can explain disownership pathologies. The explanation of the phenomenological differences between sensations in one's limbs and those in tools requires that we pay attention to the complex relation between bodily sensations and bodily ownership. I will show that the explanation given by the inflationary theorist cannot account for the phenomenological differences. Thus, there is no good reason to posit the experience of ownership. There is no experience of ownership, since there is no phenomenal content exclusively associated with ownership. Rather, the sense of ownership results from the absence of a feeling associated with loss of ownership.

My case against the presence of experiences of ownership is based on a strategy used by Paglieri (2013) to argue for the thesis that there is no specific feeling associated with free action or decision. Paglieri demonstrates that, from the fact that we can easily and reliably judge whether our actions are free, it does not follow that there is a "freedom attribute" in our experience of acting freely. The judgments are based on the absence of coercion, not on an extra ingredient of "feeling free" in our experience. Similarly, I want to argue that, from the fact that I can judge easily and reliably whether I am the owner of my experiences, it does not follow that there is an extra ingredient of "experience of ownership"; it may just be an absence of a feeling of loss of ownership. I aim to defend a default theory of judgments of ownership. This default option is to consider ourselves as owners of our experiences, with no need for any other proof or evidence from our own experience. In contrast, only a phenomenologically salient experience of loss of ownership can lift the default and force me to judge that I am not the owner of my experiences. Following Paglieri (2013), I suggest the following as desiderata of a default theory of judgments of ownership:

1. Evidence that the phenomenology specifically associated with ownership is thin and recessive and tends to be reported in ways that sound suspiciously close to ex-post reconstructions, if not outright fabrications.
2. Evidence that the lack of ownership, in contrast, associates with a clear and rich phenomenology.
3. Arguments to the effect that presence of the sense of ownership is typical and nonproblematic, whereas the absence of the sense of ownership is the exception that needs to be promptly detected, for the individuals to perform adequately.
4. Evidence that the known pathologies and distortions are adequately accounted for by the default theory.

There is agreement in the literature on the sense of ownership that the phenomenology associated with agency is thin and recessive. Even those who defend the inflationary view agree that the experience of ownership, if it does exist at all, is marginal. De Vignemont says this:

There is little doubt that if there are experiences of ownership, they are not vivid, at least not to the same extent as painful experiences, for example. Otherwise, there would be no dispute whether experiences of ownership exist or not. But the fact that they are not readily available for introspection does not imply that they do not exist.   (2013, p. 646)

In the course of arguing that sense of ownership is generated in sensory-motor processes, Tsakiris et al. also claim that:

[T]he sense of ownership and sense of agency are part of a pre-reflective experience of embodied experience. They are generated in low-level, albeit complex, sensory-motor processes. They tend to remain phenomenologically recessive or attenuated. That is, they involve a thin or minimal although not necessarily simple phenomenology.   (2007, p. 660)

O'Shaughnessy (1995) regards the sense of ownership as "attentively recessive," in the sense that it provides an awareness of the body that is tacit or implicit in the body's motor performance and results from proprioceptive feedback that functions as an integral part of the continuous movement. Thus, there seems to be widespread agreement, among those who advocate that there are experiences of ownership, that the phenomenology is thin and recessive. Furthermore, the reports of such experiences of ownership, if articulated at all, sound very close to ex-post rational reconstructions. We do not talk about ownership of bodily sensations, because there is nothing like an experience of an owner bearing a relation to a certain sensation. The body, if it is phenomenologically available in experience, appears only at the margins and thus does not appear in the report of the experience. Phenomenologists talk of body as a "zero point," "null point of orientation," or the absolute indexical "here" in relation to which things appear perspectively. Thompson says this:

The lived body cannot be reduced to another intentional object but always exceeds this kind of intentionality…experiences involve a non-object directed and implicit awareness of one's body, intransitive and pre-reflective bodily self-awareness.   (2007, p. 249)

The foregoing presents some evidence to satisfy the first desideratum for defending the default theory of the sense of ownership. First-person reports of patients suffering from somatoparaphrenia, which is characterized by a delusion of disownership of left-sided body parts provides ample evidence for the second desideratum. It is usually reported in right-brain damaged patients, with motor and somatosensory deficits, and the syndrome of unilateral spatial neglect. It sometimes occurs without associated anosognosia for motor deficits, and personal neglect. Here are reports of exchanges between patients and examiners:

EXAMINER: Whose arm is this?

A.R.: It's not mine.

EX: Whose is it?

A.R.: It's my mother's.

EX: How on earth does it happen to be there?

A.R.: I don't know. I found it in my bed.

EX: How long has it been there?

A.R.: Since the first day. Feel, it's warmer than mine. The other day too, when the weather was colder, it was warmer than mine.

EX: So, where is your left arm?

A.R.: It's under there (indefinite gesture forwards). (Bisiach et al. 1991, p. 1030)

Another report:

E: Close your eyes and tell me what you feel when I'm touching your hand.

P: That's not my hand!! ... It's not mine ... Someone left it there. I don't know who he was ... I don't know who attached it to my body.

E: Isn't it a little bit weird to have a foreign hand with you?

P: No my hand is not like this! (Invernizzi et al. 2012, p. 148)

It is interesting to note that patients are sensitive to these anomalous self-experiences, and report them voluntarily and easily, despite a greatly reduced insight into their illness (Mintz et al. 2003). Melzack (1990) describes a patient who screamed when the examiner squeezed his "alien" hand, but who still denied that this hand belonged to him. Bottini et al. (2002) also report a case of an aso-matognosic patient who was unable to report touches delivered on her left hand, which she attributed as belonging to her niece. When told that she would be touched on the left hand, she said that she felt nothing. However, when told that she would be touched on her niece's hand, her tactile anesthesia completely recovered. These cases show that bodily sensations and bodily ownership can be taken apart. This is supported by the fact that, although we can feel sensations in tools, they are phenomenologically different to sensations in one's limbs. Defenders of the inflationary view—for example, De Vignemont (2007)—argue for a complex picture to show how bodily sensations ground bodily ownership, but the account falls short of explaining the phenomenology of ownership. According to De Vignemont, sense of ownership is derived from the sensory-motor map or body schema that defines the spatial boundaries of one's own body (2007). That may well be right but notice that such an account will not count as evidence for the inflationary view, since the body schema that grounds our sense of ownership is not something that is directly available in experience. The very fact that the ground of the sense of owner-ship does not account for the phenomenology of ownership should make us doubt whether there is a phenomenology of ownership.

Furthermore, in a recent paper Hur et al. (2014) argue that there is good reason to believe that disturbances of the minimal self characterized by an abnormal sense of body, ownership, and agency are the phenomenological phenotype of schizophrenia. Bryan Charnley (1949–91) used visual metaphor and symbolism in his paintings to vividly illustrate the physical experience of schizophrenia, an illness that Charnley lived with from adolescence until his premature death in 1991. This not only gives us further evidence for a rich and vivid phenomenology associated with the lack of ownership required to satisfy the second desideratum that the patient/artist represents in his paintings, but also provides an exemplary case study for the second conjunct of the third desideratum. Some of Charnley's self-portraits are represented with thoughts and feelings floating around or exploding out of his head as a clear testament to the lack of ownership, and, insofar as it is a symptom of schizophrenia, it hampers adequate performance in everyday life.[4]

To satisfy the third desideratum, we need arguments to the effect that a presence of the sense of ownership is typical and nonproblematic, whereas the absence of the sense of ownership is anomalous. The latter needs to be promptly detected and addressed to ensure that individuals can function properly. The usual argument for this claim comes from an appeal to "immunity to error through misidentification." The fact that I experience a headache, rather than experiencing a headache and then identifying it as my own, is taken as evidence that a certain type of error is not possible in normal cases of bodily experiences. I cannot experience a headache while misidentifying whose headache it is. The "who" question never comes up at the phenomenal level because the experience is already specified with respect to ownership. Even if the experiencer is wrong about "who" the owner is—something that happens in somatoparaphrenia—the experience is already specified with respect to ownership (for example, "the hand belongs to my mother"). Cases of depersonalization seem to be evidence to the contrary here. Patients suffering from depersonalization disorder do not have any emotional response to these experiences. Feelings of detachment—not being able to feel anything, not being able to connect to people and happenings—are often mentioned in subjective reports of patients suffering from the depersonalization syndrome. For this reason, it feels *as if* the thoughts and experiences do not belong to the subject. However, patients never report that there are free-floating thoughts that lack an owner, only that a so-called "natural" affective response is not forthcoming. A subjective report from a patient:

I feel nothing—never have. When my children were born—nothing. I am not sure what love is, I have been married 30 years, it drives my husband mad when

---

[4] Bryan Charnley, available at: https://perma.cc/VM8P-E4TQ.

I talk about it. I just feel nothing—not pain, not anxiety, not happiness. I am not depressed—I am nothing.   (Baker et al. 2003, p. 432)

So, I think that the depersonalization cases do not count as evidence against the default option. This should give us some reason to think that the default option is to consider our bodily experiences as being owned by us. That is to say that there is a presumption of ownership built into one's experiences, unless there is reason to believe otherwise. My second argument for the presence of the sense of ownership as default option is based on an examination of Gallagher's claim that:

In non-observational self-awareness I do not require the mediation of a perception or judgment to recognize myself as myself. I do not need to reflectively ascertain that my body is mine, or that it is my body that is in pain or that is experiencing pleasure. In normal experience, this knowledge is already built into the structure of experience.   (2005, p. 89)

This may lead some to believe that there is some positive phenomenology or feeling associated with being the owner of one's experiences. But that would be an error. We do not find a phenomenological marker of the self in experience. Zahavi and Kriegel (2015) argue that there is no separate self-quale that one can consult in one's phenomenology in isolation from the content of consciousness. The pre-reflective self-awareness does not deliver a datum or a quality like the smell of durian. Zahavi and Kriegel claim that:

[I]t is not supposed to be any specific feeling or determinate quale at all....Our view is not that in addition to the objects in one's experiential field—the books, computer screen, half empty cup of coffee, and so on—there is also *a self-object*. Rather the point is that each of these objects, when experienced, is given to one in a distinctly first-personal way. On our view, one does not grasp for-me-ness by introspecting a self-standing quale, in the same way one grasps the taste of lemon or smell of mint.... In other words, the "me" of for-me-ness is not a separate and distinct item but rather a "formal" feature of experiential life as such.
(2015, p. 38)

This implies that pre-reflective awareness of the self does not deliver self-standing quale. In a similar vein, we might say that the pre-reflective awareness of ownership or sense of ownership is not a specific feeling or a determinate quale that we can consult in our phenomenology—an owner that we can detect in having experience. That there is an owner is just a formal feature of the structure of experience. To say that the pre-reflective sense of ownership is a formal feature of the structure of experience is to deny that there is any positive phenomenal content interlaced into the experience of ownership. But it is also to say, at the same time, that the presence of the sense of ownership is the typical case of experience.

The Charnley case study gives us some reason to think that the absence of a sense of ownership is the exception that needs to be promptly detected in order for the individuals to perform adequately. Furthermore, Parnas and Handest (2003) argue that the phenomenological manifestations of anomalous self-experience, where one's sense of bodily ownership is fragmented, are symptomatic of prodromal phases of schizophrenia and psychosis. They argue that familiarity with subtle nonpsychotic anomalies of subjective experience of one's status as the owner of one's actions, among other symptoms, is not just theoretically significant but is crucial for early differential diagnosis (Parnas & Handest 2003). The phrasings of such complaints may range from a quite trivial "I don't feel myself" or "I am not myself" to "I am losing contact with myself," or "I am becoming a monster." Another clear distortion of experience consists of a loss of bodily coherence, a sense of fragmentation accompanied by a (pre)-psychotic panic of literal dissolution ("going into pieces"). Thakkar et al. (2011) argue that their findings show that schizophrenics have a more flexible body representation and weakened sense of self, and potentially indicate abnormalities in temporo-parietal networks implicated in body ownership. Other studies—for example, Germine et al. (2013)—confirm the findings of Parnas and Handest (2003) and Thakkar et al. (2011).

The fourth, the last, desideratum concerns the adequacy of the default theory to account for known pathologies and distortions. The most striking illustrations are delusions of alien limbs, as in somatoparaphrenia where a subject disowns a limb. The default theory explains the distortion by pointing to the presence of an experience—albeit not veridical—of loss of ownership. The patient has a positive experience of some other subject as owner of the alien limb. The positive experience, although mistaken, accounts for the vividness and fine-grainedness of the delusional phenomenology. The patient has a positive experience of not being the owner of their experiences, possibly because of neurological or other mental disorders.

This completes my case for a default theory of judgments of ownership. To conclude, the default theory gives a parsimonious explanation of the known pathologies and distortions. And, as we have seen, the inflationary theorist is unable to give an adequate explanation of the phenomenological differences between sensations in one's limbs and tools. At best, it seems that the experience of ownership is a label for a solution that explains phenomenological differences between sensations in one's limbs and tools, rather than a solution that does explain the said differences. Thus, there is no good reason to posit a phenomenologically thin and recessive experience of ownership to give a single unified explanation of the phenomena alluded to by the inflationary theorists. We only need to point to the phenomenologically vivid experience of the loss of ownership to explain the pathological cases. The Rubber-Hand illusion and other phenomenological differences between sensations in one's limbs and tools can be explained by cognitivist accounts that invoke only perceptual capacities. So, we do not need to go beyond perception to posit anything more that we can know only through inference. The explanation makes evolutionary sense too: granted that the evolutionary advantage of the experience of ownership would be to alert me when I risk losing ownership of my experiences, it makes sense that the signal is set to attract my attention only when something is amiss, when I do not own my experiences. To have it otherwise would be constantly to remind one that things are as they should be. The cognitive cost is too high without much benefit: evolution will not permit wasteful expenditure of cognitive resources. The Buddhist Abhidharma philosopher can hold on to the no-ownership view without the extra burden of having to explain the phenomenology of ownership, because there is no such thing. There is nothing that it is like to be an owner of experiences.

7.5 Conclusion

This chapter argues that the no-ownership view should not be dismissed without consideration as outright absurd or incoherent. I offer a defense of the no-ownership view on behalf of Vasubandhu against these charges. The Abhidharma Buddhist philosophers are committed to denying the ownership of experiences, and thereby obliged to explain our purported experience of ownership. My experiences seemingly come with the sense that I am the one who is undergoing this experience. But is there a really an experience of ownership—namely, an experience of being a subject that underlies our sense of ownership? On behalf of Abhidharma philosophers, I argue that there is nothing that it is like to be an owner of experiences, in the sense that there is no experiential phenomenology associated with ownership. The sense of ownership is a conceptual construct.

This chapter concludes my larger argument in defense of Vasubandhu's no-self view. The no-self doctrine is so profoundly counterintuitive because it goes against the grain of our experience. The habitual sense of the self is enshrined in our sense of ownership and of agency of our thoughts, experiences, and actions as well as diachronic and synchronic unity of experiences. I have argued on behalf of the Abhidharma philosophers that the sense of self that is enshrined in these experiences is a result of construction. Philosophers will be concerned that an adequate elaboration of this radical no-self view will entail a radical revision of our cognitive framework. That is right. But the Buddhist is interested in more than just that. The motivation behind the no-self and no-person metaphysics is to induce a radical revision of our normative framework. The Buddhists claim that the no-self and no-person framework is "better" since it aims to eliminate or at least reduce suffering. Prima facie, this seems good. But is it really so? This is the question that will concern us in the next two chapters.

8

On What Matters

8.1 Introduction

"In deciding what matters, I must set aside all thoughts about my identity. The question about identity is, here, empty" (Parfit 1984, p. 284). But this line of thought was first verbalized by the Buddha and since then, by many Buddhist philosophers across cultures and times. I have argued in this book (see Chapter 2) that Abhidharma Buddhists are eliminativists about selves and persons. Since most of us contemporary philosophers do not have the soteriological and metaphysical commitments of the Buddhist, we tend to continue being enthusiastic about persons. In this chapter, I argue that this enthusiasm results from our implicit commitment to saving our actual interpersonal and intrapersonal practices and concerns, emotions, and attitudes. This commitment manifests in the desire to ground, explain, and justify our actual person-related concerns by regarding persons as ontological subjects. Revising or even reconsidering person-related practices and concerns, in the absence of selves and persons, is not an option that is explored in contemporary philosophy. In *Reasons and Persons*, Parfit flirts with eliminativism about persons but stops short because of his implicit commitment to avoiding a wholesale revision of our actual person-related practices. Contemporary philosophers, following Parfit, assume that the cost of a wholesale revision is too high, so they tend to favor preservationism rather than revisionism or even pluralism as a strategy to alternate between preservationism and revisionism depending on the context (Nichols & Shoemaker forthcoming). In this chapter, I undertake a reconsideration of person-related practices and concerns as well as interpersonal attitudes to reveal the full force of the revisionary Buddhist metaphysics.

Heretofore this book has largely defended the view that the recognition that there is no self would not undermine our ordinary conception of conscious experiences as we might have thought. We can explain the constitution and phenomenology of conscious experiences without implicating the self or self-representations of any kind. In Chapter 2, I argued that Vasubandhu's argument goes beyond eliminating selves; he is also concerned to eliminate persons. The no-persons metaphysics is not just a challenge for metaphysics, epistemology, and philosophy of mind, but also for ethics. Our person-related practices, attitudes, and concerns governed by ethical norms presuppose the existence of persons. In this chapter and the next, I show that the Abhidharma Buddhist metaphysics also commits us

Selfless Minds: A Contemporary Perspective on Vasubandhu's Metaphysics. Monima Chadha, Oxford University Press.
© Monima Chadha 2023. DOI: 10.1093/oso/9780192844095.003.0009

to a wholesale revision of our ordinary person-related practices, attitudes, and concerns. The Abhidharma Buddhists' aim is not just to change the way in which we describe and interpret the world but to change how we ordinarily interact with each other and the world we live in. The Buddhist no-self and no-person metaphysics therefore requires a major overhaul of our person-related practices and concerns.

P. F. Strawson (1959) introduces the distinction between descriptive and revisionary metaphysics: "Descriptive metaphysics is content to describe the actual structure of our thought about the world, revisionary metaphysics is concerned to produce a *better* structure" (1959, p. 9; emphasis added). This distinction is useful to get a grasp of the sense in which a revisionary metaphysics might offer us a "better" structure. Strawson sagaciously refrains from specifying the sense in which any structure is "better." It is clear, though, that Strawson was not thinking of scientists as revisionary metaphysicians; his paradigm examples were other philosophers: Descartes, Leibniz, and Berkeley. More recently, Kriegel suggests that:

It is natural to suppose that the conceptual scheme we ought to have is that which carves nature at its joints, capturing the "true" structure of reality. If so, revisionary metaphysics is effectively concerned to expose the conceptual-scheme-independent structure of reality.   (2013, p. 1)

Kriegel is wrong on both counts, however. The second claim that the "true" structure of reality is conceptual-scheme-independent is to ignore Davidson's important point that the idea of some unconceptualized "world" waiting to be organized or systematized is mistaken. The idea of "organizing" or "systematizing" something presupposes that this something already has parts or components. There is no single object, such as "the world" out there, waiting for science to organize it (Davidson 1974). The first claim, that the structure we "ought to have" is one that captures the true structure of reality, is motivated by the prevalence of scientism in contemporary philosophy. There are many ways to understand how a structure proposed by a revisionary metaphysics might be "better." It is too restrictive to regard current science (or its close philosophical cousin, Quinean naturalized epistemology) as the only model for a revisionary metaphysics. The central normative goal of Buddhism is to ameliorate suffering and that goal guides its revisionary metaphysics. This goal is prima facie worth pursuing, so a revisionism about practices motivated by the Buddhist metaphysics deserves serious consideration.

The Abhidharma Buddhist no-self and no-person revisionary metaphysics aims to produce a "better" structure that is motivated by the normative goal of eliminating, or at least reducing, suffering. So, one has to be really careful about interpreting the famous Abhidharma Buddhist saying that their metaphysics and epistemology aim at "knowing things as they *really* are." The purpose of the Buddhist revisionary metaphysics is not to describe a scheme that captures the true structure of reality. The Buddhists are concerned with the structure that allows humans to achieve the highest goal, *nirvāṇa* or enlightenment (more detail of what this means follows in the next chapter). The revised structure, in turn, entails a major reconsideration of our ordinary everyday person-related concerns and practices and interpersonal attitudes, for example, moral responsibility, praise and blame, compensation, social treatment, etc. This chapter explores the extent to which we must alter and perhaps discard some of our practical concerns in light of Buddhist revisionism. This raises a larger question for theorists of the self and person: How much weight should we give to saving our actual person-related practices and concerns and interpersonal attitudes? While I will not provide a definitive answer to this question, I hope to show that contemporary philosophers *do* give a lot of weight to saving our actual practices, concerns, emotions, and attitudes. The contrast with Buddhist revisionary metaphysics brings this implicit commitment common in contemporary philosophy into prominence. In this chapter, I am not arguing that we should change our actual practices, concerns, and attitudes, or that the Abhidharma Buddhist no-self and no-person metaphysics does succeed in presenting an all-things-considered "better" structure. I am only arguing that the Abhidharma Buddhist presents us with an alternative structure that deserves to be laid out in full together with its implications as a serious alternative. I realize that the no-self and no-persons metaphysics has major implications in the realm of moral philosophy and a question that might concern my readers: What should we do? I return to this question in the conclusion of this book.

I begin in section 8.2 with listing the similarities between Vasubandhu's and Parfit's accounts of persons. The differences in their positions emerge when we consider what effect these views about persons are likely to have on our actual person-related practices and concerns. Here we discover that Parfit and our Abhidharma Buddhists are likely to diverge. Parfit is hesitant to endorse outright eliminativism about persons because it would require a wholesale revision of our actual practices. In section 8.3, I show that Parfit's reductionist stance towards persons wavers between preservationism (Moderate Claim) and radical revisionism (Extreme Claim). But contemporary philosophers, inspired by Parfit, tend to favor the Moderate Claim and continue the project of saving our actual practices in the preservationist mode. In section 8.4, I lay out the radical revisionism entailed by endorsing a full-blown eliminativism on behalf of the Abhidharma philosophers.

8.2 Parfit and Vasubandhu

Persons as "basic particulars" were introduced in our philosophical ontology by P. F. Strawson. One of his aims in *Individuals* is to establish "the central position

which material bodies and persons occupy among particulars in general...
[to show that] in our conceptual scheme as it is, particulars of these two categories are the basic or fundamental particulars" (1959, p. 15). In the preface to
Reasons and Persons, Parfit clearly declares that although he has great respect for
descriptive metaphysics, he is, by temperament, a revisionist. In the last chapter
of *Reasons and Persons*, Parfit concludes that persons are not what we believe
them to be. Parfit summarizes his position thus:

> On this Reductionist View, persons do exist. But they exist only in the way
> nations exist. Persons, are not, as we mistakenly believe, *fundamental*. This view
> is in this sense more impersonal.   (1984, p. 445)

Parfit's critique of the entity-hood of persons, what he calls "non-reductionism,"
is well known. I will not revisit it here. Parfit's critique is usually aimed at
Cartesian dualist views but his criticism equally applies to Strawson's view of persons. Strawson conceives persons as basic particulars: "a type of entity such that
both predicates ascribing states of consciousness and predicates ascribing corpo-
real characteristics...are equally applicable to an individual entity of that type"
(1959, pp. 101–2). Strawson's concept of person is that of a distinct and independent entity thought of as embodied subject of experiences and an agent of actions.
Strawson's descriptive concept is much thinner than the normative concept of
persons due to Locke and Kant. John Locke was the first to connect issues about
personal identity with broader ethical concerns. Locke famously called "person" a
forensic term, "appropriating actions and their merit; and so belongs only to intel-
ligent agents capable of a law, and happiness, and misery" (Locke 1975 [1689],
pp. 50–1). Kant, following Locke, argued that persons possess moral capacities
and have unalienable moral status (because of having those capacities). Kant formulated the so-called *Principle of Humanity*: "So act that you treat humanity,
whether in your own person or in the person of any other, always at the same
time as an end, never merely as a means" (Kant 2002 [1785], p. 429). Strawson's
later work suggests that he would welcome such an enrichment. Although the
notion of agency (as exemplified by the structure of P-predicates) is central to
Strawson's descriptive concept, the idea of person as a moral agent becomes central in his later works, for example *Freedom and Resentment*, where he takes it for
granted that persons are deeply and naturally presupposed by our reactive-
attitude-involving practices.

   Parfit's no-entity view strips persons of their fundamental status not only in
descriptive metaphysics, but also in the domains of ethics and morality. Parfit says
that while this does not totally undermine our prudential and ethical concerns,
they need to be reconfigured in light of the reductionist view. I will return to this in
a moment. For now, I want to briefly draw attention to Parfit's claim that on the
reductionist view, persons do exist. But what does he mean by this? He says:

We do not deny that people exist. And we agree that we are not series of events—that we are not thoughts and actions, but thinkers and agents. But *this is true only because we describe our lives by ascribing thoughts and actions to people.* As I have argued, we could give a complete description of our lives that was impersonal: that did not claim that persons exist.   (1984, p. 341; emphasis added)

The talk of persons, according to Parfit, is a matter of convention, just like for our Abhidharma Buddhist Vasubandhu (see Chapter 2). As Vasubandhu would put it, "person" is only a name given to a collection of aggregates. Parfit and the Abhidharma Buddhists are reductionists about persons. Persons are nothing more than an artefact because of the way we think and talk. There are no real persons. We can continue to talk about persons in our ordinary everyday language but given that we need to drastically change our views about the nature of persons and personal identity over time, we should note that persons are only nominal existences. If Parfit and Vasubandhu are right, then the gate is open for us to reconsider and perhaps revise our person-related attitudes and practices. Abhidharma Buddhists endorse eliminativism about persons because they are not concerned with preserving our practices; they recommend their wholesale revision. Parfit comes very close to endorsing eliminativism about persons but shies away because of his uneasiness with recommending a radical revision of our actual practices.

8.3 Reductionism and Preservationism

Parfit's reductionist stance in *Reasons and Persons* wavers between the Extreme Claim and the Moderate Claim. The Extreme Claim says that our moral and prudential concerns cannot be grounded without a deep separate fact about personal identity. They are ungrounded. Period. Most of us would be perturbed by the extremity of this claim. Parfit too is worried and therefore offers the equally defensible Moderate Claim. The Moderate Claim says that our person-related attitudes and practices may well be grounded by what matters in personal identity, which Parfit identifies as "Relation R" consisting of psychological connectedness and/or continuity (1984).[1]

P. F. Strawson's (1962) essay, "Freedom and Resentment," has been interpreted as suggesting that our person-related attitudes and practices, in particular our

---

[1] Parfit defines psychological continuity in terms of overlapping chains of direct psychological connectedness (e.g., the connection between a memory and the experience of which it is a memory, between an intention and the action that carries it out, or between different temporal portions of a continuing belief, desire, or trait) that are appropriately caused.

practice of holding responsible—assigning praise or blame—is *not* something for which rational justification or grounding is needed. But we need to be more careful here. Strawson writes:

> [As to] a question about the rational justification of ordinary inter-personal attitudes in general [the attitudes from which responsibility-attributions derive],...
> I shall reply, first, that such a question could seem real only to one who had utterly failed to grasp the purport of...the fact of our natural human commitment to ordinary inter-personal attitudes. This commitment is part of the general framework of human life, not something that can come up for review.   (1962, p. 14)

Strawson's concern in his essay is to respond to incompatibilists (he calls them pessimists) who are concerned whether our practices of holding responsible can stand as they are if we acknowledge that determinism is true. He thinks that it is absurd to think that we would give up the practices, if it turned out that determinism is true. Strawson motivates his compatibilist reply by drawing attention to a distinction between practical and theoretical considerations. Strawson thinks that there is no question that our lives would be hugely impoverished if we were to give up on our practice of holding responsible, so practical considerations motivate us to preserve this practice. But the truth of determinism is a theoretical question about how things are in the world, which is insufficient to determine answers to practical questions about what we ought to do. That may well be right. Our concern with the truth or falsity of determinism does not influence our participation in the supposedly beneficial practice of holding responsible. Strawson goes further to add that the moral attitudes and the practices that express them are not simply instruments of control, justified by their efficacy. These attitudes and practices are constitutive of the moral and social nature of persons. Strawson says "it is *useless* to ask whether it would not be rational for us to do what is not in our nature to (be able to) do" (1962, p. 20). This has led many contemporary philosophers to think that Strawson is endorsing the view that moral attitudes and practices are not rationally grounded. Shoemaker writes:

> While Strawson is here concerned explicitly with what it would be rational to do if the thesis of determinism were true, *his thought clearly seems to carry over to the similar question of what it would be rational to do if certain metaphysical theses of personal identity were true.* His answer in both cases would likely be the same: asking the question about rational justification in either case fails to take seriously the deeply natural commitment we have to the practices as they stand. Indeed, constructed as we are, we simply do not have "a choice in this matter".... The question of rational grounding thus seems utterly irrelevant.
>
> (2007, pp. 348–9; emphasis added)

It is a mistake to read Strawson in this way; his thought about the irrelevance of determinism does not carry over to the metaphysical theses of personal identity. Because Strawson is careful to add that "if there were, say, for a moment open to us the possibility of such a godlike choice, the rationality of making or refusing it would be determined by quite other considerations than the truth or falsity of the *general theoretical doctrine in question*" (1962, p. 20; emphasis added). Strawson is only concerned to deny that it is not rational to wholly suspend these attitudes and practices if it were to turn out that determinism is true. But this does not rule out the possibility of choosing whether we should wholly suspend or revise our person-related attitudes and practices; the rationality of such choices would depend on other considerations. It seems to me that theoretical considerations about the nature of persons would be pretty high on the list to justify a wholesale suspension or revision of our attitudes and practices. They are not just theoretical claims about what the world is like, but a claim about the nature of beings— persons—that partake in the practices, that harbor the emotions and reactive attitudes. The "natural" commitment to these practices depends on the nature of persons. Indeed, this is the reason why Strawson discusses that the practice of holding responsible should exclude certain persons, namely those who are "immature" and "abnormal." Strawson, it seems to me, would be open to asking the question about rational justification of our practices if it were the case that persons are not what we believe them to be.

So, we need to ask, if Parfit's and Vasubandhu's reductionism about persons is right, how must we reconfigure our claims about morality and responsibility? Parfit argues that reductionism about persons requires a wholesale reconsideration of many of our attitudes including the immorality of great imprudence, desert, and commitments. Since psychological connectedness and/or continuity are a matter of degree, the strength of these connections will determine the degree to which one should hold people responsible for acting imprudently, for their past crimes and the promises they make for the future. In a sense this undercuts Siderits' reasons for why Buddhists should not eliminate persons. Siderits writes:

> Why do most Buddhists think that people should be reductionists and not elim-
> inativists? If eliminating belief in the self is important to the project of overcom-
> ing suffering, then why stop at half measures concerning the person? The answer
> is to be found in something Buddhists say concerning personal identity over a
> single lifetime. . . . One example given in this text is that of a criminal who does
> not appropriate earlier and later parts of the series. Predictably this individual
> fails to take responsibility for his past crime, sees his present punishment as
> unjustified, and persists in criminal behaviour after release. Clearly, adoption of
> the personhood concept promotes practices we wish to encourage.
>
> (2019, pp. 315–16)

Siderits appeals to practical considerations to advance the cause of Buddhist reductionism about persons. Moral responsibility no doubt is an important practical concern, but Parfit has shown that any notion of responsibility that presupposes a false conception of persons needs to be recalibrated. Rather than holding people responsible *simpliciter*, the degree of responsibility should be proportional to the degree of psychological connectedness and/or continuity. This is Parfit in his preservationist mode considering the Moderate Claim, defending a graded view of moral responsibility. If the connections between the criminal now and the individual at the time of the crime are weaker, then he deserves less punishment. This holds also true for our commitments, promises, our self-concern about our own future, and finally the fear of death. The more weakly connected our future time-slices are to our current time-slice, the more reason there is to reduce our overwhelming obsession with the well-being and longevity of our future time-slice. We have no reason to be specially concerned about our own futures, but we have reason to care for future time-slices as much as we would care for other people. Parfit would agree that one important consequence of the no-entity view is that it succeeds in "breaking barriers between people." Abhidharma Buddhists would agree that this is a step in the right direction, but perhaps we could go further.

The Moderate Claim is defended by Parfit in his more preservationist mode. Contemporary philosophers (Shoemaker 2007, 2016; Nichols & Shoemaker forthcoming; Schechtman 2010, 2014) agree with Parfit's preservationist stance. The Extreme Claim is not compatible with this preservationist stance. It suggests either suspension or at least wholesale revision of our actual practices. Contemporary philosophers therefore try to preserve the concept of persons because of its role in grounding our person-related practical concerns. Parfit's "Identity Doesn't Matter" view, I argue below, puts us on the path to eliminating rather than preserving the concept of person and wholesale revision of our actual practices rather than grounding them. More recently, Shoemaker has developed what he calls the "Identity Really *Really* Doesn't Matter" view (2016). Adopting Shoemaker's view requires us to endorse a wide-ranging pluralism about what matters in personal identity and theories about the relation between personal identity and our person-related concerns and attitudes. Shoemaker's view, I will argue, is a further step in the direction of eliminativism about persons, but again he shies away from endorsing it. Why? Because of Shoemaker's continued allegiance to preservationism about actual practical attitudes and concerns which presupposes the reality of persons as subjects of experience and agents of actions, or so I will argue.

So far so good. Parfit has helped us see that "Identity Doesn't Matter" for some practical considerations, for example, moral responsibility and prudence. What matters instead is psychological continuity and/or connectedness. Shoemaker argues that psychological continuity is not *all* that matters when we consider a wider range of person-related concerns and practices. Consider our practices of compensation with the following example from Shoemaker:

> Suppose Johann suddenly enters a fugue state. Call the radically psychologically discontinuous "fuguer" Sebastian. Suppose that I had broken Johann's wrist prior to the fugue state but that I now have the medical equipment and expertise to completely heal it and, indeed, make it stronger than before (i.e., to "rejuvenate" it). When I rejuvenate the wrist I broke, it is Sebastian's. Does what I have done count as compensation? It certainly seems so, despite the psychological discontinuity between Sebastian and Johann. This is because the kind of burden I attempted to rectify was to Johann's animal self, and while physical setbacks are, at most, merely instrumental to well-being—on any account of well-being, I think—if they persist across multiple psychological beings, they may be instrumental in reducing the well-being of whomever they are attached to. To rejuvenate the specific wrist, I broke (attached to a living human being) is to make right a burden I caused.   (2016, p. 322)

Similarly, consider the patient A who is suffering from Parkinson's disease and who has made an Advance Care Directive refusing life-sustaining treatment as well as antibiotics. A's Parkinson's disease has deteriorated significantly over the years and he is now suffering from end-stage dementia. Two months later, A contracts a life-threatening community transmitted virus. His health care team, in accordance with his wish of refusal of life-sustaining treatment, does not call an ambulance or administer antibiotics. His prudential concern in signing the directive is clearly for his future time-slice but now there is no one who is psychologically continuous with him. Biological continuity alone seems to be what matters here; psychological continuity is irrelevant. In another example, Shoemaker comes to the same conclusion when considering social treatment of severely brain-damaged relatives:

> Consider someone who, due to some traumatic brain injury, undergoes radical psychological discontinuity. She will still be treated as the owner of the pre-transformation-person's car and other property, and she will also be treated as the spouse of the pre-transformation-person's spouse, the daughter of her parent, and so forth.   (2016, p. 316)

It is possible, however, as Tierney et al. (2014) note, that social treatment and compensation can also track psychological continuity. They offer a few thought experiments to make their point. Consider this variant on their example: suppose we are able to transfer an elderly adult's entire psychological profile from her body to a new body. While the old body, which is in any case deteriorating because of aging, is destroyed, her children would presumably treat this "new" individual as their own mother, despite the lack of biological continuity. And, if an individual had caused some psychic trauma to the elderly adult before the transfer, but rectified the trauma after the transfer occurred, the elderly adult would still surely be compensated, again, despite the lack of biological continuity. In this way, Tierney et al. conclude that "it looks as though these identity-related practical concerns fail to track a singular, monistic criterion of identity, but rather follow two distinct criteria in different contexts" (2014, p. 200).

Indeed, if we consider the variety of practical concerns—anticipation, first-person recognition and concern, third-person recognition and concern, general social treatment, emotional patterns (e.g., pride and shame), compensation, and responsibility—we realize that our practical concerns do not consist of a monolithic set. There are different types of practical concerns, and while some are clearly grounded on psychological relations, some are actually grounded on others, including animalistic and humanistic relations (Shoemaker 2016). What this suggests, then, is that not only does identity not matter but also the relations Parfit thought mattered are irrelevant to some of our practical concerns (Shoemaker 2016).

Revising our pre-philosophical Strawsonian concept of person to be more like the Parfitian unified bundle of psychological states looks unstable, since several of our practical concerns turn out to put pressure on the unity of the bundle. No revision of the "person," then, can capture all of our practical concerns. And as Nichols and Shoemaker remind us:

> [D]on't forget the biggest practical concern of them all: fear of death (or the hoped-for anticipation of survival of death). As Butler noted, "Whether we are to live in a future state…is the most important question which can possibly be asked…" (Butler 1975 [1736], p. 99)….The practical concerns that often justify preservation for other concepts have much more difficulty doing so in the case of the self. And recall as well that there could be a significant practical advantage to *elimination* of the "self," namely, the therapeutic effect articulated by Buddhism.[2]   (forthcoming)

Other practical concerns, as we saw, depend on what Shoemaker calls "animalistic and humanistic relations." Psychological continuity is at least sometimes not

---

[2] Though Nichols and Shoemaker (forthcoming) are concerned with the self and want to draw a totally different conclusion from this, they would not have trouble agreeing that we can replace the self with person in this quote. The conclusion they want to draw is a provocative suggestion, what they call a radical pluralism, according to which, we can choose to be pluralists rather than preservationists or eliminativists about the self, depending on the context. I do not agree with that suggestion, but I will not argue against it here. I will press on with the argument for the claim that Buddhists, and all of us, have good reason to endorse eliminativism about selves and persons.

what is at issue when we are thinking of compensation or social treatment, but a different criterion, for example bodily continuity or biological continuity, may work in these cases. Following Shoemaker, we may add to this list: third-person reidentification and its associated sentiments, for example, why is my happiness at seeing my parents after a long time appropriate? And first-person reidentification, for example, why is it appropriate that when I look at certain photos on my mother's coffee table, I feel nostalgic? (Shoemaker 2007). What explains these feelings?

The variety and disunity of person-related concerns and attitudes suggests that no single criterion of personal identity will serve to ground all of these concerns. Some might suggest, as Tierney et al. do, that we offer plural criteria for identity. Tierney et al. settle for two criteria. They write, "empirical evidence and philosophical thought experiments indicate that judgments about personal identity are regimented by two different criteria, one in terms of psychological traits and one that largely conforms to biological criteria" (2014, p. 198). We may go further with Shoemaker and settle for a wide-ranging pluralism in the face of the disunity of our practical concerns. But Shoemaker stops short of giving up on persons and person-related concerns in the hope that there is a theory (or theories) of the relation between personal identity and our person-related practices and concerns. He says:

> [S]everal concessions may be required, including admission, perhaps, of (a) the irrelevance of certain powerful and popular criteria of personal identity for (at least some of) our practices and concerns, (b) the ultimate disunity of these practices and concerns (such that multiple types of theories of the relation between them and the metaphysics may be called for), and/or (c) the possibility of different types of rational grounding—justification and rendering-possible—where justification may actually be off the table altogether for some practices and concerns.   (2007, p. 354)

The upshot of this discussion for our purposes is that Strawsonian persons considered as *one* two-sided thing and not as *two* conjoined one-sided things—mind and body—are no longer available as one single thing to ground all of our person-related concerns. Parfitian reasons lead us to question the identity of Strawsonian persons, Shoemakerian reasons lead us to question the supposed psychological unity of Parfitian persons. What matters is not just psychological connectedness and/or continuity, but different clusters of mental and/or physical states. In other words, different clusters of mental and/or physical states play the person role in response to different practical concerns. We need persons to ground our person-related concerns and practices, but what we find are disunified clusters of mental and/or physical states playing that role. There is no real unity here that forms a whole; a person, at a time, nor over time.

What does this tell us about the concept of person? Persons are not natural kinds, there is no such thing as a "person" in nature. We routinely ascribe person-hood to mark certain clusters of mental and/or physical states as members of one or more interpersonal spheres—normative, moral, social, political, legal, cultural, community, family, etc. These spheres indicate how such clusters are to be treated. Persons, then, are at most conventional kinds as Buddhists would say or politi-cal and legal (forensic) kinds as Locke would say. Contemporary neo-Lockeans, such as Strawson, Parfit (in his preservationist mode), Olson, and Shoemaker presuppose persons and thus are concerned about questions of personal iden-tity through time and the relations between theories of personal identity and our practical concerns. If persons are merely conventional kinds, then we should ask whether having the person convention is a good thing. The Abhidharma Buddhists, I have argued in Chapter 2, give a negative answer. Persons are not useful fictions, in fact, they are as pernicious as selves. Presupposing the existence of persons as more or less persisting entities is likely to bring in all the problems that the no-self view is meant to eradicate. Perhaps we should eliminate persons, just as we should eliminate selves. But that comes at a cost. Eliminating persons will require a wholesale revision of our person-related practices and attitudes. Such a wholesale revision will take us much beyond the preservationist stance favored by contemporary philosophers. In the next section, on behalf our Abhidharma Buddhist philosophers, I explore what such a wholesale revision might look like.

8.4 Reductionism and Revisionism

The moves made by Parfit and Shoemaker seem to go a long way in shoring up eliminativism about persons, but do not take the final step. Why? Because they do not question our actual person-related practices, concerns, and attitudes. These are considered sacrosanct; they are not up for revision. In this they agree with Strawson: "the fact of our natural human commitment to ordinary inter-personal attitudes. This commitment is part of the general framework of human life, *not something that can come up for review*" (1962, p. 14; emphasis added). Strawson is not only claiming that it is hard for us to give it up. He thinks to give up these interpersonal attitudes and concerns would be to give up on our humanity. Parfit explicitly says that he is not content to be a descriptive philosopher. In the preface to *Reasons and Persons* he writes:

> Descriptive philosophy gives us reasons for what we instinctively assume, and explains and justifies the unchanging central core of our beliefs about ourselves, and the world we inhabit. I have great respect for descriptive philosophy. But by temperament, I am a revisionist....I try to challenge what we assume.

Philosophers should not only interpret our beliefs; when they are false, they should *change* them.   (1984, p. x)

Parfit has revisionist intentions, but it is his respect for descriptive metaphysics that draws him to preserving our actual person-related and practice-related concerns, and that stops him in his tracks. This is the reason for shying away from the Extreme Claim and endorsing eliminativism about persons, even though he thinks it is defensible. He thinks another claim is equally defensible: persons exist, though they are not fundamental. His preference for endorsing reductionism combined with the Moderate Claim gains traction from preservationism about our person-related practices, attitudes and concerns. Contemporary philosophers, like Shoemaker and Tierney et al., are willing to question the criteria of personal identity and the theories of the relation between personal identity and person-related concerns and practices. But they are not willing to question the person-related practices, attitudes, and concerns. I think this is also what hinders contemporary philosophers interested in Buddhism, especially Siderits and Ganeri, from endorsing eliminativism about persons. All this effort is in the service of hoping to ground our actual person-related concerns, practices, and attitudes.

But why do we regard our actual practices as sacrosanct? Why do we not want to consider revising or even jettisoning some of our ordinary person-related concerns, practices, and interpersonal attitudes? We have come so far as to believe that they cannot simply be grounded in persons or what matters in personal identity. At this point a thoroughgoing revisionist has several options. One such option not considered in contemporary philosophy is to revisit our person-related concerns, practices, and attitudes.

Abhidharma Buddhists are not content to do descriptive metaphysics in Strawson's spirit. Their aim is to propose an alternative structure, in terms of what it would take to reduce all suffering, impersonally and selflessly. Therefore, they reject not only selves but persons. And, if the consequence of this rejection is that we have to radically revise, or even discard, some of our ordinary everyday person-related practices concerns and attitudes, so be it. Abhidharma Buddhists do not have much respect for descriptive metaphysics and are also not inclined towards preservationism. As far as these Abhidharma Buddhists are concerned, person-related practices, concerns, and interpersonal attitudes are open for review and wholesale revision, if need be, in accordance with the normative goal of reducing suffering.

Shoemaker (2007) provides an expanded list of our actual person-related practices and concerns, some of these have already been discussed by Williams (1970) and Parfit (1984). Since I want to consider how a Buddhist no-self and no-person theorist might suggest a revision and perhaps elimination of some of our actual practices, it will be useful to reproduce Shoemaker's entire list here:

1. Anticipation of one's own experiences in the future.
2. Special concern for oneself in the future.
3. Anticipation of an afterlife, that is, is it possible for one to survive the death of *one's own* body, to exist in some sense.
4. Being held morally responsible only for *one's own* actions.
5. Being legitimately compensated only for sacrifices *one* has undergone.
6. Special concern for maximizing one's own well-being.
7. Being the appropriate target of various of sentiments, for example, embarrassment, pride, and regret.
8. Third-person reidentification and its associated sentiments that undergird special concern for, attitudes towards, and appropriate emotions for those in special relations to oneself.
9. First-person reidentification and its associated sentiments that undergird special concern for, attitudes towards, and appropriate emotions for one's own past or future self. (2007, pp. 317–18)

Needless to say, any such list is not exhaustive, more elements can be added to it and it may be refined further. I will address all of these in the following, though not necessarily in this order.

Let us begin with self-concern and the special concern that we have for those we love dearly before we turn to interpersonal attitudes, for example responsibility, compensation, and social treatment. The Buddhists recognize that it is a built-in pre-condition of our form of life that we have self-concern and special concern for our loved ones. That is why the Buddhists do not recommend giving up on these concerns. Rather they recommend extending similar concern to others. And they do not think that such an extension comes easy to us given our human nature; it has to be inculcated by extensive study of Buddhist texts, rational inquiry into the theses proposed within these texts coupled with meditation practices. That said, this is not to be thought of as the giving up of one's humanity but rather enlarging it. In Parfitian speak, this discovery is liberating and consoling (1984). The Buddhists agree.

To give the reader a flavor of how these meditation techniques are supposed to work and how we should consider revising our interpersonal attitudes, I focus on Buddhaghosa, an important philosopher in the Pāli Abhidhamma tradition, because he is concerned with shaping the metaphysical analysis of the Abhidharma tradition into a path for practical and therapeutic development. It is worth emphasizing that on this account there is not much difference to what the Abhidharma Buddhists would recommend. Heim (2017) explains the various analytical techniques developed by Buddhaghosa for the practice of loving kindness concentration. To begin with, Buddhaghosa says, one should consider the practical advantages of becoming filled with loving kindness, most important of which is that one becomes more tolerant of one's own and others' shortcomings and gets rid of self-loathing. It is important for beginners to the practice of loving kindness meditation to choose the first object on which to concentrate carefully. This is a tricky matter and advice from one's teacher is likely to be helpful. Buddhaghosa recommends choosing a concrete real particular person, not someone dead. Furthermore, he warns against choosing someone one intensely dislikes or likes too much, a hostile person, or a person of "the opposite sex" as the feelings one has towards such persons can be distracting, making it harder to begin. Since the content of loving kindness meditation is "may this being be happy," Buddhaghosa recommends starting with oneself is perhaps the best strategy to allow a smooth entry into the practice. The meditator can then progress in the practice by moving beyond the self to direct loving kindness towards a dearly loved one, then to a neutral person, and finally to an enemy. It is at this last point that the meditator is going to be faced with serious obstructions in the practice. Contemplating one's enemy, the meditator is likely to be overcome by anger and resentment. Buddhaghosa recognizes that these feelings are hard to dislodge but does offer practical techniques for overcoming such feelings. One of the recommended techniques is what Heim calls "resolution into elements" (2017, p. 179). The technique recommends one breaks down an enemy to a bundle of psychophysical aggregates or, further, into the material components of the body (head hair, body hairs, nails, etc.). Now ask yourself, which part is resented? There is no sensible answer to this question. If a person is seen as nothing more than a heap of constantly changing material and mental *dharmas* then the anger and resentment cannot get a foothold.

Other meditations like compassion, sympathetic joy, and finally equanimity meditations are to be practiced on the same model and are to be undertaken after completing the loving kindness meditation and in the order in which they are listed. Equanimity is different in that it retracts from the happiness and pleasure taken in the forms of love developed in the first three. Pleasure is considered as a "danger" because of its association with desires and proximity to aversion and attraction. Equanimity, on the other hand, promotes impartiality that brings with it peace, although it is not suggested that the meditator develops this with apathy or indifference. Heim does mention though that with equanimity "we may have reached the edges of what we can mean by 'love.' The breaking down of barriers it effects is coming to see all beings—dear and despised alike—as neutrals" (Heim 2017, p. 182). Equanimity is the ideal to be reached and making progress on the Buddhist Path is accomplished through successive meditations.

The point I want to draw attention to is that although attitudes of resentment and blame are difficult to dislodge because they are deeply ingrained, it is not the case that they cannot come up for review. Strawson would say reviewing attitudes of resentment and blame, which are at the core of our practices of treating each other as participants, would be to give up our humanity. Perhaps we could tinker with some reactive attitudes around the margins. The Buddhists disagree. They suggest a wholesale, but principled, revision of our practices to jettison all the *negative* reactive attitudes including those at the core. In contrast, positive reactive attitudes like forgiveness, sympathy, and compassion are to be cultivated.

Another point worth drawing attention to is that moral sentiments like pride, embarrassment, and regret are all explicitly discouraged by the Ābhidharmika philosophers, for various reasons. Pride (*atimāna*) and self-contempt (*omāna*) are derived from the root *māna* translated as conceit. Conceit is defined as:

> [F]ancying (deeming, vain imagining). It has haughtiness as characteristic, self-praise as function, desire to (advertise self like) a banner as manifestation, greed dissociated from opinionatedness as proximate cause, and should be regarded as (a form of) lunacy.[3]   (trans. Gorkom 2014, p. 84)

In this sense, conceit is taken to implicate a self-representation, and so too is its manifestation as in pride and self-contempt. And insofar as both pride and self-contempt are self-conscious emotions, they are seen as depending on a wrong view of the self. The Ābhidharmikas denounce pride and self-contempt precisely because they require representing oneself as being superior or inferior to others respectively. Surprisingly though, another self-conscious emotion *hiri* (usually translated as shame) is usually encouraged, even celebrated by the Abhidharma philosophers. This is because they do not understand *hiri* as a self-conscious emotion in the same way as philosophers and emotion theorists in the West do. *Hiri* is best understood as what we may call "anticipatory guilt" which involves contemplating various acts (e.g., lying or telling the truth), and it need not involve self-representation in the way shame and pride do (Chadha & Nichols 2019). This also offers a clue for why they discourage embarrassment and regret: both are backward-looking emotions. The Ābhidharmikas associate regret (*kukkucca*) with agitation, which increases suffering, and thus *kukkucca* is found in the group of bad or unwholesome mental factors. Heim notes that *kukkucca* is explicitly discouraged in Pāli sources. She quotes from Buddhaghosa's *Atthasālinī*, a key text in the Abhidhamma tradition: "since one cannot undo a bad deed nor do a good deed that was neglected, returning again to it in remorse is ugly" (Heim 2009, p. 246). The Abhidharma Buddhists maintain that one who is enlightened (an *arhat*) is not troubled by remorse or worry about evil deeds done in the past. So too with embarrassment construed as discomfort on account of past misdemeanor. Positive emotions, like anticipatory guilt (*hiri*) and fear of wrongdoing (*ottappa*) are forward-looking emotions which guard against wrongdoing and evil and thus are to be cultivated.

---

[3] *Atthasālinī*, Part IX, Chapter III, 256.

The overarching principle guiding these revisions is the normative goal of reducing suffering. The idea is to break down barriers among persons, to identify with others and think of others as I think of myself. After all, it is causal relations that undergird the special concern I have for my future self. But I also have the same kind of causal relations with my loved ones and other contemporary beings. Why not extend the special concern I have for my future self to others? There is no suggestion this is going to be easy, but the idea is to slowly expand the circle of me and mine to include all others. This does not require giving up on all the normal sentiments that we find ourselves with, such as anger, love, resentment, joy, shame, and pride. But only the negative ones among these sentiments like resentment, hatred, anger and negative emotions like pride and regret. The idea is to develop moral sentiments like empathy, sympathy, and compassion, all of which can be aided by identifying with other persons. Additionally, anticipatory guilt and fear of wrongdoing are encouraged as both guard against bad actions in the future.

What effect are these Buddhist meditation practices likely to have when we think of other person-related concerns like responsibility, compensation, and social treatment? For moral responsibility, the Abhidharma Buddhists would agree in principle with Parfit that psychological continuity is what matters, though the details of their account of moral responsibility are different (see Chapter 6). To restate the main point briefly, the Abhidharma Buddhist account of agency and moral responsibility involves a strategy of stepwise reduction (see also Repetti 2017). First, the discourse of enduring agents is reductively analyzed in terms of impersonal psycho-physical aggregates. On this analysis, there are no enduring selves or persons and no centralized locus of agency. Second, the psycho-physical system itself is analyzed into momentary mental and physical events, the *dharmas*. At this level of fundamental ontology, agency is explained in terms of the causal connections between the *dharmas* and between the *dharmas* and the external environment. Responsibility for the actions performed by aggregates of *dharmas* is borne by the aggregates of descendant *dharmas* in virtue of the causal chains that bind them. The Ābhidharmikas, thus, offer a purely causal account of moral responsibility. There is no room for reactive attitudes like blame and resentment, or even our legal practices for punishment.

Perhaps we can think of responsibility in terms of evanescent *dharmas*, but we cannot think of compensation in the same way. Someone might object: if we give up all notions of persons, how do we go about our daily lives of compensating one individual for the work he has done? If there is no concept of person, this practice seems to lose its point. Imagine that we actually eliminated the concept of a persisting person, such that we did not even have a notion that we could work with—it seems that we could not have a market economy. Why would I produce a good and sell it to you if I did not think that you would regard me as the same individual when it comes to paying me for the good?[4] To think about Abhidharma accounts of compensation and social treatment, we need to return to the thought embedded in Buddhaghosa's elaboration of meditation techniques. Abhidharma Buddhists urge us to think about interpersonal relations as extensions of intrapersonal relations. Parfit too wants us to think of our future selves as not that different to other people. Parfit concludes that "[w]e ought not to do to our future selves what it would be wrong to do to other people" (1984, p. 320). Parfit, in contrast, wants us to think of intrapersonal relations as extensions of interpersonal relations. This is the other way around to what I take Buddhaghosa to be suggesting. Both Buddhaghosa and Parfit consider our ordinary everyday way of thinking of relations between persons very differently from the way we ordinarily do. We tend to think of our relations with others on the model of transactions. Since the 1950s, the popularity of transactional analysis promotes thinking of all communication exchanges between people, even our intimate relations, as transactions (Berne 1958). Many of our problems, these psychologists and psychotherapists claim, come from unsuccessful transactions. I propose, on behalf of the Abhidharma Buddhists, that we reject this transaction paradigm. Think of our more intimate relations, with one's children, for example: these are not transactional. Parents (ideally) do not expect something in return. Should your children compensate you with filial piety for all you have done and are doing for them? That certainly does not seem to be the right way to think about this. When the Buddhists talk about "breaking barriers between people," the idea is to think of other people, loved ones, friends, strangers, even enemies as one thinks of one's own future self. The Buddhist practice of *dāna*, best thought of as "giving away"[5] as an ethical and soteriological virtue, is both a duty of the laity as well as an exalted "perfection" of the Bodhisattva. This practice forms the basis of lay renunciation in relinquishing attachment to material possessions and supporting the community, and as a moral ideal. The ideal for the Buddhist is that we live in a community (*saṅgha*) with no concept of private property, relinquishing all material possessions. Think of "giving away" (*dāna*) whatever goods and services one can offer to the community rather than "transacting" or "compensating" as a starting point for our everyday dealings with others. It is perhaps better to think of expanding our circle slowly. Perhaps from giving to one's own children to giving to one's students and so on. The university pays academics for teaching, but it does not seem right for academics to think that the students owe them compensation for giving them goods; it is rather a gift of knowledge that is shared with students. Markets and other financial institutions allow ordinary people like us to function in an interdependent society, but the Buddhist ideal is to take this fact of interdependence seriously so that it would lead—ultimately, in an ideal Buddhist

---

[4] I am indebted to Shaun Nichols for raising these questions.
[5] Rather than "gift-giving" which is standard in the Buddhist literature.

society—to a dissolution of markets and other financial institutions. A similar conclusion is endorsed by Graham Priest (2019).

Again, when it comes to social treatment the Abhidharma Buddhist urges us to think of all others as one would think of one's own future self. We are deeply interconnected, and thus not islands in ourselves. So, setting aside money and property for the welfare of a future self, or one's children or other loved ones to inherit, should ideally be at a par with sharing it with our contemporaries.

What then about the biggest practical concern of them all: fear of death or the hoped-for anticipation of survival of death? Buddhists do believe in rebirth without any transmigrating self: there is an afterlife. Given the metaphysics of no-selves and no-persons, rebirth sounds mysterious. How do the Buddhists square this with the idea of rebirth? If there is no "I," it is a misconception to think that I will experience pleasure or suffering in a future life. Since the very notion of self that grounds and generates our fear of death is metaphysically empty, Abhidharma Buddhists argue that fear of death should wither away (see also Parfit 1984). The doctrine of rebirth is meaningful in Buddhism, I think, insofar as it ensures that *karmic* causality is not compromised. And although rebirth and *karma* are linked together, it is *karma* that is of primary importance; rebirth is secondary. My actions, good or bad, will generate a being as different from myself in the future in this life and the ones that follow. Just as it is actually meaningless to act out of concern for one's own welfare in this life, so too it would be meaningless for the afterlife. The ethics of *karma* is thus turned on its head: the only meaningful motive for action is compassion for others. These consequences sound startling and so they should.

8.5 Conclusion

In this chapter I have explored the full consequences of adopting the Abhidharma no-self and no-person revisionary metaphysics. No-person metaphysics fails to gain traction among contemporary philosophers because although they endorse Parfit's reductionism, they favor the Moderate Claim and the preservationist attitude that accompanies it. Saving our actual practices seems to sway us in favor of preservationism. Vasubandhu is a Reductionist just like Parfit. But he goes further than Parfit to endorse the eliminativism about persons and is not perturbed by wholesale revisionism. What he is offering us with this is a new alternative that requires serious consideration by contemporary philosophers. Does Vasubandhu succeed in offering a *better* structure as promised? That is a question I will address later in the Concluding Remarks chapter. My task in this chapter was to present the radical revisionism of our ordinary practices entailed by the Buddhist metaphysics.

9

The Buddhist Path

9.1 Introduction

I do not mean to assert that the promotion of happiness should be itself the end of all actions, or even of all rules of action. It is the justification, and ought to be the controller, of all ends, but it is not itself the sole end. There are many virtuous actions, and even virtuous modes of action (though the cases are, I think, less frequent than is often supposed), by which happiness in the particular instance is sacrificed, more pain being produced than pleasure. But conduct of which this can be truly asserted, admits of justification only because it can be shown that, on the whole, more happiness will exist in the world, if feelings are cultivated which will make people, in certain cases, regardless of happiness. I fully admit that this is true; that the cultivation of an ideal nobleness of will and conduct should be to individual human beings an end, to which the specific pursuit either of their own happiness or of that of others (except so far as included in that idea) should, in any case of conflict, give way. But I hold that the very question, what constitutes this elevation of character, is itself to be decided by a reference to happiness as the standard. The character itself should be, to the individual, a paramount end, simply because the existence of this ideal nobleness of character, or of a near approach to it, in any abundance, would go farther than all things else toward making human life happy, both in the comparatively humble sense of pleasure and freedom from pain, and in the higher meaning, of rendering life, not what it now is almost universally, puerile and insignificant, but such as human beings with highly developed faculties can care to have.

(Mill 1843, VI.xii.7)

Mill wrote this as the penultimate paragraph of his *A System of Logic*. But the thought expressed here is not very different from the Bodhisattva ideal, best thought of as final stage of culmination of the Buddhist Path. The ideal is exemplified by the Buddha in his own life and since then by many Buddhists in different cultures and times. The Bodhisattva has made much progress on the Buddhist Path and is very close to being enlightened or becoming a Buddha. He has an

Selfless Minds: A Contemporary Perspective on Vasubandhu's Metaphysics. Monima Chadha, Oxford University Press.
© Monima Chadha 2023. DOI: 10.1093/oso/9780192844095.003.0010

enlightened mind (*Bodhicitta*), and vows to "be sustenance of many kinds for the realm of beings throughout space, until all have attained release" (Crosby & Skilton 1995, p. 21). A Bodhisattva has taken the most demanding vow to alleviate the suffering of all human beings. He has successfully "broken barriers between people" by realizing the truth that he is not separate from others.

It is intuitively plausible, even attractive, to suggest that the promotion of happiness in the world, or the alleviation (or reduction) of suffering is the arbiter of all that is morally valuable. Virtuous (morally good, right) actions are justified because of the promise of "more happiness" overall. But when it comes to acting in accordance with what is demanded by such "a controller of all ends," many philosophers seem to find it too demanding, if not abhorrent (Wolf 1982; Nagel 1989). Most of us value "reducing suffering overall" but it is not the only thing we value. In addition, we value our friends, family, work, projects, and so on. In this chapter, on behalf of the Abhidharma Buddhist, I undertake a close examination of the Buddhist Path and its associated Bodhisattva ideal to reveal the revisionism entailed by the Abhidharma metaphysics.

The core Buddhist teaching encapsulated in the *Four Noble Truths* is aimed at the elimination of suffering. The *Four Noble Truths* gives us meticulous practical instructions for making progress on the path culminating in enlightenment (*Nirvāṇa*). The *Eightfold Path* includes elements of wisdom and knowledge, of morality or ethical conduct, and of mental discipline: right understanding, right intent, right speech, right action, right livelihood, right effort, right mindfulness, and right concentration (see Chapter 1 for an explanation of each of these elements). These elements together tell us something general about the nature of the Path: it includes elements of conduct, knowledge, and meditation. Buddhism has been promoted as an attractive religion, a philosophy, and a way of life for those with a rational bent of mind. Many philosophers choose to ignore its non-rational features: enlightenment, insight, rebirth, omniscience, etc. For a long time, meditation was also on this list. More recently, thanks to the hype about mindfulness meditation as a cure for all kinds of human maladies, there has been a wealth of scientific and psychological research on the miracles of Buddhist meditation practices and more generally the promotion of meditation in philosophy research meetings. Some neuroscientists even try to use science to justify Buddhism by putting monks in the scanner. There are also attempts to relate Buddhist philosophy to cognitive science and the scientific study of the mind. Analytic philosophers, even those writing on Buddhist philosophy, were a bit slow in their enthusiastic endorsement of Buddhist philosophy. If anything, a famous philosopher and one of the early promoters of a dialogue between Buddhism, Western science, and contemporary Western philosophy, Evan Thompson, has recently published a book with the title: *Why I Am Not a Buddhist*. Thompson's skepticism is well-founded, but it is aimed at a recently popular version of Buddhism in the West: Buddhist modernism.

This book is not concerned with Buddhist modernism; we have been focused on Abhidharma Buddhist philosophy. In this book, I have been mainly arguing that the revisionary Abhidharma no-self and no-person philosophy can survive the most important epistemological challenges that have been leveled against it. This, for sure, is no reason to think that the Abhidharma Buddhist metaphysics, is "right" or "true" in the last analysis, but there are good enough reasons to think that it is a contender that deserves serious consideration. In the previous chapter, I showed that the revisionary Abhidharma metaphysics suggests a radical revision of our ordinary person-related practices and attitudes. In this chapter, I want to explore what is required of an individual who chooses to follow and make progress on the Buddhist Path. As we shall see, making the commitment to follow the Buddhist Path means giving up a lot that we ordinarily value in the hope of a better world in which suffering impersonally conceived is eliminated or at the very least reduced.

In section 9.2, I detail the structure of the Path as outlined in the *Abhidharmakośa-Bhāṣya* to provide a background for the ensuing discussion in this chapter. For the Abhidharma philosophers, the components of the Path—moral conduct, learning from the texts, reflection, meditation, and insight—work together to achieve the aim of abandoning the defilements (negative *dharmas*, e.g., ignorance, greed, hatred, etc.) which are the source of suffering. In section 9.3, I discuss several preliminary philosophical concerns to be faced by Buddhists recommending the Path and suggest some solutions. Then, in section 9.4, I introduce the Bodhisattva ideal. The Bodhisattvas' adventures (or misadventures as some might say) are part of the *Jātaka* tales. A brief foray into these tales to understand what it is to be a Bodhisattva, the epitome of Buddhist values, will be necessary before we can evaluate whether becoming a Bodhisattva is something we would want to aspire to. In the last and the final section of the chapter, I explore the extent to which an individual must alter his/her way of life in the light of Buddhist revisionism. As we shall see, it calls for nothing less than a major overhaul of our individual lives. This raises a further question: How should we respond to the Buddhist? While I will not provide a definitive answer to this question here, I hope what I say shows that there are considerations to resist a major overhaul. Taking a cue from Strawson, we shall assess the gains and losses to decide whether it is rational for us to embrace the Bodhisattva ideal. I will argue that a Buddhist revolution would generate significant losses to human life (as we know it).

The gains of a so-called Buddhist revolution are hard to assess. There is the promise of a world with no suffering or at least reduced suffering, which is premised on the basis of an ideal Buddhist community of monks (*sangha*). However, the *sangha* community does not exist in a vacuum. The way *sanghas* have developed in different parts of the world has been shaped by the political, social, and economic circumstances. Historically, Buddhism has thrived in parts of the world where there were complementary relationships between the *sangha* and the royalty, beginning with King Ashoka, followed by Bhutanese, Thai, and Sri Lankan royalty. An ostensibly paradoxical feature of the connection between monks and kings is that monks who have renounced the world also legitimize those who rule it, which partly explains the active role taken by monks in political movements.

There is, however, no shortage of historical examples of violence in Buddhist societies. Sri Lanka's long and tragic civil war (1983–2009), for example, involved a great deal of Buddhist nationalism. The violence against the Rohingya in present-day Myanmar is certainly related to increasingly popular campaigns in recent years to revive Myanmar's Buddhist tradition as the marker of "real" Burmese identity. Political violence in modern Thailand has often been inflected by Buddhist involvement, and there is growing evidence of complicity of Buddhist institutions in World War II-era Japanese nationalism. The facts on the ground are very different from ideal Buddhist societies that are imagined in the Buddhist texts. The histories of Buddhist societies are as checkered as most other human histories.

For a contrast case let us also briefly look at Bhutan, the only officially Buddhist country on earth. About three-quarters of Bhutan's roughly 700,000 people are Buddhists. Bhutan measures its success as a nation by Gross National Happiness (GNH) indicators, rather than more traditional measures like a nation's Gross Domestic Product (GDP) based on economic activity. GNH recognizes nine components of happiness: psychological well-being, ecology, health, education, culture, living standards, time use, community vitality, and good governance. The GNH indicators find their roots in Buddhism. Psychological well-being, for example, includes measures of meditation, prayer, nonviolence, and reincarnation. A 2012 survey by the Center for Bhutan Studies, reported by the *Washington Post*, found 51 percent of Bhutanese were found to be "not yet happy."[1] Bhutan's first comprehensive suicide survey in 2014 found that the country's suicide rate measured at roughly 20th in the world. Thus, the idealized view of Buddhist societies is at odds with real polities. It is difficult to show what might be gained by going the Buddhist way, but if these examples are anything to go by, it at least shows it is not going to be only a spectacular success story. So, it seems that we ought to be cautious about getting on the Buddhist bandwagon wholeheartedly. Or so I shall argue after we look at the losses in the last section of this chapter.

9.2 Vasubandhu's Account of the Structure of the Path and the Ideal

In the chapter on *Karma* (Action) in the *Abhidharmakośa-Bhāṣya*, Vasubandhu outlines three kinds of disciplines to be undertaken by those starting out on the Buddhist Path: *Pratimokṣa* discipline, pure discipline (arising from seeing the Truths), and discipline arising from meditation. The basic idea behind the

---

[1] Available at: https://perma.cc/W67A-AKJS.

Pratimokṣa discipline is to ensure moral restraint. The *Pratimokṣa* discipline undertaken by the laity (*upāsakas*) consists of five vows to renounce killing, stealing, illicit sex, lying, and intoxicating liquors. Even those planning to be ordained as monks start with these basic vows but have to renounce more of life's basic pleasures as they progress towards monkhood. The next category, the fasters (*upavāsasthas*), have further restrictions on times when meals can be taken and must renounce luxuries like comfortable beds and all forms of entertainment. Next come the novice monks (*śrāmaṇeras*) who must undertake to renounce all wealth in addition to everything renounced by the *upavāsasthas*. And finally, the monks (*bhikṣus*) who must undertake 250 vows according the *Abhidharmakośa-Bhāṣya*. These include celibacy for the monks and nuns, and even forbid being alone with a person of the opposite sex in the open or in seclusion. Among the 250 vows about a hundred are concerned with such matters as meals, dress, preaching, and daily behavior. Some of these details regarding the rituals to be observed by the monks are primarily aimed at the discipline of the mind, body, and speech so that the individual monks and nuns exercise moral restraint as a matter of habit. Moral restraint is a prerequisite for the Path and the various kinds of discipline to be inculcated by someone deciding to make progress on the Buddhist Path.

In Chapter 6 on "The Path and the Saints," Vasubandhu offers further details of the structure of the Path which is primarily aimed at abandoning the defilements (*kleśas*), the mental states responsible for unwholesome actions and suffering. Vasubandhu begins by noting that some defilements are removed through seeing and others through meditation suggesting that they complement each other. The Path of Seeing is what we may think of as the path of knowledge or insight; it is regarded as pure in the sense that it is unmixed with material existence. The Path of Meditation involves the body, so it is regarded as both pure and impure. Vasubandhu begins his explanation of the Path with a discussion of the *Four Noble Truths* inviting the reader to reflect on the relationship between Abhidharma theory and practice. Here, Vasubandhu defines wisdom as the "discernment of *dharmas*" (the basic constituents of reality). Chapter 1 of the *Abhidharmakośa-Bhāṣya* discusses the nature and purpose of Abhidharma, indicating how Abhidharma in the sense of theoretical discourse can lead to *prajñā* (wisdom). Vasubandhu is very emphatic that without the teachings of the Abhidharma, a student simply cannot discern the basic constituents of reality. So, theoretical knowledge of the Abhidharma (in the sense that it is derivative of the true *dharma* or teachings of the Buddha) teachings is part and parcel of the Path. But it is only in Chapter 6 that he clarifies the structure of the Path leading to enlightenment.

Whoever desires to see the Truths should first of all keep the Percepts. Then he reads the teaching upon which his Seeing of the Truths depends or he hears their meaning. Having heard, he correctly reflects. Having reflected, he gives himself up to the cultivation of meditation. With the wisdom (*prajñā*) arisen from the teaching (*śrutamayī*) for its support, there arises the wisdom arisen from reflection (*cintāmayī*), with this for its support there arises wisdom arisen from meditation (*bhāvanāmayī*).[2]   (trans. Pruden 1988, pp. 911–12)

Vasubandhu agrees here with the Abhidharma tradition more generally, according to which practices of moral conduct, learning, and thinking about the Abhidharma teaching (selflessness, impermanence, and suffering) and meditation or cultivation are crucial "spiritual exercises" of the tradition (McClintock 2010). A long commentary on this passage describes how the practice of the three types of spiritual exercises supports the passage from a conceptual and rational understanding of the nature of reality to one that is "seen" or experienced for oneself through the Path of Meditation. It is called the Path because it is more properly conceived of not as a singular experience of insight into the true nature of reality. Instead, it is repeated performance of these spiritual exercises that leads to rational understanding and internalization of the Buddhist insights. For Vasubandhu, the insight gives one the ability to discern the *dharmas* and seeing that "the *dharmas* are impermanent, suffering, empty and no-self"[3] (Pruden 1988, p. 929). To be sure, this insight is not new knowledge; these features are mentioned in the *Nikāyas* and the Abhidharma teachings which have been read, learnt, and reflected upon by the monks before they devote themselves to meditation.

How does this result in the destruction of defilements? The monk needs to eliminate craving and other defilements by eradicating their cause. This requires that the monk develops and cultivates the insight of no-self, which acts as an antidote to the false view of self, in order to free himself from craving and suffering together with its suite of defilements (greed, envy, hatred, etc.). The cultivation of selflessness (and suffering, impermanence, emptiness) goes along with the sixteen real aspects of the *Noble Truths*[4] (Pruden 1988). These sixteen aspects contradict our ordinary conceptions of objects as "lasting," "pleasant," "mine," etc. Once we rid ourselves of the false conception of self and other objects, the craving for these objects disappears. Cultivating the insight of selflessness thus annuls not only the innate false view of self, but also all the defilements that accompany it.

9.3 Preliminary Concerns and Response

The Buddhist Path presents a philosophy of enlightenment. The Path is best understood not as a single road which one traverses with fellow Buddhists but

---

[2] *Abhidharmakośa-Bhāṣya*, 6:5a–b.   [3] *Abhidharmakośa-Bhāṣya*, 6:16.
[4] *Abhidharmakośa-Bhāṣya*, 7:13a.

rather as a reticulation of various strands—moral values, ritual observances, doctrinal teachings, and contemplative exercises—into a unified network of practices focused on enlightenment. The general accounts of the Buddhist Path are described as a gradual progression from fundamental practices of generosity (*dāna*) and moral conduct (*śīla*) to the cultivation of concentration (*samādhi*) and wisdom (*prajñā*) by means of meditative development (*bhāvanā*), through the intermediary of learning and reflecting on the Buddhist teaching. There are several philosophical challenges to be faced by Buddhists who want to recommend the Path to all of us.

A first worry might be the heavy reliance on Buddhist scripture or texts—the element of faith or conviction in the authority of the Buddha or the word of Buddha. Insofar as all Buddhist schools claim to offer the right interpretation of the Buddha's words, and especially our Abhidharma philosopher Vasubandhu, the founder of the Sautrāntika (literally "those who rely upon the *sutras*") school regarded the words of the Buddha as central to his views. Vasubandhu does not shy away from criticizing fellow Buddhists, even fellow Abhidharma philosophers, on the basis that they are misinterpreting what the Buddha meant to say. This sounds way too dogmatic and dependent on faith to be of interest to a philosopher. A second concern might be the heavy reliance on meditative cultivation leading to a moment of insight that is central to the Buddhist philosophy of salvation. This dependence on experiential insight might be thought of as a kind of religious experience which is likely to be of concern to philosophers. In any case, the testimony and self-report of those who are fortunate to have such experiences shows that they become convinced of very different truths. These religious features of Buddhism—the reliance on testimony of the Buddha and experiential insight—are antithetical to a philosophical argument.

In response to this concern, it is important to keep in mind that the different wisdom practices complement each other and crisscross as components of the Buddhist Path. The Abhidharma philosophers do not draw sharp distinctions between these practices. Some elements of the Path, specifically the reliance on scriptures and meditation practices as precursors to insight, seem problematic from the point of view of analytic philosophy. I deal with them in turn. Vasubandhu lists "faith" among the auxiliaries of the Path:

> Faith (*śraddhā*), morality (*śīla*), resolution (*saṃkalpa*), exertion (*vīrya*), mindfulness (*smṛti*), concentration (*samādhi*), wisdom (*prajñā*), indifference (*praśrabdhi*), joy (*prīti*), equanimity (*upekṣā*).[5]   (trans. Pruden 1988, p. 1023)

Although faith is required in the context of the Path, there is no suggestion that it is meant to be a stand-alone or a special factor. Buddhism never promotes

---

[5] *Abhidharmakośa-Bhāṣya*, 6:68a–c.

unquestioning acceptance of the Buddhist doctrines. Rather, it requires, borrowing a concept from Karl Jaspers, "philosophical faith" (1948) to be eventually substantiated by reasoning and insight to be cultivated through meditation. The Buddha's words are meant to stand on their own philosophical cogency, not requiring his authority for legitimation. It is appropriate to remind ourselves of the oft-quoted Goldsmith verse: "O monks-Sages accept my teachings after a thorough examination and not from (mere) devotion; just like a goldsmith accepts gold only after burning, cutting, and polishing" (Thurman 1978, p. 25).

The meditative practice, conceived of as the discipline of the mind leading to internalization of Buddhist insight, seems like an important pivot in the Abhidharma description of the Path. However, insight understood as a direct, unmediated, non-conceptual knowledge of reality is founded on the totality of spiritual exercises. But it must be mentioned in this context that meditative cultivation is not admitted as a reliable source for knowledge in its own right. Vasubandhu emphasizes that the conceptual and rational understanding of the Abhidharma teachings is pivotal to the application of mindfulness meditation to support the pathway to insight (*nirvedhabhāgīya*).

Furthermore, the experiential insight is meant to be understood as "direct" experience of the teaching of the Abhidharma, previously known intellectually through learning and rational understanding. After such an experience one needs to return to the spiritual exercises which include reasoning and reflection as well as meditation to enable a reassessment and consolidation of the insight gained through cultivation. Kellner (2019) proposes that the role of insight or direct experience produced by meditation is thought to be necessary because of its presumed special power to effect a lasting transformation of consciousness; it is not, as recently claimed, thought to corroborate or confirm the validity of any preceding reasoning (Adam 2016). The reasoning is not incomplete and the inferences from the teachings drawn are not in need of further validation. Rather, the inferential reasoning is limited insofar as it can only produce conceptual certainty. By itself it is not sufficient to remove the deep misconceptions in the mind, for example, the false belief in the self. Thus, reflective reasoning is incapable of transforming consciousness in the way that is necessary from a soteriological perspective. The latter is accomplished by meditation and insight.

The role of the brief experiential insight is to "directly experience" or equivalently "see" for oneself. The notion of "seeing," I think, is best treated as metaphorical. It is not to be thought of as "new knowledge" or confirmation available through transcendental insight or revelation. The idea is that through meditative concentration on one's own bodily or mental states (Vasubandhu's detailed example is concentrating on breathing) one can internalize the characteristics of the real: that the *dharmas* are impermanent, suffering, no-self. Tom Tillemans (2013) has argued that some Buddhist thinkers, Dharmakīrti and Kamalaśīla in particular, sought to emphasize the epistemic continuity between the rational and non-rational practices of reasoning and cultivation. Vasubandhu can easily fit into this camp. Tillemans has argued that meditative cultivation in this sense does not make a significant epistemic contribution over and above philosophical reasoning (2013). Brigit Kellner goes further to claim that for Kamalaśīla:

> Conceptual certainty is not regarded as sufficiently strong to remove the deep-seated misconception of the mind, but this is more like psychological or phenomenological insufficiency, not one of strength of evidence... inference is not in need of confirmation. In other words, post-conceptual gnosis functions as a particularly powerful antidote to deeply rooted mental obstacles that need to be uprooted on the path to liberation; it is not some kind of privileged unassailable evidence.   (2020, p. 70)

The point of this discussion is to show that the opposition between rational (inferential) and non-rational (meditation) practices within the Buddhist tradition is not as stark as in some other religions.

9.4 Concerns About the Boddhisattva Ideal

Bodhisattva vows rest on the commitment to put others on a par with oneself. It is a statement about the willingness to postpone one's own well-being, even the achievement of the highest good, enlightenment, for the sake of relieving the suffering of others. This vow requires tremendous self-control and the Bodhisattva has perhaps made considerable progress on the Path to reach the point of being ready to take such a vow. But even novice monks and nuns starting out must undertake some other vows that might seem pretty demanding, and sometimes pointless. For example, celibacy, giving up one's family, one's friends, fasting, eating at restricted times, and having restricted amounts of food, wearing certain garments in specific ways, etc. For the novice as well as for the experienced monk there is no room for anything but inculcating wisdom, compassion, generosity, and so on, all in the service of alleviating suffering. Other things that we value, for example friendship and our own projects, are valuable only to the extent that they contribute to the Buddhist value. So, friendship is encouraged in the Buddhist circles but only being friends with the wise monks who can be thought of as role models. Insofar as the Buddhist Path is presented as an option available to all of us, we might want to consider whether this is what we want to pursue. Some of our concerns about the Bodhisattva ideal might echo Susan Wolf's qualms about moral saints, but it goes further in an important respect. Wolf (1982) is concerned about the dominance of moral values. I agree with her that the dominance of moral values is a legitimate concern, but it becomes much more serious when the dominance is coupled with value monism: the highest and only value for the Bodhisattvas is to pursue the single moral goal of alleviating suffering of all beings. But before we raise these concerns, it is worth getting a better understanding of the Bodhisattva ideal and its place in Abhidharma Buddhism.

Although the Bodhisattva is promoted as the ideal of the perfect person in Buddhism, Vasubandhu and the Abhidharma Buddhist tradition more generally talk about many other kinds of persons, namely *Śrāvakas* (hearers), *Pratyekabuddhas* (ascetics), and *Arhats* (those who have reached enlightenment), classified according to their capacities and the means they employ, including the Path they choose for the attainment of Buddhahood. In the Abhidharma tradition, there exists no clear hierarchy among these perfect persons. Contrarily, the Mahāyāna tradition is very clear in exalting the Bodhisattvas as the highest among the perfect persons. In this section, I will focus on the Bodhisattva ideal not only because it is found in all Buddhist traditions, but also because it is the only ideal extensively elaborated in the Indian Buddhist narrative literature, the *Jātaka* tales, making it the most popular and sought for ideal. The *Jātaka* tales are part of the canon of sacred Buddhist literature depicting the earlier incarnations (human as well as animal) of the being who would become Siddhartha Gautama, the first Buddha.

The Bodhisattva vow is a commitment to give up one's own well-being and enlightenment for the sake of others. A Bodhisattva (like the first Buddha) is a person who inculcates the six *paramitas* (perfections): generosity, discipline, patience, exertion, meditation, and insight, all in the effort to liberate all beings from suffering. Put simply in these terms, it is easy to see why it is the highest ideal promoted by the Buddhist. The *Jātaka* tales celebrate innumerable deeds of virtue and compassion performed by the Buddha during his previous lives. But a significant number of these tales involve astonishing and gruesome acts of bodily sacrifice: in his birth as King Sibi, for example, the Buddha gouged out his eyes and gave them to a blind man; in his birth as Prince Mahasattva, he threw himself off a cliff in order to feed a starving tigress; in his birth as King Maitribala, he encouraged five demons to feed on his flesh and blood; in his birth as King Candraprabha, he cut off his own head on behalf of a greedy brahman; in his birth as a hare, he jumped into a fire in order to feed a hungry traveler; and in his birth as an elephant, he removed his own tusks and presented them to an evil hunter. Such stories serve to illustrate, in the starkest possible way, the great selflessness and compassion exemplified by the Buddha during his many lives as a Bodhisattva. These stories are to be thought of as the finest examples of the perfection of generosity or giving (*dāna*), they intend to be instructive and inspiring, but they seem outright offensive and puerile. And it gets worse. The most celebrated *Jātaka* tale is about the last incarnation as Prince Viśvaṃtarā before he attains Buddhahood. According to this tale, on becoming the King, Viśvaṃtarā not only gave away the kingdom's most prized possessions, including the white elephant, to his rival kingdoms, but also proceeded to give away his wife and children to a life of slavery to wicked Brahmins. Modern readers are likely to be incensed by such stories and would not be mistaken if they find such an ideal abhorrent rather than something that they would want to aspire to. This reaction to the stories is understandable but a bit more needs to be said here in order to bring out the didactic role of these tales.

The valorization of over the top gift giving may seem scandalous to us but these stories are set in the context of promoting Buddhist values in opposition to the traditional Hindu values. The Hindu *Dharmaśāstras* (Treatises on Duties) list one's responsibilities to oneself, to the family, and as a member of society in terms of one's caste (*varna*) and stage of life (*āśrama*). According to *Dharmaśāstras*, the Bodhisattva king belongs to the *kṣatriya* (warrior) caste and thus has duties to protect his kingdom and subjects, and duties towards his wife and children to provide for their needs. Renunciation of the kind celebrated by the Buddhist is directly opposed to the traditional Hindu goals and way of life. According to the latter, enlightenment is to be achieved by the disinterested performance of one's *Dharmaśāstric* duty. Many of the Bodhisattva stories reveal this tension with traditional Hindu values and are meant to promote the Buddhist value of giving (*dāna*) as much superior to the traditional Hindu values.

The *Jātaka* tales sound gruesome when first encountered; the self-sacrifice and generosity of the Bodhisattva are extreme. The discomfort felt by the modern reader is not totally missed in the Buddhist literature. Even though these stories are exalted as examples of the six perfections, this status is sometimes contested in the contemporary literature on Buddhism. Reiko Ohnuma (2000) helpfully classifies the opposition to the Bodhisattva's gift of body into internal and external opposition. The "internal" opposition occurs within the stories themselves where various characters voice their opposition by dissuading the Bodhisattva or trying to dissuade the recipient from taking the gift. The "external" opposition occurs within the exegetical or commentarial literature where these stories are discussed. Both the internal and external opposition point to certain doctrinal inconsistencies that are revealed in the Bodhisattva's extreme sacrifices. Ohnuma (2000) discusses many issues arising out of the extreme nature of the sacrifice portrayed in what she calls "the gift of the body stories." I highlight two such tensions which apply more generally to extreme examples of sacrifice exalted in the Bodhisattva stories.

The internal opposition is exemplified within the story itself where various ministers and the Queen try to dissuade the Bodhisattva King by reminding him of his duty towards his subjects and kingdom as well as his duties towards various members of the family. The basic complaint is that the Boddhisattva can bring about greater good if he does not indulge in extreme self-sacrifice as in cutting off his head and so on. Sometimes even so-called "deities" step in to dissuade the

Bodhisattva. But all of this comes to naught because the Bodhisattva cannot be dissuaded. In response to these requests the Bodhisattva proudly cites the uniqueness and excellence of his gifts. In one story, the Bodhisattva responds by stating how he has become superior to other Bodhisattvas by virtue of the excellence of the gifts he has offered and thus overtaken them in the pursuit of Buddhahood. In the Sanskrit version of the story of King Candraprabha, the Bodhisattva's rebuke of the deity expands to include a well-known Buddhist mythological figure as well:

> For it was right here, deity, that I sacrificed myself to a tigress, and thus outdistanced Maitreya, who had set out [for Buddhahood] forty eons before. Maitreya Bodhisattva was outdistanced by a single gift of my head.
>
> (Quoted in Ohnuma 2000, p. 53)

This is surprising to say the least. The Bodhisattva is meant to be a paragon of selflessness and compassion. Pride (*abhimāna*), on the other hand, is rooted in the conceit of the self (*māna*), one of the most dangerous conceits that a Buddhist surely must rid himself of. Ohnuma writes, "[t]hus, the 'selfless' Bodhisattva is not so 'selfless' after all, and it is this paradox that seems to be exposed in the argument of his opponents" (2000, p. 57). Furthermore, it seems by denying the greater good, the Bodhisattva is not living in accordance with the vow of liberating all others. He seems to be more concerned by the "personal excellence" to be achieved by indulging in the greatest sacrifice. A further inconsistency which relates to this paradox has to do with the Bodhisattva vow of "being reborn" until all beings are liberated from suffering. It seems that the Bodhisattva is likely relying on a robust notion of rebirth which is hard to distinguish from the Hindu notion of reincarnation: the same self being reborn. If there is no self, then it remains an open question whether the same Bodhisattva is reborn. Is the person who takes the vow the same as the person who keeps the vow? This question is difficult for the Buddhist no-self theorists to answer.

The external opposition is highlighted in the external opposition to the stories in the commentarial tradition. Viśvaṃtarā's extreme gifts are discussed in the commentarial literature. King Milinda asks the Buddhist monk Nāgasena a series of questions about Viśvaṃtarā's gift (Horner 1964): Do all Bodhisattvas give away their wives and children?[6] Do they do so with their wives' and children's consent? Why don't they give themselves away instead? How do they acquire merit by causing anguish to others? The King argues against excessive or extreme gifts by citing examples where too much of a good thing turns out to be harmful, e.g., excessive rainfall damages crops. The monk Nāgasena answers by offering other

---

6 *Milindapanha*, 186.

examples where extreme manifestations are good, for example, the sun dissipates darkness because it is exceedingly bright. This is hardly a reply, but a red herring, to the King's genuine concerns about the excessive nature of the gifts. The concern here points to a conflict arising between the Buddhist exaltation of a Bodhisattva's compassion and its exaltation of other virtues like wisdom and equanimity. This concern is widely discussed in the literature. For example, Buddhaghosa, as we saw in the previous chapter, encourages the meditator to develop loving kindness first toward himself, then toward a friend, then toward a neutral person, and finally toward an enemy. The meditator must ultimately strive to "break the barriers between people" so that no distinctions between them are possible. Buddhaghosa provides a hypothetical case where if a friend, a neutral person, and an enemy were all being attacked by a robber who wished to kill one of them, the one who has broken down all barriers would be completely unable to choose which of the four people should be killed. Buddhaghosa specifically rules out the option of the meditator sacrificing himself to the killer in order to save the other three, since that would indicate a preference for the others over oneself, and thus a lack of true equanimity. Loving kindness and compassion are important to begin with, but in the Buddhist hierarchy of virtues they are lower, and therefore must ultimately be transcended by equanimity, the highest virtue. And again, Sàntideva in his famous *Bodhicaryāvatāra* (A Guide to the Bodhisattva's Way of Life) expresses ambivalence about the gift of the body. At several places he warns against attachment to the body as one's own, colorfully calling it a "contraption full of shit!,"[7] and also suggests that giving of the flesh is no different from the giving away of food and other possessions.[8] But he also warns that the Bodhisattva should not give away his body or life to an unworthy recipient for an inferior purpose. A Bodhisattva should not sacrifice his life for someone who lacks compassion (like the greedy brahmin in the story), but he should do so for someone whose intentions are equivalent to his own. In this way, nothing will be lost.[9] The conflict between the Buddhist values of compassion, on the one hand, and wisdom and equanimity, on the other hand, seems to be at the heart of what makes these Buddhist thinkers uncomfortable about the Bodhisattva's excessive gifts.

Ohnuma (2007) remarks that the internal and the external opposition is not just motivated by the doctrinal inconsistencies but also, at least in part, by visceral concerns that are ultimately the source of the discomfort. This links to another source of discomfort that derives from the fact that the Bodhisattva ideal opens Buddhist ethics to the Demandingness Objection (Williams 1973). Williams raises the objection against utilitarianism. The central idea behind the objection is that utilitarianism demands unacceptably much of an agent. Being moral, properly understood, is not the only thing that matters to beings like us; we also

---

[7] *Bodhicaryāvatāra*, 5.61 and 5.70.   [8] *Bodhicaryāvatāra*, 7.25–6.
[9] *Bodhicaryāvatāra*, 5.86–7.

care about family, friends, and other non-moral projects. Indeed, the kind of demandingness that Williams has in mind in objecting to utilitarianism is much tamer than the demandingness imposed by the Bodhisattva vows. Insofar as becoming a Bodhisattva and eventually a Buddha is something that is possible, and indeed something which we should all aspire to, we can claim Buddhism asks unacceptably much. In what follows, I suggest how the Buddhist might respond to the Demandingness Objection. The Buddhist reply to this objection also provides a potential response to the perceived doctrinal inconsistencies that Ohnuma has delineated.

First, it is worth emphasizing that Abhidharma Buddhists are not suggesting that becoming a Bodhisattva is the only ideal; the sacrifices made by other kinds of perfect persons, namely, *Śrāvakas* (hearers), *Pratyekabuddhas* (ascetics), and *Arhats* (enlightened beings) are perhaps not as demanding as the extreme sacrifices required by the Bodhisattva. After all, the various vows and sacrifices are directly aimed at the one's own well-being. They are liberated from suffering and achieve enlightenment. In contrast, the Bodhisattva vows require him to suffer through many rebirths until all other beings are liberated from suffering. The Bodhisattva vows are extremely demanding. Vasubandhu is aware of this and in one of the rare discussions in the Buddhists texts, he addresses the Demandingness Objection. Why do the Bodhisattvas, once they have undertaken the resolution to obtain supreme *Bodhi* (enlightenment), take such a long time to obtain it?

> Because supreme Bodhi is very difficult to obtain: one needs great accumulation of knowledge and merit and innumerable heroic works…One would understand that the Bodhisattva searches out this Bodhi so difficult to obtain, if this were the sole means of arriving at enlightenment; but such is not the case. Why then do they undertake this infinite labour? For the good of others, because they want to become capable of pulling others out of the great flood of suffering. But what personal good do they find in the good of others? *The good of others is their own good*, because they desire it.[10]
>
> (trans Pruden 1988, pp. 480–1; emphasis added)

Vasubandhu acknowledges that it is difficult to understand why anyone would want to take the Bodhisattva vows, especially if there are other, presumably easier, ways of achieving enlightenment. Vasubandhu's answer is that the Bodhisattva does not make a distinction between his own good or well-being and that of all others, he identifies his well-being with the well-being of all others. There is, of course, the further question about how such an identification is possible. His reply:

---

[10] *Abhidharmakośa-Bhāṣya*, 3.93–4.

Persons devoid of pity and who think only of themselves believe with difficulty in the altruism of the Bodhisattvas; but compassionate persons understand it easily. Don't we see that certain persons, who lack compassion, find pleasure in the suffering of others even when it is not to their benefit? In the same way one must admit that the Bodhisattvas, established in compassion, find pleasure in doing good to others without any egoistic concerns. Don't we see that some persons, ignorant of the true nature of the conditioned *dharmas* that constitute their fabricated self are attached to these *dharmas* through the force of habit, as completely lacking in self as these *dharmas* are, and suffer a thousand pains by reason of this attachment? In the same way one must admit that the Bodhisattvas, through the force of habit, detach themselves from the *dharmas* that constitute the fabricated self, no longer consider these *dharmas* as "me" and "mine", increase compassionate solicitude for others, and are ready to suffer a thousand pains because of others.

In a few words, there is a certain category of persons, who, indifferent to what concerns them personally, are happy through the well-being of others, and are unhappy through the suffering of others. For them, to be useful to others is to be useful to themselves....an excellent person, through his personal suffering, looks out for the well-being and destruction of suffering of others, for he suffers the suffering of others.[11]   (trans. Pruden 1988, p. 481)

Here, Vasubandhu is pointing to the psychological transformation brought about by realizing the truth of the Abhidharma teachings of no-self. There is no separate self, all we are is an everchanging flux of momentary *dharmas* causally connected with past and future *dharmas*. All boundaries between people are fabricated resulting from a false belief in an enduring and separate self. Selfish interests and a special concern for our own well-being have no basis in reality but are the result of self-delusion. Bodhisattvas on this picture are those excellent persons who have been successful in "breaking barriers between themselves and others" so that they are able to identify the suffering of others as their own suffering. The Abhidharma Buddhist philosophers believe that such radical psychological transformation is possible, although it is by no means easy. It requires a combination of learning the teachings of Abhidharma, analysis and reasoning to support the Buddhist teachings, cultivation of meditation practices and experiential insight, followed by further analysis of the experiential insight achieved through meditation to consolidate those experiences as part of one's psyche. This radical transformation equips the Bodhisattva not only to let go of ordinary egoistic concern with "me" and "mine" but to be able to identify with the well-being of others as one's own well-being.

---

[11] *Abhidharmakośa-Bhāṣya*, 3.94a.

Vasubandhu's response to the Demandingness Objection is to say that judged from the perspective of a practitioner who has already made considerable progress on the Path the Bodhisattva ideal is not too demanding. The Bodhisattva's mind is freed from greed, anger, hatred, and other unwholesome roots; rather it is overflowing with compassion, empathy, and equanimity. What we ordinary people find demanding, regarding all others with the compassion and care we afford to ourselves and those dear to us, comes naturally to the transformed Bodhisattva. But for the novice who is beginning on the Path, and the experienced monk who is yet to achieved enlightenment (*Bodhi*), this is no comfort. Once the psychological transformation has been achieved, the Demandingness Objection is defused. However, the demands made on the novice who embarks on the Buddhist Path are not excessive. The demands made in the preparatory stages of the Path are very different from the demands on the practitioner who has made considerable progress. It is as simple as giving away food to begin with, as an act of generosity, to develop your psychological muscles right up to the point where giving away all of one's wealth and worldly possessions, one's limbs or indeed one's life just comes naturally to the adept practitioner. The Demandingness Objection perhaps has maximum force for the case of the ordained monk who has not yet cultivated the perfections of compassion, empathy, equanimity, and so. The ordained monk suffers the all too familiar pushes and pulls of past loves and comforts, while scrupulously adhering to the demands and burden of the many vows. Whatever discomfort is experienced by ordained monks is to be dismissed by the Buddhist doctrine as a result of the delusion of an enduring and separate self. He just has to take refuge in the thought that he has not made adequate progress. As he progresses further on the path, the discomfort will gradually fade away.

This same response can do double duty to explain away the doctrinal inconsistencies pointed out by Ohnuma. The Bodhisattva ideal presents a package deal which results in a transformation of one's beliefs, desires, and values. Once the distinction between the self and other has been totally overcome (if indeed it is possible) the apparent tension between "personal excellences" and "excellences" fades away. The same can be said about the apparent tension between values of compassion, equanimity, and wisdom. They seem to pull in opposite directions in that they seem to prescribe different courses of action, but again these tensions are only experienced by those who have not achieved enlightenment. The novice and the ordained monk will no doubt feel they have to choose between conflicting courses of action, but the conflict is only a result of the delusion of an enduring separate self.

9.5 Is the Bodhisattva Ideal Worth Pursuing?

Even if we grant Vasubandhu that such psychological transformation can be achieved by all of us and that it is indeed possible after we really internalize the Abhidharma no-self teaching, we might still worry whether that it is something we would want to aspire to. This points to a more general worry: Is it best for us to choose the Buddhist Path? Abhidharma Buddhists, of course, think that it is, for it ultimately leads to eliminating or at least reducing suffering. Prima facie, Buddhism presents a promising alternative, but is it one we should embrace wholeheartedly? The details of the Path also mean that we reject most of what we ordinarily recognize as pleasurable (watching the sunset on a summer's evening while enjoying a drink with friends, or going to the movies, or a concert, etc.) as only "seeming" pleasures. "Seeming," because sensory pleasures lead to craving for more of the same. And craving is the root of suffering. In the last analysis, according to the Buddhist, existence in this world is bound up with suffering (First Noble Truth) and the Buddhist Path (Fourth Noble Truth) is the way to achieve a release from suffering (*nirvāṇa*). A release from suffering, on this picture, entails a rejection of this world. Are we really convinced that the torments of the Bodhisattva Path are better, all things considered, than being in the world? Our Buddhist is a monist about values, moral principles, moral judgments, emotions: all of these are to be guided by the one golden aim—eliminating or reducing suffering overall. The problem here is what Nagel labels "the Draconian solution" to the problem of the meaning of life:

[T]o deny the claims of the subjective view, withdraw from the specifics of individual human life as much as possible, minimize the area of one's local contact with the world and concentrate on the universal. Contemplation, meditation, withdrawal from the demands of the body and of society, abandonment of exclusive personal ties and worldly ambition—all this gives the objective standpoint less to be disengaged from, less to regard as vain. I gather this response is recommended by certain traditions, though I don't know enough to be sure that it isn't a caricature: the loss of self in the individual sense is thought to be required by the revelations of an impersonal view, which takes precedence over the view from here. And apparently it is possible for some individuals to achieve this withering away of the ego, so that personal life continues only as a vehicle for the transcendent self, not as an end in itself.

I cannot speak from experience, but this seems to me a high price to pay for spiritual harmony. The amputation of so much of oneself to secure the unequivocal affirmation of the rest seems a waste of consciousness. I would rather lead an absurd life engaged in the particular than a seamless transcendental life immersed in the universal. Perhaps those who have tried both would laugh inscrutably at this preference. It reflects the belief that the absurdity of human life is not such a bad thing. There are limits to what we should be prepared to do to escape it—apart from the point that some of these cures may be more absurd than the disease.   (1989, pp. 218–19)

Most of us are in the same position as Nagel; we think this is too high a price to pay. There is a limit to what we are prepared to do to escape the existential fact of suffering that the Buddhist wants us to believe. If this is the only way out, most of us would be tempted to stay in and deal with the ups and downs of life as we go through it.

Some of us might be moved by the kinds of concerns raised by Susan Wolf. Bodhisattva is much like the *Loving Saint* described by Wolf as the utilitarian ideal, whose own well-being simply consists in the well-being of others (1982). Wolf is concerned with whether the Loving Saint, insofar as he is the obsessed do-gooder, is boring, humorless, bland, and no fun to be with. What is missing in the saint's life are the non-moral virtues: a robust sense of humor, a refined musical or artistic ability, culinary acuity, and athletic prowess. That seems right; the Bodhisattva has all the Buddhist moral virtues and to such an extreme degree that all the non-Buddhist and non-moral virtues are crowded out as well as any personal interests and characteristics that we generally think contribute to a healthy, well-rounded, richly developed character. Perhaps this shows that a Bodhisattva would not be an attractive ideal, certainly not someone that you would want to have as part of your family or friends. A Loving Saint, or Bodhisattva, might not be a good cook or an artist, but he could still be an admirable person. The Bodhisattva vows might allow a person to develop some of his own talents and qualities, and perhaps there is room to continue some of his own projects, but they will all have to be in the service of the greater good. Anything that a Bodhisattva does like saving his child rather than a stranger or finishing his book on Buddhism, etc., is done only because it will be in the service of reducing suffering. But, says Wolf, even when Bodhisattva allows himself to pursue his projects, he will be tempted to justify his action by appeal to his sole moral principle to legitimize his preference. Williams would complain that this is "one thought too many" (1981, p. 18). Most of us would agree that the only justification for saving one's child rather than a stranger from drowning is that it is one's child. Any further appeal to "reducing suffering overall" is beside the point. The Bodhisattva's situation is worse. Insofar as a Bodhisattva is only moved by the sole motivation of reducing suffering and continues to dismiss all human motivations as insignificant, he cannot appeal to anything like "it's my child" and "It's best overall in such situations for each to prioritize one's own." Terms like "my" and "own" carry no moral weight for the Buddhist; if anything, adding them to the justification should ring warning bells against promoting our own interests. The Bodhisattva would value his projects, talents, and relationships only as means to reducing suffering, and be willing to sacrifice them as soon as another project or relationship could reduce more suffering. A Bodhisattva's "shallow appreciation" which allows only instrumental value for projects, talents, and relationships reveals that a Bodhisattva person lacks integrity in Williams' sense of the term (1981), insofar as integrity is defined in terms of commitments that people identify with most deeply as constituting who they are. In the same vein, Wolf writes:

But a desire to be as morally good as possible is not likely to take the form of one desire among others which, because of its peculiar psychological strength, requires one to forego the pursuit of other weaker and separately less demanding desires. Rather, the desire to be as morally good as possible is apt to have the character not just of a stronger, but of a higher desire, which does not merely successfully compete with one's other desires but which rather subsumes or demotes them.... In other words, the ideal of a life of moral sainthood disturbs not simply because it is an ideal of a life in which morality unduly dominates. The normal person's direct and specific desires for objects, activities, and events that conflict with the attainment of moral perfection are not simply sacrificed but removed, suppressed, or subsumed. The way in which morality, unlike other possible goals, is apt to dominate is particularly disturbing, for it seems to require either the lack or the denial of the existence of an identifiable, personal self.   (1982, pp. 423–4)

The Bodhisattva will not be moved by these considerations; loss of integrity is not going to worry him. Integrity and other identity conferring commitments or indeed any values, desires, projects, relationships, etc., delineating an identifiable personal self are to be rejected by the Buddhists. The Buddhist should resist the appeal to "identification" in the sense it is used by the Deep-Self theorists (Wolf 1987) as it illicitly smuggles in the problematic notion of self.

All identifications are false identifications in that they imply the assumption of a self that grounds separateness between persons. The Buddhist does not buy into this individualistic conception of values which places importance on what "I" value. There is no such "I," therefore it is a mistake to talk about "my" values. Any conception of personal values flows from ignorance about the true nature of oneself and the world. There is, according to the Buddhists, only one value which is to minimize suffering, impersonally conceived. Becoming a Bodhisattva then requires a cognitive and psychological transformation which alters one's beliefs, desires, and values. Thus, being a Bodhisattva is best thought of as development of one's own moral character so that one is naturally disposed to putting the welfare of all ahead of one's own welfare. So, compassion, sympathy, loving kindness, etc., are all emotions that are to be inculcated as one moves towards the highest moral perfections of equanimity and detachment which are essential for making progress on the Path to become a Bodhisattva and, eventually, a Buddha. This kind of moral perfection is not in the least compatible with self-perfection or development of one's personal excellences.

Any repugnance that we feel towards such an ideal stems from the sense that it demands us to sacrifice too much of what we ordinarily take to be valuable. For a Bodhisattva only one thing is valuable: minimizing suffering (even at the cost of sacrifice of one's own life). Wolf is not concerned by the fact that the Utilitarian or

Kantian conception of value is monistic; her complaint is that the dominance of moral values cannot coexist with the best one can achieve. I think the problem becomes more serious if we combine dominance of moral values with value monism, as the Buddhists do. There is only one value that matters and that is minimizing suffering, and that value trumps all other considerations. The attraction of monism is its simplicity, it delivers a single fundamental moral value. It gives us a common currency for decision-making. Monism seems to rule out the complexity and conflict that is part of our moral experience. Pluralism is attractive because it shows that there are genuine incommensurabilities and discontinuities in value comparisons; there is no single uber value which dictates how all other values are to be ranked. These incommensurabilities and discontinuities are the basis of genuine moral conflict and regret which are certainly part of our moral experience. Recent empirical work confirms that our ethical experience is of apparently irreducible plural values (Gill & Nichols 2008).

Most of us value much more than just reducing suffering. We value our family friends and colleagues, our projects, and talents even though we are aware that some of these may indeed put us in moral danger. Cocking and Kennett (2000) argue that friendship in some cases may make demands on us that are likely to lead us morally astray, yet friendship is valuable in its own right, nonetheless. The case can be extended to romantic love and family relationships. Those of us who care deeply about our own projects are often led "morally" astray by failing to do the best we can to alleviate world poverty or pursuing any other moral cause because of lack of time and/or forgetfulness. These relationships or projects are valuable for me, they are mine. Buddhist no-self and no-person metaphysics robs these special relations of their significance and value because the notions of "me" and "mine" are ultimately grounded in the false belief in the self.

Abhidharma Buddhists believe that normative moral distinctions and motivations are primarily derived from emotion or sentiment rather than (practical) reason. Hence, the Abhidharma Buddhists emphasize inculcating the so-called positive emotions that will promote their sole normative goal of eliminating or at least reducing suffering for all. Buddhists, too, are sentimentalists of a kind, though surprisingly, this has not been discussed in the literature on Buddhist ethics except a fleeting mention by Slote (2018). It is worth noting that the Abhidharma list of positive and agreeable emotional responses tracks morally right actions whereas aversive responses track morally wrong actions. For example, aversive emotional responses to the suffering of others are implicated in violence and the wrongness of killing. This much sounds right but the Buddhist vows are likely to extend this imperative against killing even to killing in self-defense, killing in war, abortion, etc., since the same aversive emotional response is likely to accompany such cases. However, most of us think that killing in self-defense, war, and abortion are not clearly "morally" wrong and killing in these situations is permissible. To refer back to the Bodhisattva story, being generous towards strangers is accompanied by agreeable feelings and surely is morally right, perhaps even praiseworthy but not when it is pushed to the extreme limit in giving away one's own children in slavery. Most of us would agree that this is morally wrong, even if the Bodhisattva's perfected emotional responses suggest otherwise. It is easy to see that these kinds of cases will multiply and offer easy counterexamples against the proposed one-to-one matching between positive emotional responses and moral rightness and negative emotional responses and moral wrongness.

This suggests that the Buddhists are required to extirpate a whole lot of normal human emotions. Anger has to go and together with it blame and resentment, only to be replaced by patience and compassion for the perpetrators of crime. Regret has to go too, only to be replaced by anticipatory guilt and fear of wrongdoing. The Abhidharma Buddhists have no place for backward-looking emotions and disagreeable emotions that cause pain. But many of us think that anger and regret, blame and resentment are not only morally justifiable, but also an important part of the social fabric of our society. Nichols (2014) offers historical evidence to show that anger and vengeance play a role in sustaining punishment norms. He also argues that punishment, in turn, secures cooperation. Jettisoning our punishment norms comes at a huge loss to society.

Eliminating selves and persons in the sense of breaking barriers between people seemingly entails nothing less than a revolution. We need to be cautious about wholeheartedly embracing a Buddhist revolution if we think about losses and gains to our lives (as we know them). We might think that embracing the no-self and no-person view has revisionary consequences for epistemology and philosophy of mind, but it seems that the consequences are much more revolutionary when we think about our ordinary practices and values. Perhaps this is what leads ancient Pudgalavādins and contemporary philosophers to salvage at least a conventional notion of persons. I think that they need to be clear that they are not prepared to go where the Buddhist arguments lead them; rather they want to minimize their losses by jumping the Buddhist ship before it takes them too far afield.

9.6 Conclusion

This chapter suggests that the proposed Buddhist revolution will generate significant losses for our ordinary individual lives (as we know them). In saying this, I am not suggesting that in embracing Buddhism with its accompanying ideal of making progress on the Buddhist Path is not worthwhile. Some progress on the Buddhist Path might actually improve our lives. But pursuing the highest ideal, becoming a Bodhisattva, is perhaps taking it too far. It seems like an extreme that the Buddhist, by her own lights, should avoid rather than valorize.

Concluding Remarks

This book offers a new interpretation of Vasubandhu as presenting a no-self and no-person metaphysics. In the *Abhidharmakośa-Bhāṣya*, Vasubandhu argues that selves and persons are only nominal existences; they do not do any causal work. My interpretation of Vasubandhu departs from contemporary philosophers' writings on Buddhism in two ways. First, Vasubandhu is not just an eliminativist about the self, but also an illusionist about the sense of self and all kinds of self-representation. Second, Vasubandhu is not just an eliminativist about the self, but also about persons.

The first point raises concerns about the adequacy of Abhidharma explanations for a wide range of experiential and cognitive phenomena. I have tried to meet these challenges by developing and refining the Abhidharma explanations using resources from contemporary philosophy and cognitive sciences. If some of the arguments in this book succeed, then we have explanations for key phenomena—episodic memory, synchronic unity of experiences, sense of ownership, and sense of agency—without implicating any self-representations. This constitutes my defense of the Abhidharma Buddhist ontology of mind.

The second point concerns the normative implications of Vasubandhu's no-self and no-person metaphysics. Abhidharma Buddhist metaphysics is motivated by the normative goal of eliminating, or at least reducing, suffering. This goal seems well worth pursuing. A natural concluding move for the book would be to endorse the normative implications and let the revisionary metaphysics drive our moral practices. But when we lay out the entailments of the no-person metaphysics, they seem, at the very least, unpalatable, if not downright absurd. These revisionary implications for our normative commitments, I think, give us reason to pause.

Since Strawson's landmark 1962 essay, "Freedom and Resentment," there has been a tendency in contemporary philosophy to regard person-related practices as sacrosanct, "not something that can come up for review." I do not agree with Strawson that our person-related practices are not up for review. Abhidharma Buddhists argue that most of us have false beliefs about our own nature and identity over time. They also argue that when we give up these false metaphysical beliefs, we need to also revise our moral beliefs and practices. I am also not in favor of the wholesale revision of our ordinary person-related practices entailed by Vasubandhu's metaphysics. There is a general methodological lesson to draw

Selfless Minds: A Contemporary Perspective on Vasubandhu's Metaphysics. Monima Chadha, Oxford University Press.
© Monima Chadha 2023. DOI: 10.1093/oso/9780192844095.003.0011

here: neither our person-related practices nor our theories of personal identity are immune to revision.

Following Parfit (1984), most contemporary philosophers aim to establish the true metaphysics of selves and persons before applying it to ethics. In contrast, Marya Schechtman (2010, 2014) argues that the metaphysics of selves and persons should be constrained by our ethical concerns and practices. I recommend that we build theories of "what we are" and "how we should live" that are mutually constrained by some form of a wide reflective equilibrium. The qualification "wide" is important especially in the context of cross-cultural philosophy. We improve our prospects of making progress in philosophy when we are willing to engage with comprehensive worldviews that rest on intuitions and insights from widely disparate intellectual cultures, contexts, and times. Strawson and Vasubandhu have both been highly influential in their respective philosophical circles. This book has brought them into dialogue with one another on the most fundamental questions in philosophy: What are we? And how we should live? My hope is that we can learn more about metaphysics of identity and ethics and be stimulated to develop new approaches to each of them, when we consider them not in isolation, and not from the standpoint of any one particular philosophical tradition.

References

Primary Texts

Buddhaghosa (ca. 450 AD). *Atthasālini*. Translation (2005 [1942]): B. Ñāṇamoli, *The Fount of Meaning (Atthasālinī) by Buddhaghosa Ācariya*. Island Hermitage Library: Dodandūwa. Partially typed, partially handwritten, ms. on *Asl*. 36–114.

Buddhaghosa (ca. 450 AD). *Visuddhimagga*. Translation (1991): B Ñāṇamoli, *The Path of Purification: Visuddhimagga by Bhadantācariya Buddhaghosa*. Kandy: Buddhist Publication Society.

Kamalaśīla (ca. 740 AD). *Tattvasaṃgrahapañjikā* [Commentary on the Compendium of Reality]. Translation (1986 [1937–3]): G. Jha, *The Tattvasaṃgraha of Śāntarakṣita With the Commentary of Kamalaśīla* (Vols. 1–2). Delhi: Motilal Banarsidass.

Śāntarakṣita (ca. 725 AD). *Tattvasaṃgraha* [Compendium of Reality]. Translation (1986 [1937–9]): G. Jha, *The Tattvasaṃgraha of Śāntarakṣita With the Commentary of Kamalaśīla* (Vols. 1–2). Delhi: Motilal Banarsidass.

Śāntideva (ca. 800 AD). *Bodhicaryāvatāra* [Bodhisattva's Way of Life]. Translation (1995): K. Crosby & A. Skilton, *The Bodhicaryāvatāra*. New York: Oxford World's Classics.

Utpaladeva (ca. 900 AD). *Īśvarapratyabhijñākārikā* [Recognition of the Lord with the Author's Commentary]. Translation (2002 [1994]): R. Torella, *The Īśvarapratyabhijñākārikā of Utpaladeva with the Author's Vṛtti*. Delhi: Motilal Banarsidass.

Vasubandhu (ca. 430 AD). *Abhidharmakośabhāṣyam* [Treasury of Abhidharma]. Translations: L. Pruden (1988), *Abhidharmakośabhāṣyam*. Berkeley: Asian Humanities Press; M. Kapstein (2001), Vasubandhu and the Nyāya Philosophers on Personal Identity. In *Reason's Traces* (pp. 347–91). Somerville, MA: Wisdom Publications.

Vasubandhu (ca. 430 AD). *Karmasiddhiprakarana* [Treatise on Action]. Translation (1987): L. Pruden, *Karmasiddhiprakarana: Treatise on Action by Vasubandhu*. Berkeley: Asian Humanities Press.

Vātsyāyana (ca. 400 AD). *Nyāya-sūtra and Nyāya-bāṣya* In A. Thakur (Ed.), *Gautamīya-nyāya-darśana with Bhāṣya of Vātsyāyana*. Delhi: Indian Council of Philosophical Research. Translations: M. Gangopadhyaya (1982), *Gautama's Nyāya-sūtra with Vātsyāyana's Commentary*. Calcutta: Indian Studies; M. Dasti & S. Phillips (Eds.) (2017), *The Nyāya-Sūtra: Selections with Early Commentaries*. Indianapolis: Hackett.

Texts Without Authors

Majjhima Nikāya: The Middle Length Discourses of the Buddha: A Translation of the Majjhima Nikaya. Translation (1995): B. Ñāṇamoli & B. Bodhi. Boston: Wisdom Publications.

Milinda Pañha: Milinda's Questions. Translation (1963–4): I. B. Horner, 2 volumes. Bristol: Pali Text Society.

Saṃyutta Nikāya: The Connected Discourses of the Buddha. Translation (2000): B. Bodhi. Boston: Wisdom Publications.

Yogācārabhūmi. Edition (1957): V. Bhattacharya. Calcutta: University of Calcutta.

Other Published Works

Adam, M. T. (2016). Philosophy, Meditation, and Experience in the Great Debate at Bsam Yas. *Journal of the International Association of Buddhist Studies*, 39, 351–74.

Alais, D., & D. Burr. (2004). The Ventriloquist Effect Results from Near-Optimal Bimodal Integration. *Current Biology*, 14, 257–62.

Alsmith, A. (2015). Mental Activity and the Sense of Ownership. *Review of Philosophy and Psychology*, 6(4), 881–96.

Anscombe, G. E. M. (1962). On Sensations of Position. *Analysis*, 22(3), 55–8.

Audi, P. (2012). Grounding: Toward a Theory of the In-Virtue-Of Relation. *The Journal of Philosophy*, 109(12), 685–711.

Baker, D., E. Hunter, N. Lawrence, N. Medford, C. Patel, M. Senior,...A. S. David (2003). Depersonalisation Disorder: Clinical Features of 204 Cases. *The British Journal of Psychiatry*, 182(5), 428–33.

Bartlett, F. C. (1932). *Remembering: A Study in Experimental and Social Psychology*. Cambridge: Cambridge University Press.

Bayne, T. (2008a). The Unity of Consciousness and the Split-Brain Syndrome. *The Journal of Philosophy*, 105, 277–300.

Bayne, T. (2008b). The Phenomenology of Agency. *Philosophy Compass*, 3(1), 182–202.

Bayne, T. (2009). Unity of Consciousness. *Scholarpedia*, 4(2), 7414.

Bayne, T. (2010). *The Unity of Consciousness*. Oxford: Oxford University Press.

Bayne, T. (2011). The Sense of Agency. In F. Macpherson (Ed.), *The Senses* (pp. 355–74). New York: Oxford University Press.

Bayne, T. (2014). The Multisensory Nature of Perceptual Consciousness. In D. J. Bennett & C. S. Hill (Eds.), *Sensory Integration and the Unity of Consciousness* (pp. 15–36). Cambridge, MA: MIT Press.

Bayne, T., & E. Pacherie (2014). Consciousness and Agency. In J. Clausen & N. Levy (Eds.), *Springer Handbook of Neuroethics* (pp. 211–30). Dordrecht: Springer.

Benoit, R. G., K. K. Szpunar, & D. L. Schacter (2014). Ventromedial Prefrontal Cortex Supports Affective Future Simulation by Integrating Distributed Knowledge. *Proceedings of the National Academy of Sciences*, 111, 16550–5.

Bermúdez, J. (2011). Bodily Awareness and Self-Consciousness. In S. Gallagher (Ed.), *The Oxford Handbook of the Self* (pp. 157–79). Oxford: Oxford University Press.

Bermúdez, J. (2015). Bodily Ownership, Bodily Awareness, and Knowledge Without Observation. *Analysis*, 75, 37–45.

Berne, E. (1958). Transactional Analysis: A New and Effective Method of Group Therapy. *American Journal of Psychotherapy*, 12, 735–43.

Berntsen, D. (2021). Involuntary Autobiographical Memories and Their Relation to Other Forms of Spontaneous Thoughts. *Philosophical Transactions of the Royal Society B*, 376(1817), 20190693.

Bertelson, P. (1988). Starting from the Ventriloquist: The Perception of Multimodal Events. In M. Sabourin, F. I. M. Craik, & M. Robert (Eds.), *Advances in Psychological Science* (Vol. 2, pp. 419–39). Hove: Psychology Press.

Bertelson, P. (1999). Ventriloquism: A Case of Crossmodal Perceptual Grouping. *Advances in Psychology*, 129, 347–62.

Bisiach, E., M. L. Rusconi, & G. Vallar (1991). Remission of Somatoparaphrenic Delusion Through Vestibular Stimulation. *Neuropsychologia*, 29(10), 1029–31.

Blackburn, P. (1994). *The Oxford Dictionary of Philosophy*. Oxford: Oxford University Press.

Blanke, O., & T. Metzinger (2009). Full-Body Illusions and Minimal Phenomenal Selfhood. *Trends in Cognitive Sciences*, 13, 7–13.

Bodhi, B. (2000). *The Connected Discourses of the Buddha: A New Translation of the Samyutta Nikaya*. Boston: Wisdom Publications.

Bottini, G. E., E. Bisiach, R. Sterzi, & G. Vallar (2002). Feeling Touches in Someone Else's Hand. *Neuroreport*, 13(2), 249–52.

Brison, S. J. (1999a). Trauma Narratives and the Remaking of the Self. In M. Bal, J. Crewe, & L. Spitzer (Eds.), *Acts of Memory* (pp. 39–54). Hanover: University Press of New England.

Brison, S. J. (1999b). The Uses of Narrative in the Aftermath of Violence. In C. Card (Ed.), *Essays in Feminist Ethics and Politics* (pp. 200–25). Lawrence: University Press of Kansas.

Brison, S. J. (2003). *Aftermath: Violence and the Remaking of a Self*. Princeton: Princeton University Press.

Butler, J. (1736). *The Analogy of Religion*, "Appendix I: Of Personal Identity." Reprinted in Perry 1975, pp. 99–106.

Calvert, G. A., B. E. Stein, & C. Spence (Eds.) (2004). *The Handbook of Multisensory Processing*. Cambridge, MA: MIT Press.

Cardinali, L., A. Zanini, R. Yanofsky, A. C. Roy, F. de Vignemont, J. C. Culham, & A. Farnè (2021). The Toolish Hand Illusion: Embodiment of a Tool Based on Similarity with the Hand. *Scientific Reports*, 11(1), 1–9.

Chadha, M. (2013). Self in Early Nyāya: A Minimal Conclusion. *Asian Philosophy: An International Journal of the Philosophical Traditions of the East*, 23(1), 24–52.

Chadha, M. (2015). Time-Series of Ephemeral Impressions: The Abhidharma-Buddhist View of Conscious Experience. *Phenomenology and the Cognitive Sciences*, 14(3), 543–60.

Chadha, M., & S. Nichols (2019). Self-Conscious Emotions Without a Self. *Philosophers' Imprint*, 19(38).

Chakrabarti, A. (1982). The Nyāya Proofs for the Existence of the Soul. *Journal of Indian Philosophy*, 10, 211–38.

Chakrabarti, A. (1992). I Touch What I Saw. *Philosophy and Phenomenological Research*, 52(1), 103–16.

Chakrabarti, A., & R. Weber (Eds.) (2015). *Comparative Philosophy Without Borders*. London: Bloomsbury Publishing.

Cinel, C., G. W. Humphreys, & R. Poli (2002). Cross-Modal Illusory Conjunctions Between Vision and Touch. *Journal of Experimental Psychology, Human Perception, and Performance*, 28, 1243–66.

Cocking, D., & J. Kennett (2000). Friendship and Moral Danger. *Journal of Philosophy*, 97(5), 278–96.

Conway, M. A. (2001). Sensory Perceptual Episodic Memory and Its Context: Autobiographical Memory. *Philosophical Transactions of the Royal Society of London B*, 356(1413), 1375–84.

Conway, M. A. (2005). Memory and the Self. *Journal of Memory and Language*, 53(4), 594–628.

Conway, M. A., J. A. Singer, & A. Tagini (2004). The Self and Autobiographical Memory: Correspondence and Coherence. *Social Cognition*, 22(5), 491–529.

Cousins, L. (1991). The 'Five Points' and the Origins of the Buddhist Schools. In T. Skorupski (Ed.), *The Buddhist Forum II* (pp. 27–60). London: School of Oriental and African Studies, University of London.

Cox, C. (1995). *Disputed Dharmas: Early Buddhist Theories on Existence—An Annotated Translation of the Section on Factors Dissociated from Thought from Saṅghabhadra's Nyāyānusāra*. Tokyo: Studia Philologica Buddhica XI.

Crosby, K., & A. Skilton (1995). *The Bodhicaryavatara: A Guide to the Buddhist Path of Awakening*. Oxford: Oxford University Press.

Csikszentmihalyi, M. (1978). Intrinsic Rewards and Emergent Motivation. In M. R. Lepper & D. Greene (Eds.), *The Hidden Costs of Reward: New Perspectives on the Psychology of Human Motivation* (pp. 205–16). Hillsdale: Erlbaum.

Dainton, B. (2000). *Stream of Consciousness: Unity and Continuity in Conscious Experience.* London: Routledge.

Damasio, A. (2012). *Self Comes to Mind.* New York: Vintage Books.

Dasti, M., & S. Phillips (Eds.) (2017). *The Nyāya-Sūtra: Selections with Early Commentaries.* Indianapolis: Hackett.

Davids, T. W. R. (Trans.) (1969 [1890]). *The Questions of King Milinda (Sacred Book of the East, 35).* Delhi: Motilal Banarsidass.

Davidson, D. (1974). On the Very Idea of a Conceptual Scheme. *Proceedings and Addresses of the American Philosophical Association,* 47, 5–20.

Davis, J. H. (2016). 'The Scope for Wisdom': Early Buddhism on Reasons and Persons. In S. Ranganathan (Ed.), *The Bloomsbury Research Handbook of Indian Ethics* (pp. 127–54). London: Bloomsbury Academic.

De Gelder, B., & P. Bertelson (2003). Multisensory Integration, Perception, and Ecological Validity. *Trends in Cognitive Sciences,* 7(10), 460–7.

De Haan, E. H. F., P. M. Corballis, S. A. Hillyard, C. A. Marzi, A. Seth, V. A. F. Lamme,... Y. Pinto (2020). Split-Brain: What We Know Now and Why This is Important for Understanding Consciousness. *Neuropsychology Review,* 30(2), 224–33.

De Vignemont, F. (2007). *Habeas Corpus:* The Sense of Ownership of One's Own Body. *Mind & Language,* 22(4), 427–49.

De Vignemont, F. (2013). The Mark of Bodily Ownership. *Analysis,* 73(4), 643–51.

De Vignemont, F., & P. Fourneret (2004). The Sense of Agency: A Philosophical and Empirical Review of the 'Who' System. *Consciousness and Cognition,* 13(1), 1–19.

Dehaene, S., & L. Naccache (2001). Towards a Cognitive Neuroscience of Consciousness: Basic Evidence and a Workspace Framework. *Cognition,* 79(1–2), 1–37.

Dehaene, S., C. Sergent, & J. P. Changeux (2003). A Neuronal Network Model Linking Subjective Reports and Objective Physiological Data During Conscious Perception. *Proceedings of the National Academy of Sciences,* 100, 8520–5.

Della Sala, S., C. Marchetti, & H. Spinnler (1991). Right-Sided Anarchic (Alien) Hand: A Longitudinal Study. *Neuropsychologia,* 29(11), 1113–27.

Della Sala, S., C. Marchetti, & H. Spinnler (1994). The Anarchic Hand: A Fronto-Mesial Sign. In G. Boller & J. Grafman (Eds.), *Handbook of Neuropsychology* (Vol. 9, pp. 233–55). Amsterdam: Elsevier.

Dennett, D. (1992). The Self as a Center for Narrative Gravity. In F. Kessel, P. Cole, & D. Johnson (Eds.), *Self and Consciousness: Multiple Perspectives* (pp. 103–15). Hillsdale: Erlbaum.

Dreyfus, G. (1997). *Recognizing Reality: Dharmakirti's Philosophy and Its Tibetan Interpretations.* New York: SUNY Press.

Dreyfus, G. (2011a). Is Mindfulness Present-Centred and Non-Judgmental? A Discussion of the Cognitive Dimensions of Mindfulness. *Contemporary Buddhism,* 12(1), 41–54.

Dreyfus, G. (2011b). Self and Subjectivity: A Middle Way Approach. In M. Siderits, E. Thompson, & D. Zahavi (Eds.), *Self, No-Self? Perspectives from Analytical, Phenomenological, and Indian Traditions* (pp. 114–44). Oxford: Oxford University Press.

Dreyfus, G. (forthcoming). *But Aren't We Conscious? A Buddhist Reflection on the Hard Problem.*

Dreyfus, G., & E. Thompson (2007). Asian Perspectives: Indian Theories of Mind. In P. Zezalo, M. Moscovitch, & E. Thompson (Eds.), *The Cambridge Handbook of Consciousness* (pp. 89–114). Cambridge: Cambridge University Press.

Duvarci, S., & K. Nader (2004). Characterization of Fear Memory Reconsolidation. *Journal of Neuroscience*, 24(42), 9269–75.

Edelglass, W., & J. Garfield (2009). *Buddhist Philosophy: Essential Readings*. Oxford: Oxford University Press.

Efron, R. (1967). The Duration of the Present. *Annals of the New York Academy of Sciences*, 138(2), 713–29.

Eltschinger, V. (2010). Dharmakīrti. *Revue Internationale de Philosophie*, 3, 397–440.

Eltschinger, V. (2014). Is There a Burden-Bearer? The Sanskrit Bhārahārasūtra and Its Scholastic Interpretations. *Journal of the American Oriental Society*, 134(3), 453–79.

Farah, M. J. (1994). Visual Perception and Visual Awareness after Brain Damage: A Tutorial Overview. In C. Umlità & M. Moscovitch (Eds.), *Attention and Performance XV: Conscious and Nonconscious Information Processing* (pp. 37–76). Cambridge, MA: MIT Press.

Frith, C. (1992). *The Cognitive Neuropsychology of Schizophrenia*. Hillsdale: Erlbaum.

Fulkerson, M. (2011). The Unity of Haptic Touch. *Philosophical Psychology*, 24(4), 493–516.

Gaesser, B., & D. L. Schacter (2014). Episodic Simulation and Episodic Memory Can Increase Intentions to Help Others. *Proceedings of the National Academy of Sciences*, 111(12), 4415–20.

Gallagher, S. (2000). Philosophical Conceptions of the Self: Implications for Cognitive Science. *Trends in Cognitive Sciences*, 4(1), 14–21.

Gallagher, S. (2005). *How the Body Shapes the Mind*. Oxford: Oxford University Press.

Gallagher, S. (2012). Multiple Aspects in the Sense of Agency. *New Ideas in Psychology*, 30(1), 15–31.

Gallagher, S., & D. Zahavi (2012). *The Phenomenological Mind*. London: Routledge.

Ganeri, J. (2000). Cross-Modality and the Self. *Philosophy and Phenomenological Research*, 61(3), 639–57.

Ganeri, J. (2001). *Philosophy in Classical India*. London: Routledge.

Ganeri, J. (2004). An Irrealist Theory of Self. *The Harvard Review of Philosophy*, 12(1), 61–80.

Ganeri, J. (2007). *The Concealed Art of the Soul*. New York: Oxford University Press.

Ganeri, J. (2011). Subjectivity, Selfhood, and the Use of the Word 'I'. In M. Siderits, E. Thompson, & D. Zahavi (Eds.), *Self, No-Self? Perspectives from Analytical, Phenomenological, and Indian Traditions* (pp. 176–92). Oxford: Oxford University Press.

Ganeri, J. (2012a). *The Self: Naturalism, Consciousness, and the First-Person Stance*. Oxford: Oxford University Press.

Ganeri, J. (2012b). Buddhist No-Self: An Analysis and Critique. In I. Kuznetsova, J. Ganeri, & R.-P. Chakravarthi (Eds.), *Hindu and Buddhist Ideas in Dialogue: Self and No-Self* (pp. 63–76). London: Ashgate.

Ganeri, J. (2017). *Attention, Not Self*. Oxford: Oxford University Press.

Garfield, J. (2015). *Engaging Buddhism: Why Does Buddhism Matter to Philosophy?* Oxford: Oxford University Press.

Germine, L., T. L. Benson, F. Cohen, & C. I. L Hooker (2013). Psychosis-Proneness and the Rubber Hand Illusion of Body Ownership. *Psychiatry Research*, 207(1), 45–52.

Gethin, R. (1992). *The Buddhist Path to Awakening: A Study of Bodhi-Pakkhiyā Dhammā*. Leiden: Brill.

Gethin, R. (1998). *The Foundations of Buddhism*. Oxford: Oxford University Press.

Gill, M. B., & S. Nichols (2008). Sentimentalist Pluralism: Moral Psychology and Philosophical Ethics. *Philosophical Issues: A Supplement to Noûs*, 18(1), 143–63.

Gold, J. (2015). *Paving the Great Way: Vasubandhu's Unifying Buddhist Philosophy*. New York: Columbia University Press.

Gold, J. (2021). Vasubandhu. In E. N. Zalta (Ed.), *The Stanford Encyclopedia of Philosophy* (Spring 2021 Edition). Online: https://plato.stanford.edu/archives/spr2021/entries/vasubandhu/.

Goodman, C. (2004). The Treasury of Metaphysics and the Physical World. *Philosophical Quarterly*, 54(216), 389–401.

Goodman, C. (2016). Uses of the Illusion of Agency: Why Some Buddhists Should Believe in Free Will. In R. Repetti (Ed.), *Buddhist Perspectives on Free Will: Agentless Agency* (pp. 34–44). New York: Routledge.

Gorkom, N. V. (2014). *Cetasikas*. 2nd ed. London: Zolag.

Greenwald, A. G. (1980). The Totalitarian Ego: Fabrication and Revision of Personal History. *American Psychologist*, 35(7), 603–18.

Gupta, A. S., M. A. van der Meer, D. S. Touretzky, & A. D. Redish (2010). Hippocampal Replay Is Not a Simple Function of Experience. *Neuron*, 65(5), 695–705.

Hallisey, C. (1996). Ethical Particularism in Theravāda Buddhism. *Journal of Buddhist Ethics*, 3, 32–43.

Heim, M. (2009). The Conceit of Self-Loathing. *Journal of Indian Philosophy*, 37(1), 61–74.

Heim, M. (2017). Buddhaghosa on the Phenomenology of Love and Compassion. In J. Ganeri (Ed.), *The Oxford Handbook of Indian Philosophy* (pp. 171–89). Oxford: Oxford University Press.

Hill, C. (2018). Unity of Consciousness. *Wiley Interdisciplinary Reviews: Cognitive Science*, 9(5), e1465.

Hoel, E. (2021). The Overfitted Brain: Dreams Evolved to Assist Generalization. *Patterns*, 2(5), 100244.

Horner, I. B. (Ed.) (1964). *Milinda's Questions: Milindapanha*. London: Pali Text Society.

Hötting, K., & B. Röder (2004). Hearing Cheats Touch, But Less in Congenitally Blind than in Sighted Individuals. *Psychological Science*, 15(1), 60–4.

Hume, D. (1975 [1739]). *A Treatise of Human Nature*. Edited by L. A. Selby-Bigge, 2nd ed. revised by P. H. Nidditch. Oxford: Clarendon Press.

Humphreys, G. W., & M. J. Riddoch (1993). Interactions Between Object and Space Systems Revealed Through Neuropsychology. In D. E. Meyer & S. Kornblum (Eds.), *Attention and Performance XIV: Synergies in Experimental Psychology, Artificial Intelligence, and Cognitive Neuroscience* (pp. 143–62). Hillsdale: Erlbaum.

Hur, J. W., J. S. Kwon, T. Y. Lee, & S. Park (2014). The Crisis of Minimal Self-Awareness in Schizophrenia: A Meta-Analytic Review. *Schizophrenia Research*, 152(1), 58–64.

Invernizzi, P., M. Gandola, D. Romano, L. Zapparoli, G. E. Bottini, & E. Paulesu (2012). What is Mine? Behavioral and Anatomical Dissociations Between Somatoparaphrenia and Anosognosia for Hemiplegia. *Behavioral Neurology*, 26(1–2), 139–50.

Jackson, F. (1998). *From Metaphysics to Ethics: A Defence of Conceptual Analysis*. Oxford: Oxford University Press.

James, W. (1983 [1890]). *The Principles of Psychology*. Cambridge, MA: Harvard University Press.

Jaspers, K. (1948). *Der Philosophische Glaube*. Zürich: Artemis.

Jeannerod, M., & E. Pacherie (2004). Agency, Simulation and Self-Identification. *Mind & Language*, 19(2), 113–46.

Jha, G. (Ed.) (1984). *The Nyāya-Sūtras of Guatama with the Bhāsya of Vātsyāyana and the Vārttika of Uddyotakara*. Delhi: Motilal Banarsidass.

Johansson, R. (1985). *The Dynamic Psychology of Early Buddhism*. London and Malmo: The Scandinavian Institute of Asian Studies.

Kant, I. (1998 [1787]). *Critique of Pure Reason*. Translated and edited by P. Guyer & A. Wood. Cambridge: Cambridge University Press.

Kant, I. (2002 [1785]). *Groundwork for the Metaphysics of Morals*. Translated by A. Wood. New Haven: Yale University Press.

Kapstein, M. (2001). *Reason's Traces: Identity and Interpretation in Indian and Tibetan Buddhist Thought*. Boston: Wisdom Publications.

Kellner, B. (2019). Buddhist Philosophy and the Neuroscientific Study of Meditation. *Newsletter of the American Philosophical Association*, 19(1), 36–40.

Kellner, B. (2020). Using Concepts to Eliminate Conceptualization: Kamalaśīla on Non-Conceptual Gnosis (nirvikalpajñāna). *Journal of the International Association of Buddhist Studies*, 43, 39–80.

Kellner, B., & J. A. Taber (2014). Studies in Yogācāra-Vijñānavāda Idealism I: The Interpretation of Vasubandhu's Viṃśikā. *Asiatische Studien*, 68(3), 709–56.

Kentridge, R. W. (2004). Spatial Attention Speeds Discrimination Without Awareness in Blindsight. *Neuropsychologia*, 42(6), 831–5.

Kentridge, R. W., C. A. Heywood, & L. Weiskrantz (1999). Attention Without Awareness in Blindsight. *Proceedings of the Royal Society of London B*, 266(1430), 1805–11.

Kirberg, M. (2022). Neurocognitive Dynamics of Spontaneous Offline Simulations: Re-conceptualizing (Dream) Bizarreness. *Philosophical Psychology*, 1–30.

Klein, S. B. (2013). Making the Case That Episodic Recollection is Attributable to Operations Occurring at Retrieval Rather than to Content Stored in a Dedicated Subsystem of Long-Term Memory. *Frontiers in Behavioural Neuroscience*, 7, 3.

Klein, S. B. (2014a). Sameness and the Self: Philosophical and Psychological Considerations. *Frontiers in Psychology: Perception Science*, 5, 29.

Klein, S. B. (2014b). Autonoesis and Belief in a Personal Past: An Evolutionary Theory of Episodic Memory Indices. *Review of Philosophy and Psychology*, 5(3), 427–47.

Klein, S. B. (2015a). What Memory Is. *Wiley Interdisciplinary Reviews: Cognitive Science*, 6(1), 1–38.

Klein, S. B. (2015b). The Feeling of Personal Ownership of One's Mental States: A Conceptual Argument and Empirical Evidence for an Essential, but Underappreciated, Mechanism of Mind. *Psychology of Consciousness: Research, Practice, and Theory*, 2(4), 355–76.

Klein, S. B. (2016). Lost Feeling of Ownership of One's Mental States: The Importance of Situation Patient R.B.'s Pathology in the Context of Contemporary Theory and Empiricism. *Philosophical Psychology*, 29(4), 490–3.

Kriegel, U. (2013). The Epistemological Challenge of Revisionary Metaphysics. *Philosophers' Imprint*, 13(12), 1–30.

Krueger, J. W. (2011). The Who and the How of Experience. In M. Siderits, E. Thompson, & D. Zahavi (Eds.), *Self, No-Self? Perspectives from Analytical, Phenomenological, and Indian Traditions* (pp. 27–55). Oxford: Oxford University Press.

Kuznetsova, I. (2012). Utpaladeva's Conception of Self in the Context of the Ātmavāda-Anātmavāda Debate and in Comparison with Western Theological Idealism. *Philosophy East and West*, 62(3), 339–58.

Ladavas, E., R. Paladini, & R. Cubelli (1993). Implicit Associative Priming in a Patient with Left Unilateral Neglect. *Neuropsychologia*, 31(12), 1307–20.

Le Poidevin, R. (2011). The Temporal Prison. *Analysis*, 71(3), 456–65.

Levi, P. (1996). *Survival in Auschwitz*. New York: Simon & Schuster.

Lewis, D. (1972). Psychophysical and Theoretical Identifications. *Australasian Journal of Philosophy*, 50(3), 249–50.

Lewis, D. (1995). Should a Materialist Believe in Qualia? *Australasian Journal of Philosophy*, 73(1), 140–4.

Locke, J. (1975 [1689]). *An Essay Concerning Human Understanding*. Edited by P. H. Nidditch. The Clarendon Edition of the Works of John Locke. Oxford: Oxford University Press.

Loftus, E. F. (2003). Our Changeable Memories: Legal and Practical Implications. *Nature Reviews: Neuroscience*, 4(3), 231–4.

LoLordo, A. (2019). Introduction. In A. LoLordo (Ed.), *Persons: A History* (pp. 1–16). Oxford: Oxford University Press.

McAdams, D. P. (2001). The Psychology of Life Stories. *Review of General Psychology*, 5(2), 100–22.

McClintock, S. (2010). *Omniscience and the Rhetoric of Reason: Śāntarakṣita and Kamaśīla on Rationality, Argumentation, and Religious Authority*. Boston: Wisdom.

McGurk, H., & J. MacDonald (1976). Hearing Lips and Seeing Voices. *Nature*, 264(5588), 746–8.

McKinnon, N. (2003). Presentism and Consciousness. *Australasian Journal of Philosophy*, 81(3), 305–23.

Martin, M. G. F. (1992). Sight and Touch. In T. Crane (Ed.), *The Contents of Experience: Essays on Perception* (pp. 199–201). Cambridge: Cambridge University Press.

Martin, M. G. F. (1995). Bodily Awareness: A Sense of Ownership. In J. Bermúdez, A. Marcel, & N. Eilan (Eds.), *The Body and the Self* (pp. 267–89). Cambridge, MA: MIT Press.

Mellor, C. S. (1970). First Rank Symptoms of Schizophrenia: I. The Frequency in Schizophrenics on Admission to Hospital II. Differences Between Individual First Rank Symptoms. *The British Journal of Psychiatry*, 117(536), 15–23.

Melzack, R. (1990). Phantom Limbs and the Concept of a Neuromatrix. *Trends in Neurosciences*, 13(3), 88–92.

Mendis, N. K. G. (2007). *Anatta-lakkhana Sutta: The Discourse on the Not-Self Characteristic* (translation from Pali). Online: https://www.accesstoinsight.org/tipitaka/sn/sn22/sn22.059.mend.html.

Metzinger, T. (2003). *Being No One: The Self-Model Theory of Subjectivity*. Cambridge, MA: MIT Press.

Meyers, K. L. (2017). The Dynamics of Intention, Freedom, and Habituation According to Vasubandhu's Abhidharmakośabhāsya. In J. H. Davis (Ed.), *A Mirror is for Reflection: Understanding Buddhist Ethics* (pp. 239–56). Oxford: Oxford University Press.

Mill, J. S. (1843). *A System of Logic*. London: Parker.

Mintz, A. R., K. S. Dobson, & D. M. Romney (2003). Insight in Schizophrenia: A Meta-Analysis. *Schizophrenia Research*, 61(1), 75–88.

Nagel, T. (1989). *The View from Nowhere*. Oxford: Oxford University Press.

Neisser, U. (1988). Five Kinds of Self-Knowledge. *Philosophical Psychology*, 1(1), 35–59.

Neurath, O. (1959). Protocol Sentences. In A. J. Ayer (Ed.), *Logical Positivism* (pp. 199–208). New York: The Free Press.

Nichols, S. (2008). Imagination and the I. *Mind & Language*, 23(5), 518–35.

Nichols, S. (2014). Episodic Sense of Self. In J. D'Arms & D. Jacobson (Eds.), *Moral Psychology and Human Agency: Philosophical Essays on the Science of Ethics* (pp. 137–55). Oxford: Oxford University Press.

Nichols, S., & D. Shoemaker (forthcoming). The Embattled 'Self': Elimination or Preservation?

O'Callaghan, C. (2008). Seeing What You Hear: Cross-Modal Illusions and Perception. *Philosophical Issues*, 18(1), 316–38.

O'Callaghan, C. (2017a). *Beyond Vision: Philosophical Essays*. Oxford: Oxford University Press.

O'Callaghan, C. (2017b). Enhancement Through Coordination. In B. Nanay (Ed.), *Controversies in Philosophy of Perception* (pp. 109–20). London: Routledge.

O'Shaughnessy, B. (1995). Proprioception and the Body Image. In J. Bermúdez, A. Marcel, & N. Eilan (Eds.), *The Body and the Self* (pp. 175–203). Cambridge, MA: MIT Press.

Obeyesekere, G. (1991). Myth, History and Numerology in the Buddhist Chronicles. In H. Bechert (Ed.), *The Dating of the Historical Buddha Part 1* (pp. 152–82). Göttingen: Vandenhoeck & Ruprecht.

Ohnuma, R. (2000). Internal and External Opposition to the Bodhisattva's Gift of His Body. *Journal of Indian Philosophy*, 28(1), 43–75.

Ohnuma, R. (2007). *Head, Eyes, Flesh and Blood: Giving Away the Body in Indian Buddhist Literature*. New York: Columbia University Press.

Olson, E. T. (1998). There Is No Problem of the Self. *Journal of Consciousness Studies*, 5(5–6), 645–57.

Olson, E. T. (2007). *What Are We? A Study in Personal Ontology*. Oxford: Oxford University Press.

Olson, E. T. (2009). Self: Personal Identity. In W. P. Banks (Ed.), *Encyclopedia of Consciousness*. Amsterdam: Elsevier/Academic Press.

Oteke, C. (1988). *'Ich' und das Ich: Analytische Untersuchungen zur Buddhistisch-Brahmanischen Ātmankontroverse*. Stuttgart: Franz Steiner Verlag.

Pacherie, E. (2006). Towards a Dynamic Theory of Intentions. In S. Pockett, W. P. Banks, & S. Gallagher (Eds.), *Does Consciousness Cause Behavior? An Investigation of the Nature of Volition* (pp. 145–67). Cambridge, MA: MIT Press.

Pacherie, E. (2007). Sense of Control and Sense of Agency. *Psyche*, 13(1), 1–30.

Paglieri, F. (2013). There's Nothing Like Being Free: Default Dispositions, Judgments of Freedom, and the Phenomenology of Coercion. In A. Clark, J. Kiverstein, & T. Vierkant (Eds.), *Decomposing the Will* (pp. 136–59). New York: Oxford University Press.

Parfit, D. (1984). *Reasons and Persons*. Oxford: Oxford University Press.

Parkin, A. J. (1996). The Alien Hand. In P. W. Halligan & J. C. Marshall (Eds.), *Method in Madness: Case Studies in Cognitive Neuropsychiatry* (pp. 173–83). Hove: Psychology Press.

Parnas, J., & P. Handest (2003). Phenomenology of Anomalous Self-Experience in Early Schizophrenia. *Comprehensive Psychiatry*, 44(2), 121–34.

Peacocke, C. (1999). *Being Known*. Oxford: Clarendon Press.

Perry, J. (1977). Frege on Demonstratives. *Philosophical Review*, 86(4), 474–97.

Phillips, I. (2010). Perceiving Temporal Properties. *European Journal of Philosophy*, 18(2), 176–202.

Pickard, H. (2014). Stories of Recovery: The Role of Narrative and Hope in Overcoming PTSD and PD. In J. Z. Zadler, B. Fulford, & C. W. van Staden (Eds.), *The Oxford Handbook of Psychiatric Ethics* (pp. 1315–27). Oxford: Oxford University Press.

Pockett, S. (2002). On Subjective Back-Referral and How Long it Takes to Become Conscious of a Stimulus: A Reinterpretation of Libet's Data. *Consciousness and Cognition*, 11(2), 144–61.

Pockett, S. (2003). How Long is 'Now'? Phenomenology and the Specious Present. *Phenomenology and the Cognitive Sciences*, 2(1), 55–68.

Pribram, K. H. (1999). Brain and the Composition of Conscious Experience. *Journal of Consciousness Studies*, 6(5), 19–42.

Priest, G. (2019). Marxism and Buddhism: Not such Strange Bedfellows. *Journal of the American Philosophical Association*, 4(1), 2–13.

Pruden, L. (1987). *Karmasiddhiprakarana: Treatise on Action by Vasubandhu*. Berkeley: Asian Humanities Press.

Pruden, L. (Ed.) (1988). *Abhidharmakośabhāṣyam*. English translation of Poussin, Louis de la Vallée (1923–1931 [1980]), *L'Abhidharmakośa de Vasubandhu*, Bruxelles: Institut Belge des Hautes Études Chinoises. Berkeley: Asian Humanities Press.

Quine, W. V. O. (1960). *Word and Object*. Cambridge, MA: MIT Press.

Rafal, R. (1997). Balint Syndrome. In T. Feinberg & M. Farah (Eds.), *Behavioral Neurology and Neuropsychology* (pp. 337–56). New York: McGraw-Hill.

Repetti, R. (2017). What Do Buddhists Think About Free Will? In J. H. Davis (Ed.), *A Mirror is for Reflection: Understanding Buddhist Ethics* (pp. 257–76). New York: Oxford University Press.

Ronkin, N. (2005). *Early Buddhist Metaphysics: The Making of a Philosophical Tradition*. London: Routledge-Curzon.

Ronkin, N. (2018). Abhidharma. In E. N. Zalta (Ed.), *The Stanford Encyclopedia of Philosophy*. Online: https://plato.stanford.edu/archives/sum2018/entries/abhidharma/.

Schacter, D. L. (2012). Adaptive Constructive Processes and the Future of Memory. *American Psychologist*, 67(8), 603–13.

Schacter, D. L., & D. R. Addis (2007). On the Constructive Episodic Simulation of Past and Future Events. *Behavioral and Brain Sciences*, 30(3), 331–2.

Schacter, D. L., S. A. Guerin, & P. L. St. Jacques (2011). Memory Distortion: An Adaptive Perspective. *Trends in Cognitive Sciences*, 15(10), 467–74.

Schechter, E. (2012). The Switch Model of Split-Brain Consciousness. *Philosophical Psychology*, 25(2), 203–26.

Schechtman, M. (2010). Personhood and the Practical. *Theoretical Medicine and Bioethics*, 31(4), 271–83.

Schechtman, M. (2014). *Staying Alive: Personal Identity, Practical Concerns, and the Unity of a Life*. Oxford: Oxford University Press.

Schmithausen, L. (1987). *Ālaya-vijñāna: On the Origin and the Early Development of a Central Concept of Yogācāra Philosophy*. Tokyo: International Institute for Buddhist Studies.

Schwitzgebel, E. (2008). The Unreliability of Naive Introspection. *Philosophical Review*, 117(2), 245–73.

Sekar, K., W. M. Findley, D. Poeppel, & R. R. Llinás (2013). Cortical Response Tracking the Conscious Experience of Threshold Duration Visual Stimuli Indicates Visual Perception Is All or None. *Proceedings of the National Academy of Sciences*, 110(14), 5642–7.

Shams, L., Y. Kamitani, & S. Shimojo (2000). What You See is What You Hear. *Nature*, 408(6814), 788.

Shimojo, S., & L. Shams (2001). Sensory Modalities Are Not Separate Modalities: Plasticity and Interactions. *Current Opinion in Neurobiology*, 11(4), 505–9.

Shoemaker, D. (2007). Personal Identity and Practical Concerns. *Mind*, 116(462), 317–57.

Shoemaker, D. (2011). Moral Responsibility and the Self. In S. Gallagher (Ed.), *The Oxford Handbook of the Self* (pp. 487–519). Oxford: Oxford University Press.

Shoemaker, D. (2016). The Stony Metaphysical Heart of Animalism. In S. Blatti & P. Snowdon (Eds.), *Animalism* (pp. 303–28). Oxford: Oxford University Press.

Shoemaker, S. (1984). Self-Reference and Self-Awareness. In S. Shoemaker (Ed.), *Identity, Cause and Mind: Philosophical Essays* (pp. 6–18). Cambridge: Cambridge University Press.

Siderits, M. (1997). Buddhist Reductionism. *Philosophy East and West*, 47(4), 455–78.

Siderits, M. (2006). Buddhas as Zombies: A Buddhist Reduction of Subjectivity. In M. Siderits, E. Thompson, & D. Zahavi (Eds.), *Self, No Self? Perspectives from Analytical, Phenomenological, and Indian Traditions* (pp. 308–32). Oxford: Oxford University Press.

Siderits, M. (2007). *Buddhism as Philosophy*. Indianapolis: Hackett.

Siderits, M. (2011). Buddhist Non-Self: The No Owner's Manual. In S. Gallagher (Ed.), *The Oxford Handbook of the Self* (pp. 297–315). Oxford: Oxford University Press.

Siderits, M. (2013). Buddhist Paleocompatibilism. *Philosophy East and West*, 63(1), 73–87.

Siderits, M. (2014). Causation, "Humean" Causation and Emptiness. *Journal of Indian Philosophy*, 42(4), 433–49.

Siderits, M. (2015). *Personal Identity and Buddhist Philosophy: Empty Persons*. London: Routledge.

Siderits, M. (2019). Persons and Selves in Buddhist Philosophy. In A. LoLordo (Ed.), *Persons: A History* (pp. 301–25). Oxford: Oxford University Press.

Sierra, M., D. Baker, N. Medford, & A. S. David (2005). Unpacking the Depersonalization Syndrome: An Explanatory Factory Analysis on the Cambridge Depersonalization Scale. *Psychological Medicine*, 35(10), 1523–32.

Slote, M. (2018). Sentimentalist Virtue Ethics. In N. E. Snow (Ed.), *The Oxford Handbook of Virtue* (pp. 343–58). Oxford: Oxford University Press.

Slotnick, S. D., & D. L. Schacter (2004). A Sensory Signature That Distinguishes True from False Memories. *Nature Neuroscience*, 7(6), 664–72.

Snowdon, P. (2009). "Persons" and Persons. *Organon F*, 16(4), 449–76.

Snowdon, P. (2018). Wittgenstein and Naturalism. In K. M. Cahill & T. Raleigh (Eds.), *Wittgenstein and Naturalism* (pp. 15–32). London: Routledge.

Soroker, N., N. Calamaro, & M. Myslobodsky (1995a). "McGurk Illusion" to Bilateral Administration of Sensory Stimuli in Patients with Hemispatial Neglect. *Neuropsychologia*, 33(4), 461–70.

Soroker, N., N. Calamaro, & M. Myslobodsky (1995b). Ventriloquism Effect Reinstates Responsiveness to Auditory Stimuli in the "Ignored" Space in Patients with Hemispatial Neglect. *Journal of Clinical and Experimental Neuropsychology*, 17(2), 243–55.

Sripada, C. (2015). Self-Expression: A Deep-Self Theory of Moral Responsibility. *Philosophical Studies*, 173(5), 1203–32.

St. Augustine (2003 [1467]). *City of God*. Translated by H. Bettenson. London: Penguin Classics.

Stoesz, W. (1978). The Buddha as Teacher. *Journal of the American Academy of Religion*, 46(2), 139–58.

Strawson, G. (1999). The Self. In S. Gallagher & J. Shear (Eds.), *Models of the Self* (pp. 1–24). Exeter: Academic Imprint.

Strawson, G. (2000). The Phenomenology and Ontology of the Self. In D. Zahavi (Ed.), *Exploring the Self* (pp. 39–54). Amsterdam: John Benjamins.

Strawson, G. (2003). What is the Relation Between an Experience, the Subject of an Experience, and the Content of the Experience? *Philosophical Issues*, 13, 279–315.

Strawson, G. (2007). Why I Have No Future. *The Philosophers' Magazine*, 38, 21–6.

Strawson, G. (2015). When I Enter Most Intimately into What I Call Myself. In P. Russell (Ed.), *The Oxford Handbook of David Hume* (pp. 269–92). Oxford: Oxford University Press.

Strawson, G. (2017). *The Subject of Experience*. Oxford: Oxford University Press.

Strawson, P. F. (1959). *Individuals*. London: Methuen.

Strawson, P. F. (1962). Freedom and Resentment. In G. Watson (Ed.), *Agency and Answerability*. Oxford: Oxford University Press.

Strawson, P. F. (1966). *The Bounds of Sense: An Essay on Kant's Critique of Pure Reason*. London: Methuen.

Taber, J. A. (1990). The Mīmāṃsā Theory of Self-Recognition. *Philosophy East and West*, 40(1), 35–57.

Taber, J. A. (2012). Uddyotakara's Defense of a Self. In I. Kuznetsova, J. Ganeri, & R.-P. Chakravarthi (Eds.), *Hindu and Buddhist Ideas in Dialogue* (pp. 97–114). Farnham: Ashgate.

Tappen, J., C. Williams, S. Fishman, & T. Touhy (1999). Persistence of the Self in Advanced Alzheimer's Disease. *IMAGE Journal of Nursing Scholarship*, 31(2), 121–5.

Thakkar, K. N., H. S. Nichols, L. G. McIntosh, & S. Park (2011). Disturbances in Body Ownership in Schizophrenia: Evidence from the Rubber Hand Illusion and Case Study of a Spontaneous Out-of-Body Experience. *PLoS One*, 6(10), 1–9.

Thompson, E. (2007). *Mind in Life: Biology, Phenomenology, and the Sciences of Mind*. Cambridge, MA: Harvard University Press.

Thompson, E. (2014). *Waking, Dreaming, Being: Self and Consciousness in Neuroscience, Meditation, and Philosophy*. New York: Columbia University Press.

Thompson, E. (2020). *Why I Am Not a Buddhist*. New Haven: Yale University Press.

Thorpe, S., D. Fize, & C. Marlot (1996). Speed of Processing in the Human Visual System. *Nature*, 381(6582), 520–2.

Thurman, R. (1978). Buddhist Hermeneutics. *Journal of the American Academy of Religion*, 46(1), 19–39.

Tierney, H. (2020). The Subscript View: A Distinct View of Distinct Selves. In T. Lobrozo, J. Knobe, & S. Nichols (Eds.), *Oxford Studies in Experimental Philosophy* (pp. 126–57). Oxford: Oxford University Press.

Tierney, H., C. Howard, V. Kumar, T. Kvaran, & S. Nichols (2014). How Many of Us Are There? In J. Sytsma (Ed.), *Advances in Experimental Philosophy of Mind* (pp. 181–202). London: Bloomsbury.

Tillemans, T. J. (2013). Yogic Perception, Meditation, and Enlightenment: The Epistemological Issues in a Key Debate. In S. M. Emmanuel (Ed.), *A Companion to Buddhist Philosophy* (pp. 290–306). Chichester: John Wiley & Sons.

Tillemans, T. (2021). Dharmakīrti. In E. N. Zalta (Ed.), *The Stanford Encyclopedia of Philosophy* (Spring 2021 Edition). Online: https://plato.stanford.edu/archives/spr2021/entries/dharmakiirti/.

Torella, R. (2002 [1994]). *The Īśvarapratyabhijñākārikā of Utpaladeva with the Author's Vṛtti: Critical Edition and Annotated Translation*. Delhi: Motilal Banarsidass.

Treisman, A. (2003). Consciousness and Perceptual Binding. In A. Cleermans & C. Frith (Eds.), *The Unity of Consciousness: Binding, Integration, and Dissociation* (pp. 95–113). Oxford: Oxford University Press.

Tsakiris, M. S., S. Schütz-Bosbach, & S. Gallagher (2007). On Agency and Body-Ownership: Phenomenological and Neurocognitive Reflections. *Consciousness and Cognition*, 16(3), 645–60.

Tulving, E. (1993). What is Episodic Memory? *Current Directions in Psychological Science*, 2(3), 67–70.

Tulving, E. (2005). Episodic Memory and Autonoesis: Uniquely Human? In H. S. Terrace & J. Metcalfe (Eds.), *The Missing Link in Cognition: Origins of Self-Reflective Consciousness* (pp. 3–56). Oxford: Oxford University Press.

Tye, M. (2003). *Consciousness and Persons: Unity and Identity*. Cambridge, MA: MIT Press.

Van Kesteren, M. T., M. Rijpkema, D. J. Ruiter, & G. Fernández (2010). Retrieval of Associative Information Congruent with Prior Knowledge is Related to Increased Medial Prefrontal Activity and Connectivity. *Journal of Neuroscience*, 30(47), 15888–94.

Waldron, W. (2003). *The Buddhist Unconscious: The Alaya-Vijñana in the Context of Indian Buddhist Thought*. London: Routledge.

Walton, D. (1995). *Arguments from Ignorance*. Philadelphia: Pennsylvania State University Press.

Warren, H. C. (1896). *Buddhism in Translations* (Vol. 3). Cambridge, MA: Harvard University Press.

Watson, A. (2014). The Self as a Dynamic Constant: Rāmakaṇṭha's Middle Ground Between a Naiyāyika Eternal Self-Substance and a Buddhist Stream of Consciousness-Moments. *Journal of Indian Philosophy*, 42(1), 173–93.

Watson, G. (2006). The Problematic Role of Responsibility in Contexts of Distributive Justice. *Philosophy and Phenomenological Research*, 72(2), 425–32.

Westerhoff, J. (2010). Abhidharma Philosophy. In W. Edelglass & J. Garfield (Eds.), *The Oxford Handbook of World Philosophy* (pp. 193–204). Oxford: Oxford University Press.

Westerhoff, J. (2019). Nāgārjuna. In E. N. Zalta (Ed.), *The Stanford Encyclopedia of Philosophy* (Fall 2020 Edition). Online: https://plato.stanford.edu/archives/fall2020/entries/nagarjuna.

Williams, B. (1970). The Self and the Future. *The Philosophical Review*, 79(2), 161–80.

Williams, B. (1973). *The Problems of the Self: Philosophical Papers 1956–1972*. Cambridge: Cambridge University Press.

Williams, B. (1981). *Moral Luck: Philosophical Papers, 1973–1980*. Cambridge: Cambridge University Press.

Williams, B. (2000). Philosophy as a Humanistic Discipline. *Philosophy*, 75(294), 477–96.

Williams, P. M. (1981). On the Abhidharma Ontology. *Journal of Indian Philosophy*, 9, 227–57.

Wilson, A., & M. Ross (2003). The Identity Function of Autobiographical Memory: Time is on Our Side. *Memory*, 11(2), 137–49.

Winecoff, A., J. A. Clithero, R. M. Carter, S. R. Bergman, L. Wang, L., & S. A. Huettel (2013). Ventromedial Prefrontal Cortex Encodes Emotional Value. *The Journal of Neuroscience*, 33(27), 11032–9.

Wittgenstein, L. (1975). *Philosophical Remarks*. Oxford: Blackwell.

Wolf, S. (1982). Moral Saints. *The Journal of Philosophy*, 79(8), 419–39.

Wolf, S. (1987). Sanity and the Metaphysics of Responsibility. In F. D. Schoeman (Ed.), *Responsibility, Character, and the Emotions: New Essays in Moral Psychology* (pp. 46–62). Cambridge: Cambridge University Press.

Woods, J. (1915). The Yoga-Sūtras of Patañjali as Illustrated by the Comment Entitled the Jewel's Lustre of Maniprabhā. *Journal of the American Oriental Society*, 34, 1–114.

Zahavi, D. (2003). Inner Time-Consciousness and Pre-Reflective Self-Awareness In D. Welton (Ed.), *The New Husserl: A Critical Reader* (pp. 157–80). Bloomington: Indiana University Press.

Zahavi, D. (2005). *Subjectivity and Selfhood: Investigating the First-Person Perspective*. Cambridge, MA: MIT Press.

Zahavi, D. (2012). The Time of the Self. *Grazer Philosophische Studien*, 84(1), 143–59.

Zahavi, D., & U. Kriegel (2015). For-me-ness: What it is and What it is not. In D. O. Dahlstrom, A. Elpidorou, & W. Hopp (Eds.), *Philosophy of Mind and Phenomenology: Conceptual and Empirical Approaches* (pp. 36–53). London: Routledge.

Index

For the benefit of digital users, indexed terms that span two pages (e.g., 52–53) may, on occasion, appear on only one of those pages.